THE NEW GENERATION IN MEIJI JAPAN

KENNETH B. PYLE

THE NEW GENERATION
IN MEIJI JAPAN

Problems of Cultural Identity, 1885–1895

Stanford University Press, Stanford, California

Stanford University Press, Stanford, California
© 1969 by the Board of Trustees of the
Leland Stanford Junior University
Printed in the United States of America
ISBN 0-8047-0697-2
Original edition 1969
Last figure below indicates year of this printing:
90 89 88 87 86 85 84 83 82 81

for Anne

ACKNOWLEDGMENTS

THIS BOOK is a revision of my doctoral dissertation, which was presented at The Johns Hopkins University during 1965–66. In the course of its writing I was helped by many people and institutions to whom I wish to record my thanks.

Preparation and research were made possible through the financial support of the Ford Foreign Area Fellowship Program, the Office of Education of the United States Government, the Graduate Fellowship Committee of The Johns Hopkins University, the East Asian Studies Committee of Stanford University, and the Modern Japan Seminar of the University of Washington.

I am deeply indebted to Professors Matsumoto Sannosuke of Tōkyō Kyōiku University and Kawazoe Kunimoto of Waseda University, and to Professor Ōsone Shōsuke and Mr. Kamikawa Rikuzō, both formerly of the Inter-University Center for Japanese Language Studies in Tokyo, for tutoring during my stay in Japan from 1961 to 1964.

Portions of the book benefited from presentation to the Japan Seminars at Harvard and the University of Washington; and I am grateful also to Robert J. C. Butow and Marius B. Jansen for their encouragement and help. Stanford University Press deserves special thanks for its care and efficiency in the making of this book.

I have long awaited an opportunity to express my gratitude to two former teachers and advisers, Ernest R. May of Harvard and C. Vann Woodward of Yale, who introduced me to the study of history. My greatest debt is to Thomas C. Smith of Stanford, who has given me far too generously of his time. Although a Hopkins graduate student, I studied for several years under Professor Smith; and it was he who suggested the topic of this study and guided my work on it at every stage.

Finally, my heaviest obligations are to my parents, Mr. and Mrs. Hugh G. Pyle; to my parents-in-law, Mr. and Mrs. William P. Henszey; and above all to my wife, Anne, for so many things that I cannot here begin to name them.

K.B.P.

CONTENTS

THE NEW GENERATION IN MEIJI JAPAN

INTRODUCTION

IN 1868 A PARTY within Japan's warrior aristocracy seized power and embarked upon a revolutionary program that transformed the nation. Rejecting traditionalistic proposals for overcoming the political crisis provoked by Commodore Perry in 1853, these warrior revolutionaries liquidated the Tokugawa system, abolished the privileges of their own class, and remorselessly sacrificed elements of Japanese tradition. They met the challenge of Western power by dismantling the old structure and by building a new political and social order inspired by the civilization of their Western adversaries. In the course of their active leadership, from 1868 through the turn of the century, Japan made the transition from a predominantly agrarian to a nearly industrial economy. Of such a period in history Jacob Burckhardt once wrote, "The historical process is suddenly accelerated in terrifying fashion. Developments which otherwise take centuries seem to flit by like phantoms in months or weeks, and are fulfilled."[1] Indeed an Englishman who came to live in Japan in 1873 observed, less than two decades later, that the swift pace of change "makes a man feel preternaturally old; for here he is in modern times,

---

[1] Superscript numbers refer to the Notes (pp. 207–22), primarily citations of sources and relevant collateral material. Footnotes, generally more substantive in nature, are designated by asterisks (*) and daggers (†).

... and yet he can himself distinctly remember the Middle Ages. . . . Thus does it come about that . . . we ourselves feel well-nigh four hundred years old."[2]

The leaders of the revolution swept away the warrior aristocracy's sources of power and privilege: its exclusive right of arms-bearing and officeholding and its superior education and distinctive culture.[3] They lowered the legal barriers that had traditionally divided society into four classes; abolished restrictions on occupation, residence, food, and dress upon which this legal division depended; liquidated the warrier's monopoly of office by throwing open positions in the bureaucracy to members of all classes; ended his exclusive right to arms by making service in a new national army compulsory for all classes; and undermined his privilege of a superior education by creating a universal public education system. Lacking means to maintain his distinctive way of life, the warrior was compelled to compete with commoners in a world where success depended heavily on acquiring the skills and understanding of a new culture.

The new leaders did away with the old baronies and created a highly centralized government with power sufficient to meet the social and economic challenge of the West. They fashioned an industrial policy that required rapid assimilation of a new technology. The new government retained foreign engineers, technicians, and teachers; promoted translation; and established training programs both in Japan and abroad. Education was radically altered to produce personnel qualified for the tasks of an industrial age. Already modified in the late Tokugawa period, the classical curriculum gave way in the new school system to the study of Western languages, scientific and technical training, and a variety of other disciplines whose content was adopted from Western education.

By emphasizing developments in the century before Perry's arrival, recent scholarship has provided some understanding of the remarkable responsiveness of Japanese society to the

Western challenge. But historians nonetheless continue to be impressed by the scope and pace of change after 1868. "The result," one has recently remarked, "was a generation of sweeping and breathless change such as history had rarely seen until this century."[4] A major survey of modern world history concludes that the change undergone by Japan in the Meiji period (1868–1912) "still stands as the most remarkable transformation ever undergone by any people in so short a time."[5]

Though this revolution upon which the Meiji leadership embarked in 1868 saved Japan from national disaster such as was experienced nearly everywhere else in Asia, it exacted a fearful cost in historical and cultural dislocation, and thus in psychological strain. It caused the generation born in the years after Perry's arrival—the generation that was growing up amidst this revolutionary social and cultural change—to endure extraordinary mental agonies. Lafcadio Hearn, a teacher in Japan during the years we shall be studying, was a sensitive observer of these agonies. He wrote in 1894 that the Japanese student urged himself

to efforts in excess of his natural powers, with the frequent result of mental and moral enervation. The nation has entered upon a period of intellectual overstrain. Consciously or unconsciously, in obedience to sudden necessity, Japan has undertaken nothing less than the tremendous task of forcing mental expansion up to the highest existing standard; and this means forcing the development of the nervous system. For the desired intellectual change, to be accomplished within a few generations, must involve a physiological change never to be effected without terrible cost. In other words, Japan has attempted too much; yet under the circumstances she could not have attempted less.[6]

The purpose of this work is to examine the impact of these abrupt changes upon the thought of young Japanese in the new age. We shall focus upon the first generation of Japanese to attend the new Western-oriented schools of higher learning and the ways in which their attraction to Western culture affected their national self-image.

For many Japanese in this period of intense national consciousness, alienation from their own cultural heritage posed perplexing dilemmas. Building a powerful industrial nation required supplanting much of Japanese tradition with techniques and practices borrowed from the West. Young Japanese were troubled by the implications of this process, for the very modernity they sought had in some sense to be regarded as alien in origin. They were in fact painfully sensitive to the self-effacement that cultural borrowing implied. They saw in Westernization the destruction of Japanese identity. Youth is typically attracted to the new; but was not the joy of innovation greatly lessened if the "new" was not really new, but merely borrowed or imitated?

But what was the alternative? Japanese uniqueness could be defined only in terms of the old and the traditional. Yet was it not the old and the traditional that would have to be discarded if the nation was to modernize and survive? And were not the old and the traditional bitterly symbolic of national impotence? Our concern here is with the attempts that young Japanese made in the 1880's and 1890's to resolve these dilemmas—to escape their historical predicament, to reconcile the conflicting needs of cultural borrowing and national pride, to be both modern and Japanese.

We shall concentrate our attention on two rival groups of young intellectuals who, over the course of a decade, debated issues raised by rapid cultural change. The critical decade began in 1885 with the publication of an influential book proclaiming the emergence of a new generation of "Meiji youth." Its author, Tokutomi Sohō, urged youth to seek total Westernization of Japanese society along the lines of nineteenth-century liberal doctrine. Only thus, he argued, could Japan become a strong industrial nation, the equal of the Western powers. To propagate his ideas, Tokutomi organized in 1887 a group of bright, literate young men who called themselves the Min'yūsha (Friends of the Nation).* Tokutomi became a leading spokesman for the new generation; and the Westernism advocated in Min'yūsha periodicals enjoyed for a time great vogue among educated young Japanese.

As the decade wore on, however, the ideas of a rival group gained increasing appeal. The declared purpose of the Seikyō-sha (Society for Political Education), founded in 1888, was the preservation of Japan's cultural autonomy. Although its members—the most prominent were Miyake Setsurei, Kuga Katsunan, and Shiga Shigetaka—were imbued with Western values and committed to the adoption of many Western institutions, they believed that only by maintaining a distinct cultural identity could Japanese feel equal to Westerners and recover their national pride. In their writings they sought to define Japan's uniqueness and to formulate an independent Japanese role in international society.

The controversy between the Min'yūsha and the Seikyōsha attracted national attention because it involved fundamental issues that divided the hearts and minds of a great many Japanese. The problem of cultural identity has been a continuing one in modern Japan, but it has perhaps never been more intense nor more openly confronted than it was in the years we shall study here.

Before taking up the ideas of these two groups, which we shall do separately in Chapters 2 and 3, we must reconstruct the framework of generational change in the 1880's in order to understand the outlook of Meiji youth and, in particular, to understand why the concern for cultural identity was so intense for them.

* The Glossary (pp. 223–24) gives Japanese characters for many of the names and terms used in the text.

Chapter One

THE NEW GENERATION

IT WAS, in some ways, the best of times for Japanese youth. The period of sweeping change following Perry's arrival brought a fresh climate that favored ambition, vitality, and new destiny. Suddenly the old restraints were removed. Shut to the rest of the world for over two centuries, Japan now opened herself to rejuvenating influences. Destruction of the restrictive Tokugawa system created a new environment unexpectedly sympathetic and responsive to the exuberance and experimentation of youth. Young Japanese grew up in a social order that was unfinished and evolving, where innovation, new discovery, and creative thought were prized.

The rapid tempo of change tended to produce marked differences of outlook between generations. Among youth who, in the first decades of the Meiji period, were financially able to go to the cities and attain the higher reaches of education, there developed a self-awareness and a feeling of identity as a generation. It is this group of young men, whom I shall call "the new generation," that we shall be concerned with in this book. Among them there was a widely shared feeling that—despite filial traditions—the knowledge and responses of the adult generation were unsuited to a time of unprecedented reform. *Kokumin no tomo,* a magazine published by young Japanese in the 1880's and 1890's, proclaimed that "today's elders are already useless to society. In a progressive age they are unfortunately a troublesome burden."[1] A tract entitled *Discourse on Youth*, written in 1887 by Ozaki Yukio (1859–1954), a young Japanese later to become a great statesman, admitted that societies ordinarily depend upon both the creative impulses of the young and the conservative impulses of the older generation; but he argued that because Japan was in a period of vast reconstruction, "today's Japan belongs to youth, not to old people."[2] The magnitude of change in the early Meiji period—especially the loosening of family ties, the appearance of new occupational groups, and the influx of a new culture—served to create for youth opportunities of self-expression and social advancement scarcely imaginable in the Tokugawa period.

Change kindled a sense of liberation and confidence among members of the new generation; but it also brought them agonizing uncertainties. Until their early teens, the young Japanese we shall deal with in this study received traditional, Confucian-oriented training at home and in private academies. Thereafter, in the newly established schools, they were taught by Western instructors, tutored in freshly translated Western texts, and proselytized by newly arrived missionaries. Graduates of these schools entered society with divided minds: they felt themselves torn between the familiar, comfortable values of their childhood and the new, liberating values of their later education. The conflict of old and new values denied young Japanese the emotional security afforded by identification with the aims of an ordered culture. "What *is* today's Japan?" one recent graduate of a new Western-oriented school asked in 1888. "The old Japan has already collapsed, but the new Japan has not yet risen. What religion do we believe in? What moral and political principles do we favor? It is as if we were wandering in confusion through a deep fog, unable to find our way. Nothing is worse than doubt or blind acceptance."[3]

Serious problems of cultural identity were created by this conflict of historical experience and changing times. This chapter examines these problems in light of the major formative influences on the outlook of young Japanese.

I

The independent outlook of the new generation developed only as economic and cultural change loosened the bonds of the traditional family. So long as the ties of family authority stayed tight—as they had through most of the Tokugawa period—ideological conflict between generations was unlikely. Let us briefly consider the nature of traditional family authority, the ways in which it was weakened, and how its erosion contributed to an independent outlook among young Japanese of the new generation.[4]

In Tokugawa Japan the family bore the primary responsibility for transmitting the cultural heritage from generation to generation.[5] The family began the child's training in the basic forms of civilized living by teaching him the importance of sex distinctions and relative age, by shaping his attitudes of obedience to and respect for authority, and by instilling in him the transcendent importance of family and community over individual welfare. School and community aided family in the task of socialization, but theirs was a secondary, complementary role; they reinforced the basic lessons taught in the family. There was little in the wider, adult world to undermine an instinctive confidence in the patterns of behavior the young man had learned at home as a child.

Aside from its prominent role in socialization, the family played an important part in vocational training. During the Tokugawa period, notwithstanding some occupational mobility, the normal expectation was that a son would follow in his father's occupation. Thus the basic skills of the family occupation were taught and practiced at home. In the case of the warrior, it was expected that much of his vocational education would come from outside the family in fief schools; but this study, rooted in moral training, was a natural extension of the training begun in the family.

The solidarity of the traditional family was assured, above all, by the economic interdependence of its members. Occupations attached to families, not to individuals, because the family was the unit of production. The cooperative effort of all its members was required to produce the family income. The typical and safest course for a son was to follow the occupation of the family, whose training, capital, and help in time of need were crucial for his survival. In a restrictive economy, the power to withhold inheritance of the family trade afforded the father a powerful sanction. There was "a strong reason why the son should accept the authority of his father, since revolt left him little prospects of a livelihood outside the family occupation."[6]

The family's immutable authority, its compelling symbols, and its cohesion discouraged youthful independence. The legal, ritual, ideological, economic, and emotional ties of kinship secured a solidarity that thwarted the development of an explicit youth consciousness or ideology.* So long as a young man's occupational role and social orientation were acquired within the family, continuity between generations was assured.

The revolutionary change of the mid-nineteenth century broke this continuity. It did so in many ways, but most clearly in two: first, the abolition of feudal restrictions on choice of

---

* There were in fact young people's groups in Tokugawa Japan, but they were organized in ways that reinforced the values of the hierarchical family. In the villages such groups had their own rigid internal hierarchy. Yanagida Kunio points out that in Satsuma and other places the group's hierarchy reflected relative status of the members' families in the village. Elsewhere, however, it was more often based on relative age. Yanagida Kunio, *Meiji bunka shi: fūzoku hen*, in Kaikoku, XIII, 306. (For complete authors' names, titles, and publication data see the Bibliography, pp. 225–32.) See also Harumi Befu, "Village Autonomy and Articulation with the State," *Journal of Asian Studies*, XXV, 1 (1965), 30–31.

occupation established the freedom to choose one's vocation; and second, the adoption of a new industrial technology created a great number of new occupational groups. In such ways events of the early Meiji period initiated changes that led to a gradual decline in the power of the family's symbols, a shrinking in the scope of its activities, and a weakening of its authority. Processes by which society transmitted its heritage across generations, and so assured its own continuity, were increasingly disrupted. The "continuous world" of family, community, and school was broken.[7]

The decisive experience in demarcating the new generation was, I believe, attendance in the new schools of higher learning. Nowhere did youth feel so deeply the impact of the converging forces of change as in these Western-oriented schools. Traditionally, as we have seen, a child's education had begun at home with instruction in the family's work and in the conduct of life; formal schooling had simply extended that instruction. Thus within the workings of an integrated, unified cultural order, the school had a secondary, complementary role.

After 1868, tasks were imposed upon the new educational system that brought it into conflict with the traditional role of the family. The new schools became agents of cultural and social revolution. As education took on the burden of imparting a knowledge and understanding of Western culture and thereby preparing the young for occupations in an industrial society, the family's role in vocational training declined. Success in the new era depended much less on traditional skills acquired in the family than on the mastery of some aspect of the new learning, such as mechanical engineering, French law, double-entry bookkeeping, or English conversation.[8] Technological development created an increasing number of occupational groups that depended upon an accumulation of technical knowledge, the transmission of which lay beyond family competence.

Thus a young man's role in life was not necessarily set at birth; opportunities beyond his immediate inheritance lay all about, to be grasped with ability, education, and effort. As new avenues of advancement opened, youth strove, often with impressive results, to rise in the world, to be better than their fathers. Opportunity of course was not equal. Economic and status considerations made it difficult for poor peasant youth to acquire advanced education; prestige, cultural tradition, and economic means favored youth of warrior stock. The paths of social ascent, practically speaking, were open only to young men financially able to go to the cities and attain the higher reaches of education.

Among the latter there developed a youthful independence unimaginable as long as inheritance of the family occupation was the normal expectation. In the new schools they prepared for careers that had as yet no clear guidelines, careers whose patterns they and not their parents would determine. The schools provided training that opened the way to new professions in industry, finance, journalism, education, and the bureaucracy, where economic ties to the family were weaker and material independence a possibility.

Journalism, for example, offered unusual opportunity to recently educated young men, for it was they who possessed the knowledge and understanding of Western civilization that the reading public demanded. A prominent young journalist, Taguchi Ukichi (1855–1905), observed in 1888 that young Japanese in the field of journalism had dislodged their elders. Recent school graduates, he pointed out, despite their lack of business experience, had established new publications and had taken control of many old ones. (Taguchi himself was an early example: he began publishing the influential *Tōkyō keizai zasshi* in 1879 at the age of 24.) Their success, he concluded, lay with their advantage of a better grounding in Western studies.[9]

In addition to superseding the functions of the family in

vocational training, the new schools disrupted the family's role in elementary socialization, for the values and ideas taught and practiced in the Western-oriented education were often at variance with those learned at home. Schools promoted spiritual freedom by drawing students out of stifling familistic environments and into an open, professedly egalitarian setting. "Heaven," wrote the leading educator of the new age, "did not create men above men, nor put men under men."[10] By encouraging relationships based on achievement rather than ascription—a tendency that had begun in the fief schools during the late Tokugawa period, but which gained strong confirmation from the revolutionary events after 1868—the new schools weakened, or at least called into question, the values of the hierarchical family. "In human society," explained a representative publicist of the 1870's, "all men, from prince and minister at the top to peasant and merchant at the bottom, are human beings of equal worth. . . . The only distinction . . . is between those who, having learning and ability, are useful to society, and those who are not."[11]

The schools in another way undermined traditional gradations of status. Owing to the disappearance of an aristocratic culture after 1868, "all classes of Japanese," in Thomas Smith's valuable phrase, "were born cultural equals" in the Meiji period.[12] And the cultural revolution, I would add, was sometimes a leveler of age-groups as well as of classes. As long-established institutions were weakened or replaced, the authority of age was undermined. Parents as well as children faced the world anew. Since graduates of the Western schools were often the best prepared for the new professions, young Japanese, and not their elders, were often "the effective guides to a new world, and they thereby gained a strange, anomalous authority,"[13] an authority sometimes difficult to reconcile with the traditional structure of social life.

The journalist Yamaji Aizan (1864–1917) tells of an incident from his childhood that illustrates how swift social and cultural change weakened traditional deference to age. Recalling his primary school experience, he writes that the sudden demand for teachers trained in Western studies meant that frequently a young man scarcely out of his teens, hastily educated in a new normal school, would be appointed principal. Seeing this young principal lording his suddenly acquired authority over classics teachers of an older generation could only weaken respect for age. "To those brought up in the strict social order under the Bakufu," wrote Yamaji, "it must indeed have been an odd spectacle."[14]

Confident of their superior education, members of the new generation assumed themselves better qualified than their elders for contemporary tasks. This attitude was not new. Fukuzawa Yukichi (1835–1901), for example, a generation earlier, had had something of the same feeling. "We students," he wrote, recalling his school days in the 1850's, "were conscious of the fact that we were the sole possessors of the key to knowledge of the great European civilization. However much we suffered from poverty, whatever poor clothes we wore, the extent of our knowledge and the resources of our minds were beyond the reach of any prince or nobleman of the whole nation. If our work was hard, we were proud of it."[15]

Such pride was equally strong and more widespread in the new generation. Japan, it seemed, was being wholly transformed; and many youth were convinced that education in the new schools destined them to complete the reforms the previous generations had only begun. In the tract on youth already mentioned, Ozaki Yukio observed that societies seeking adjustment to rapidly changing or completely new circumstances had to rely on youth for the critical function of revitalization. In an age requiring rapid adoption of Western civilization, he continued, young Japanese by their new education were especially suited to perform this function. Older people, on the other hand, "brought up in an entirely Oriental atmosphere, find Western civilization difficult to understand."

Ozaki was confident that his generation of Japanese would cultivate the notion of "self-responsibility" (*jinin no kokoro*) and would fulfill its destiny of leadership.[16]

One finds this concern with self-direction, self-reliance, and self-respect expressed repeatedly in the writings of the new generation. It was one manifestation of the independent outlook developing among well-educated young men; it also represented an explicit attack on the dependence, submission, and group identification stressed by the traditional ethic. Among students in the new schools, where exposure to foreign ideas was direct and where an ethic emphasizing objective criteria of skill prevailed over kinship criteria, an attitude critical of traditional vertical relations of dependence—of child on parents, retainer on lord, pupil on teacher, present on all past generations—manifested itself in impulsive, self-assertive conduct. Take the example of Futabatei Shimei (1864–1909). The rebelliousness of the novelist during his youth typifies the self-willed behavior of many in the new generation. As a boy of fifteen he found himself in disagreement with a public political position taken by the principal of an academy where he was studying. At once he went to the office of the principal to argue the point with him; and when the latter scolded Futabatei for his disrespect, the boy impulsively withdrew from the academy. Soon afterward, he entered the government-sponsored foreign-language school. Five years later, approaching graduation, Futabatei disputed an administrative reorganization of the school and again withdrew.[17] Nearly all the major figures dealt with in this study were involved in similar incidents.

More than impulse was involved in these incidents. In the writings of the new generation one finds an idealization of inner-directed conduct whereby one ought to act according to internalized principles of right and wrong rather than in conformity with immediate social environment; one should rely on his own efforts, knowledge, and skills rather than on the

joint effort of the group; one ought to accept responsibility
for his own actions rather than seek security and guidance in
the group. This ideal, which Futabatei expressed as a major
theme of his first novel, *Ukigumo,* sanctioned the independent
outlook among young Japanese in the new generation.

One must not exaggerate the suddenness with which this
kind of behavior appeared. R. P. Dore has shown that, despite
efforts to prevent it, competitiveness had already been developing in late Tokugawa education, that "for all the emphasis on collective goals in the [Tokugawa] ideology there was
little in the actual experience of the young samurai to develop
a 'team spirit' and everything to encourage individualistic self-
assertion." In practice the self-assertion was a distinctive kind
of individualism. Kamishima Jirō has characterized it as *"tai-
gunshūteki*—individual self-assertion toward *the group.* It was
not a self-sufficient individualism but one which depended on
the group's existence, since it was primarily a desire to secure
recognition and admiration from the group and power within
it."[18] This type of conduct enjoyed stronger sanctions during
the Meiji period, of course, and as a result became more pro-
nounced.

II

The destruction of the restrictive Tokugawa system and the
dispersion of its aristocratic culture, by calling into question
the axiomatic values of the family, offered many youth new
opportunities of self-expression and social advancement. But
change also brought new and painful uncertainties. A young
man's entrance into society, so natural in Tokugawa days,
fixed as it had been by traditions and secured within the broad
structure of family activities, now lost its certainty. As change
disrupted the once smooth transfer of life patterns from generation to generation, the security and ease with which youth
had ordinarily located themselves in Tokugawa society disappeared. An independent but sensitive youth like Ebina Danjō

(1856–1937), for example, could confess to a feeling of loneliness owing to the "lack of spiritual understanding between me and my parents."[19] The parents, moreover, were suffering their own disruptions. Fathers of many in the new generation were displaced from occupations in mature life by the sudden abolition of status distinctions. In his novel *Yoakemae*, Shimazaki Tōson (1872–1943) describes the traumatic effect that the political and social change had upon his father, an effect that contributed to the father's eventual insanity. The novelist Natsume Sōseki (1867–1916) describes the attempt of the adult generation to live by traditional values in the modern world as like waging "war against oneself."[20] In the new age, then, growing up became a difficult, disturbing, unsettling experience: the thinking and experience of previous generations provided no certain precedents for new tasks; and the disintegrative effects of change on the older generation were in turn reflected in insecurities among the young. "A youngster of sixteen," wrote a leading young journalist in 1887, "confronts problems of life (*seikatsuteki no mondai*) that his ancestors, even his elders today, never imagined."[21] Disoriented at a sensitive stage of life by the rapid pace of social change and by the confusion of the adult generation, youth entered society uncertain of their bearings.

Cultural discontinuities aggravated the condition. Formal education, which during most of the Tokugawa period had played a role complementary to the family's in cultural transmission, was abruptly reconstituted as an agent of cultural revolution. As a result, the roles of family and school were brought into conflict—one transmitting inherited culture, the other imparting a culture at variance with the old—creating in youthful thinking a radical cleavage between traditional and modern, Japanese and Western. Lafcadio Hearn observed such uncertainty among the schoolboys he taught in the 1890's. He saw how they were stirred when members of the parental generation who visited the school spoke to them of their ancestors, of loyalty and honor, and of decay of the ancient spirit.

But after one such occasion a student mused to Hearn: "No matter how good the old morality was, we cannot follow any such moral law and preserve our national independence and achieve any progress.... We must forsake our past."[22] The young Japanese gained through his education a vision of values beyond those of his immediate culture and acquired a sense of separateness from the social world about him: he felt himself detached from the social order and impelled to question the traditional way of life. Unconscious acceptance of his trusted early surroundings was undermined; and his sudden experience of incongruity between the old ways and the new values learned in Western-oriented schools shattered trust in his immediate world.

This lack of spiritual surety among youth was the result not simply of acquiring a broader cultural perspective; it came as well with growing awareness of the vulnerability of the traditional social order and its peculiar morality. The treaties signed with Western powers at the end of the Tokugawa period imposed for the first time in history extensive limitations on the sovereignty of the Japanese state. This national humiliation was at first blamed on the ineptness and weakness of the Tokugawa system and in this sense was viewed as a political and military failure. The ensuing effort to build a powerful new industrial order, however, required supplanting much of the traditional culture with techniques and practices borrowed from the West. As the bureaucracy and the military, commerce, industry, and education fell under the sway of the Western example, the humiliation of the unequal treaties which had earlier been ascribed to the bankruptcy of the old regime was increasingly, in the decades after 1868, laid to the failings of the traditional culture. Young Japanese therefore found in the national experience a confirmation of their belief that the knowledge, traditions, and responses of previous generations were unreliable guides to the future, and that a sharp break with the past was necessary.

The adult generation had experienced tensions between old

and new, traditional and modern, but their tensions had never been so wrenching as those that the new generation now felt.[23] Among Japanese coming to manhood at Perry's arrival there had not been prevalent the anxious self-doubt or the pained introspection that one now found in the new generation. Perhaps this was because they had not felt in their upbringing the full force of cultural change; they had grown up in a rapidly changing but not yet "broken" world.[24] In their youth, the values and institutions of the old society had still commanded respect and conviction. The radical cleavage between traditional and modern that developed in the outlook of the new generation therefore provides a dramatic example of how contrasting experiences may "serve to demarcate one age group from another in intellectual history."[25]

The attempt to live according to new values that were "not insensibly acquired in childhood as part of the natural order of things, but learned, usually late, as part of a self-conscious quest for appropriate forms of behavior"[26] was often distressing. Kozaki Hiromichi (1856–1938), who became a leading Christian educator, tells in his autobiography of the mental agony he suffered as a young man: "The year and a half spent as a Christian inquirer is the unhappiest period of my life. The rational part of me rebelled against taking the decisive step; yet to turn away from Christianity and be content with Confucianism would leave my spirit of inquiry unsatisfied. This dilemma so wrought on me that I had a nervous breakdown."[27] The writings of others, such as the brooding Kitamura Tōkoku (1869–94), who took his own life, tell of the melancholia and mental turmoil of their youth.[28] Tokutomi Sohō, whom we shall discuss in the succeeding chapter, related in his autobiography that "mental sickness" (nōbyō) was widespread among students in the 1870's and 1880's.[29] Writing of the same period, Lafcadio Hearn concluded that "the social and moral experience of one race could not be either suddenly or gradually substituted for that of another with happy re-

sults. . . . The youths, on whose capacity the future of the country would depend, were being seriously overworked. Many of
the brightest and the most earnest had died under the strain.
Most of the larger Middle Schools throughout the country had
lost some of their most promising students. Brain disorders
were not uncommon."[30]

The sensitivity of youth to the cleavage between Japanese
and Western was heightened by the rapid growth of national
consciousness. They grew up at a time when the new government was seeking to strengthen itself by deliberately fostering
a sense of belonging to the nation: the establishment of modern communications, a national conscript army, and a national
education system were designed in part to raise allegiances to
the national level. The Meiji leaders hoped to modify traditional loyalties to the family and to the local community by
encouraging the individual to identify above all with the nation. There was a natural growth of national consciousness,
too, with the emergence of Japan as a nation-state in competition with other nation-states and with the influx of Westerners
and Western culture. Moreover political issues in the 1870's
and 1880's focused attention on the nation, for prior to the
promulgation of a constitution in 1889 the new political framework was still taking shape and was the subject of widespread
debate.

But though national consciousness thus permeated the
thinking of the new generation, national pride did not. On
the contrary, discovery of their nationality was often embarrassing to youth: comparison with the Western culture to
which they were attracted only underlined the failings of their
own cultural heritage. Many young Japanese turned their
backs on the past, even rejected history outright, and in this
way sought to conceal the source of their shame. Erwin Baelz,
a German doctor who arrived in Japan in 1876 to teach at
Tokyo University, relates in his diary the embarrassment he
discovered among his students over their cultural heritage:

"The cultured among them are actually ashamed of it. 'That was in the days of barbarism,' said one of them in my hearing. Another, when I asked about Japanese history, bluntly rejoined: 'We have no history. Our history begins today.' "[31] The English scholar Basil Hall Chamberlain, a long-time resident in Japan, warned Westerners in 1891: "Whatever you do, don't expatiate, in the presence of Japanese of the new school, on those old, quaint, and beautiful things Japanese which rouse our most genuine admiration. . . . Speaking generally, the educated Japanese have done with their past. They want to be somebody else and something else than what they have been and still partly are."[32]

It was the historical predicament of youth to be caught in a confrontation of circumstances that intensified the awareness of their heritage and at the same time stigmatized it. Their formal education and their advancement in the world were almost entirely bound up with the acquisition of technical skills and ways of thought adopted from an alien culture. For those who went on to higher education, departure from the inherited occupational and social roles became a common experience. Traditional skills became outdated; old ways of organizing and viewing social life became problematic and controversial. This process, entailing as it did a sudden loss of trust in the immediate world and in its transmitters and interpreters, left Japanese youth with no sure sense of their identity. What did it mean to be a Japanese in the modern world? For the young, unless positive, prideful responses could be found—answers that could give reassuring substance to their national consciousness—their heightened self-awareness could lead to self-destructive doubt and shame. What young Japanese had to come up with if they were to locate themselves confidently and securely in the world was some viable conception of their history, some meaningful way of relating the past to the present and future. This quest forms the major theme of my study.

The new generation emerging in the 1880's expressed two divergent answers to this need for historical orientation. One response was to liken the revolutionary transformation of Japan to historical development in the West, to see Japan as following a path of social advancement discernible in the history of more advanced Western nations, to regard this process as a fixed, universal pattern of development to which all progressing nations conformed. All around them young Japanese could find confirmation of this view of their history. They saw unfolding in their environment trends discernible in the history of Western nations: the disappearance of a feudal aristocratic regime, the emergence of a nation-state endowing its people with extensive civic rights, the transition from an agrarian to an industrial economy, a growing faith in science, reason, and progress. Japan, according to this view, was remaking herself in conformity with universal laws of human progress; as she advanced she inevitably would become more like Western societies. This interpretation made the experience of youth less bewildering: it helped to mend the radical cleavage in their minds between the old and the new, the traditional and the modern. There were, however, troubling implications in this identification with Western history and traditions. Cultural borrowing, though not new in the Japanese experience, in the latter part of the nineteenth century posed peculiar dilemmas: its coincidence with mounting national consciousness wounded self-esteem. If the goals and values of Japanese society were defined entirely in Western terms, all cultural autonomy would be lost; seen in this perspective, the process would become self-effacing and destructive of integrity. Moreover, in the 1880's and 1890's impatience with Western extraterritorial privilege in Japan and the transference of European rivalries and ambitions to East Asia intensified the dilemmas: to advocate Westernization in the heyday of Western imperialism could well be construed as submission, even treachery.

The alternative response of young Japanese was to argue the compatibility of progress and cultural autonomy and to seek something in their national past that they and the world could esteem as uniquely Japanese, something of their own that need not be sacrificed in the course of modernization. There was no ready consensus in the new generation concerning what was redeemable from its heritage; nor at the outset was there any enthusiasm for salvaging the traditional culture, since youth themselves were beneficiaries of its passing. The national consciousness of the new generation, however, prodded the search. Building a powerful industrial nation required supplanting much of Japanese tradition with techniques and practices borrowed from the West. To compensate for their loss, "to own the ground they stood on,"[33] young Japanese began to seek some way in which they might define their uniqueness.

Two combative groups of young intellectuals representing these divergent responses will be the subject of our study. Over the course of nearly a decade they argued the great issues that confronted the nation in the late nineteenth century. Despite their opposition, the groups were not so polarized as they and their adherents supposed: their members shared a common framework of concerns and expectations that distinguished them as belonging to the same age group. Their debate therefore mirrored the spiritual conflicts of a generation.

Chapter Two

MEIJI YOUTH AND WESTERNISM

BY THE 1880's, the reform ardor of the Meiji leaders had begun to wane; because the new social order was already becoming established, they were disinclined to hold up their revolutionary example for emulation by the new generation. They
had by now instituted many of the revolutionary proposals of
their youth: the abolition of the rigid Tokugawa social order,
the organization of a national conscript army, the establishment of universal education with a reformed curriculum, the
introduction of new technology, and the successful promotion
of an ambitious industrial policy. Although completion of the
remaining major reforms—including the drafting of a constitution, the codification of law, and the establishment of parliamentary institutions—still occupied government, the ruling group, now entering their fifties and purged of liberal elements, was increasingly concerned with eliminating instability
and reestablishing order and unity in political life.*

---

* Itō Hirobumi recalled that "we were just then [about 1880] in an age of transition. The opinions prevailing in the country were extremely heterogeneous
and often diametrically opposed to one another. We had survivors from former
generations who were still full of theocratic ideas and who believed that any
attempt to restrict an imperial prerogative amounted to something like high
treason. On the other hand there was a large and powerful body of the younger
generation educated at a time when the Manchester theory was in vogue, and
who in consequence were ultra-radical in their ideas of freedom.... A work
entitled *History of Civilization,* by Buckle, which denounced every form of gov-

The increasing conservatism in government circles was re-
pugnant, as we shall see in this chapter, to many politically
conscious members of the new generation, whose hopes for a
reformation of Japanese society were still unsatisfied. Nakae
Chōmin (1847–1901), admired by young Japanese for his progressive views and for his translation of Rousseau's *Contrat
Social*, commented in 1887 that the leaders of the Meiji government could no longer inspire the younger generation. In
ordinary times, by virtue of their position and their accomplishments, they would be honored by the young; but in this
age of unprecedented reform, he said, their ideas had become
outdated.[1]

Even Fukuzawa Yukichi, whose Westernism had attracted
young Japanese in the 1870's, seems to have been no longer
the spiritual leader of youth he had once been.[2] Fukuzawa, for
his part, writing in 1882, confessed dismay at the brashness of
the new generation, at its temerity in discussing national politics and its disrespect for its elders. But he conceded that youth
might justifiably point to the rebellious behavior of his own
generation as precedent for their independence; and he concluded stoically that the intemperance of youth must be tol-
erated, since it was a consequence of the political revolution
his own generation had initiated.[3]

Many members of the new generation hoped for a "spiritual
revolution" that would go beyond institutional change to
reform basic habits of thought and reshape patterns of behavior; and these young Japanese felt that the adult generation
did not understand the need for such a revolution. Yamaji
Aizan complained in 1890 that national progress made thus
far had been material, whereas spiritual values had been ne-

---

ernment as an unnecessary evil, became the great favorite of students of all the
higher schools, including the Imperial university. But those same students
would not have dared to expound the theories of Buckle before their own conservative fathers. At that time we had not arrived at the stage of distinguishing
clearly between political opposition on the one hand and treason to the established order on the other." Quoted in Sansom, pp. 347–48.

glected. It was useless, he said, to try to adopt Western parliamentary institutions if politicians were still thinking like feudal lords.[4] Kozaki Hiromichi wrote in 1887 that "we must rid
ourselves of Oriental traits," adding "I hope we shall learn all
of the ways of the West. We must not, in this progressive reform movement, simply adopt the externals of Western customs; we must go further and reform people's minds as well."
Many Japanese had adopted Western styles of living, Western
diet and clothing, yet they remained "Oriental in disposition
as before."[5]

Perhaps the most widely recognized spokesman for the new
generation emerging in the 1880's was Tokutomi Soho (1863–
1957). He captured the imagination of many Japanese youth
by expressing their enthusiasm for building a progressive Western society in Japan, and his writings and the journals he
edited self-consciously delineated the cleavage between generations. The development of his ideas as a young man, their
wide acceptance, and their subsequent metamorphosis illus-
trate various basic aspects of the search for a cultural identity.
This chapter traces the origins of Tokutomi's early thought
and examines its widespread appeal for the new generation.

I

Tokutomi Iichirō—in his adult life he came to be known
more often by his pen name, Tokutomi Soho—was born in
1863 in a village midway between the castle towns of Kumamoto and Kagoshima on the southern island of Kyushu.[6] He
was the elder son in a family of wealthy peasants who for generations had occupied important local administrative offices
in the Kumamoto domain. Tokutomi's ancestors had inter-
married with other moneyed village families to form a lineage
group that enjoyed many of the characteristic privileges of
samurai: they possessed the right to bear surnames, wear
swords, and study at the fief school. Yet they were not authentic
samurai; they remained in the countryside where their pres-

tige and power were rooted, protecting and promoting their landed interests.

"Gōnō," as wealthy peasants were called, were an anomalous social group difficult to accommodate within the traditional structure of Tokugawa society. Neither commoners nor aristocrats, "the country gentry," Tokutomi once wrote, "tasted the bitterness of commoners under a feudal system without becoming servile, and savored the sweetness of feudal warriors without becoming arrogant."[7] Better educated and more prosperous than many warriors, gōnō were often frustrated by a class system that restricted their advance. Such frustration caused Tokutomi's grandfather to pour great effort into the education of his sons, apparently in the hope of enhancing their prospects.[8]

As it happened, their opportunity arose out of ties with reform-minded samurai. Several of Tokutomi's kinship group were students and followers of Yokoi Shōnan (1809–69), who played a prominent part in the national political movements of the period following Perry's arrival.[9] The second son of a Kumamoto warrior family of modest rank, Yokoi established a private school in Kumamoto, where he began to develop his ideas of reform. Partly because of his emphasis on loyalty to the imperial institution, Yokoi fell into disfavor with his domain's conservative ruling council, and prudent samurai of his own fief avoided him. But he did attract an enthusiastic following among samurai from neighboring fiefs and among wealthy peasant youth. His first pupils were Tokutomi's father and uncles, who later helped him finance his school and other reform projects and accompanied him on his travels.[10] Yokoi, who married Tokutomi's aunt, became an advisor first to reformers within the shogunate and then to the young warriors who led the overthrow of the Tokugawa system.

Pragmatic, prodded by disaffection, receptive to new thought, and curious about the sources of Western strength, Yokoi was uninhibited in his thinking about the crisis in

Japanese foreign relations. He early rejected a policy of national isolationism, believing that the nation's future required
the adoption of Western technology, the establishment of a
great navy, and the development of foreign trade. He evinced
an interest in many Western institutions; and his primary
concern was for parliamentary government, which he thought
would make possible and encourage a wider participation in
Japanese government.

Tokutomi emphasizes in his autobiography the influence
that Yokoi had on his own ideas; and one suspects that Yokoi's
views were in turn influenced by the reform predilections of
his wealthy peasant allies. Yokoi's admiration of Western institutions made him, finally, a target of xenophobic warriors;
he was assassinated in 1869.

Although the social distance between gōnō and samurai was
narrowing, as the collaboration of Tokutomi's family with
Yokoi had demonstrated, psychological and cultural distinctions between the two classes persisted. Tokutomi felt such
distinctions in painful childhood experiences. In 1870, when
he was seven,* his family moved from its village homestead to
Kumamoto, where his father had been appointed to a high
position in the reformed domain administration. Warrior
children there scorned his breeding, and taunted him for his
countrified ways. Tokutomi was never able to forget their dis-
dainful attitude, and it is easy to suppose that memories of
such experiences may have contributed to the anti-aristocratic
bias of his early thought.[11]

Perhaps more than any other social group, wealthy peasants
stood to gain from the cultural revolution that followed 1868.
Lacking a secure position within inherited cultural traditions,
they nonetheless did possess the qualities and means to become
the arbiters of the new culture. Practical-minded, they early
showed an interest in Western technology. Tokutomi's father

---

* Ages in this book are computed according to Western practice.

helped to finance a trip that Yokoi's two nephews took to America in 1866 to study Western science; and at about the same time, Tokutomi's uncle, Takezaki Ritsujirō, established a large experimental farm outside of Kumamoto, where he tested Western farming methods. In subsequent years the family promoted factories, newspapers, churches, and other new cultural institutions. Undoubtedly, the enthusiasm of these wealthy peasants for Western learning stemmed in part from the opportunity it offered them to obliterate cultural barriers to their advance.

One of the most ambitious projects in which Tokutomi's family played a leading role was the establishment in 1871 of the Kumamoto School for Western Studies, one of the earliest schools of its kind in Japan.[12] The hope of Tokutomi's father and of other reformers who had gained control of the domain following the Restoration was that by training their brightest students in the new learning and by preparing them for positions of national leadership they might project Kumamoto into the forefront of national politics. They hired Captain Leroy Lansing Janes, a graduate of West Point, to serve as headmaster and to teach English, science, mathematics, and world history.

The founders placed one restriction on the curriculum: it was not to include the study of Western ethics. Janes was told when he arrived from America that traditional Japanese ethics would be taught in conjunction with the new Western learning and that Tokutomi's uncle, Takezaki Ritsujirō, would lecture the students regularly from Confucian texts. Though they were leaders in adopting the technical and practical learning of the West, Tokutomi's family took pride in their Confucian erudition: both his father and his uncle, who had his own academy in Kumamoto, where Tokutomi studied before entering the School for Western Studies, were regarded as Confucian scholars. Tokutomi's formal education, prior to entering the School for Western Studies, had emphasized Chinese and native classics. He found, however, that when he began at the new school, the *Analects* and *Greater Learning* seemed antiquated.[13]

The distinction between the utilitarian and the ethical teachings of Western culture—a clean distinction in the outlook of the adult generation—proved difficult to transmit to the students. Their curiosity, their attraction to the Western learning, and their respect for the new teacher proved too great to confine within the bounds of practical learning alone. Also, by the time Tokutomi entered the school in 1875, Janes (whose father-in-law was a Congregational minister) had, in spite of his instructions, begun to proselytize. Tokutomi, caught up in the fervor that swept the school, joined thirty-four of his classmates in an avowal of Christian faith in a ceremony atop Mount Hanaoka outside Kumamoto.

Their declaration precipitated a sharp conflict with the parental generation. Yokoi Shōnan's son was among those who took the oath, and we are told that his mother (Tokutomi's aunt) threatened to take her own life if he would not recant. A compromise was reached in family council when the son agreed not to become a preacher![14] One student, Ebina Danjō, even though his father began fasting, refused to renounce his new belief, finding justification for his disobedience in the teachings of Wang Yang-ming. According to the Wang Yang-ming School, if one was serving his country he should follow the dictates of his own conscience, even if such action involved a violation of conventional filial piety.[15] It was in terms of its value to the community that these youth justified their new faith—and their rejection of parental authority. Their oath itself declared that the propagation of Christianity served the nation by discarding outmoded ways of thought.

Tokutomi's parents were not so wrathful as some of the others, but they were angry enough to destroy his Bible and hymnal.[16] He was, at thirteen, younger than many of the others who signed the oath (Ebina was twenty, Yokoi's son nineteen).

His recollection years later was that he had merely followed the example of his older classmates; he had been too young, he said, to have had any understanding of the oath.[17] However that may have been, we can conjecture that the incident implanted in his mind the beginnings of a youth consciousness that he was subsequently to articulate as an explicit ideology.

Conflict over the Hanaoka oath forced the closure of the School for Western Studies in the autumn of 1876, and Tokutomi's parents sent him to Tokyo to continue his education. But following a short period of study at an English-language school, Tokutomi, heedless of his parents' will, joined several of his former Kumamoto schoolmates at Dōshisha, a new school established in Kyoto under American missionary auspices. In the spring of 1878, when he returned to Kumamoto for the first time in over two years, his outspoken Christian views embarrassed his parents and brought rebuke from their friends. He nevertheless returned to Kyoto later in the same year, accompanied by his younger brother, Roka, who also entered Dōshisha.[18]

Western-oriented schools such as Dōshisha imparted to students cut off from familistic environments the tastes and understanding of the new culture. Niijima Jō, Dōshisha's first president, greatly influenced the young Tokutomi's outlook. Niijima had traveled in Europe and America, had studied at Andover, Amherst, and Andover Theological Seminary, and had returned to Japan confident that if "we want to make our country the equal of civilized nations we must not stop with imitating the externals of civilization; we must strive for its essence."[19] With this aim in mind, he helped found Dōshisha as a private school that would introduce Christianity to young Japanese. Inspired by the warmth and compassion of his mentor, Tokutomi was baptized by Niijima in 1878; and although he was never comfortable with Christian dogma, he had grown convinced that the adoption of Western ethics and values was imperative for Japan's progress as a civilization.

Tokutomi studied at Dōshisha for over three years; but in the spring of 1880, following his involvement in a student dispute with school authorities over an administrative reorganization, he decided to withdraw from the school. Restless, and ambitious to begin a career in journalism (he had read newspapers avidly for several years), he returned to Tokyo; but once there he discovered that without experience or the proper introductions he could not find a position. In the fall of 1880 he reluctantly returned to his home in Kumamoto, where he began teaching in a private school. He later recalled that he came almost at once into disagreement with the traditional views of an older teacher. Self-willed, and confident of his own education, Tokutomi decided in 1882 to establish his own school in Kumamoto, where he would emphasize the study of Western society, politics, and history.[20]

He was only nineteen when his new school opened; and, self-consciously intent upon encouraging youthful independence, he deliberately created an informal atmosphere that would contrast with traditional classroom formality. Tokutomi encouraged his students to call him by his given name (Iichirō San); and rather than set school regulations himself, he asked the students to draw up their own rules and to govern themselves.[21] He often traveled with his students during school vacations, as in the summer of 1884, when he accompanied several of them to Tosa, where they visited with other youth groups. Enrollment in his school grew rapidly to over one hundred and included youth from many parts of Kyushu.[22]

In addition to his teaching, Tokutomi was involved for a time in the People's Rights Movement. Disaffection toward the oligarchy and demands for parliamentary government spread rapidly in the early 1880's, and the adoption of Western liberal theory gave the emergent party movement an ideological attraction for youth. During 1882 Tokutomi went twice to Tokyo in hopes of meeting the leaders of the movement. On his second trip, serving as representative of the Kumamoto political factions opposing the government oligarchy, he met several of the movement's ideologues, including Nakae Chōmin, Baba Tatsui, and Taguchi Ukichi. Itagaki Taisuke, the head of the Liberal Party (Jiyūtō), discussed his views at length with Tokutomi, apparently regarding the young schoolmaster as a potential follower with influence among Kyushu youth.[23]

II

Tokutomi spent the years 1880 to 1886 in Kumamoto. In terms of intellectual development, this was the most significant period of his life. Teaching others stimulated him to intense, thoughtful study; it led him to reflect on his experiences and those of his pupils and so increased his awareness of the particular outlook of his own age group; it provoked thought on the changing content and purpose of education and on the relation of his generation to the nation's future. His lectures drew on notes from his Dōshisha classes and on the writings of Macaulay, Tocqueville, and Guizot. He read extensively from Spencer, Mill, and Rousseau; from Cobden, Bright, and the Manchester School; and he sought to digest their views and to relate them to the lives of young Japanese.

From his experiences as a student and as a young schoolmaster came the idea for his first important piece of writing, a long essay written in 1885 entitled "Education of Youth in Nineteenth Century Japan." He submitted the essay to Taguchi Ukichi, editor of the prominent *Tōkyō keizai zasshi* (Tokyo Economist) and a publicist with wide influence in political and business circles, who agreed to publish it.* Soon after,

---

* A year earlier, in 1884, Tokutomi had published and circulated at his own expense two short treatises. One was an attack on Confucian morals; the other was a discussion of the qualities that Japanese politicians would have to develop in preparation for the new parliamentary system to be initiated in 1890. Among those who read the second essay was Taguchi, who wrote Tokutomi that he had "not seen such writing since the Restoration." Tokutomi, then just twenty-one, was long grateful for his encouragement. Tokutomi Iichirō, *Jiden*, p. 192.

Tokutomi expanded the essay and published it in book form under the title *Youth of the New Japan*.[24]

Tokutomi's book emphasized that revolutionary change had opened a gulf in understanding and sympathy between the "old men of Tempō" (Tempō is the period 1830–44, during which most of the Restoration leaders were born) and the "youth of Meiji." Young and old were also frequently in conflict in Western society, he observed, but their differences were not so great as in Japan, where the pace of change had been more rapid. The "old people of the feudal age" could not understand the problems of youth in the new Japan: "A youngster of sixteen confronts problems of life (*seikatsuteki no mondai*) that his ancestors, even his elders today, never imagined." Tokutomi argued that to meet challenges unprecedented in the experience of the adult generation, youth must develop habits of independence and self-reliance. "Your great foe," he told youth, "may well be the old people whom you have always loved and respected. . . . They are relics of yesterday's world; you are masters of the future."[25]

Youth of the New Japan was concerned with what constituted proper education for this new generation. Before 1868 the feudal order, governed by a "dictatorship of social custom," had oppressed education and stifled progressive thought. Confucian scholarship was like a "hothouse flower" or a "rare curio," ornamental and diverting but of no practical value; and education had been confined to shallow moral training designed to uphold feudal society. The overthrow of the Tokugawa system had brought with it a shift in the nature of education from inculcating Confucian morality to providing technical and vocational training. But Tokutomi argued that this reform was deficient in one major respect: it had neglected to build a spiritual foundation for the new practical education.[26]

He was not alone in his apprehension. A great many commentators on education deplored the single-minded concern with vocational instruction set forth in the preamble of the

Education Act of 1872, which stated that the purpose of education was to enable a student to "make his way in the world, employ his wealth wisely, make his business prosper, and thus attain the goal of life."[27] Although many writers objected to this view of learning as an investment in worldly success, there were differences in the remedies they offered.

In all, Tokutomi discerned four schools of thought regarding the future of Japanese education. The first he called the "reactionary" view (*fukkoshugi*); it was held by men of an older generation who wished to revive the education of the feudal age, preferring the *Kojiki* and the Chinese classics to the writings of Spencer, Darwin, and Macaulay. Tokutomi disposed of this view quickly: Japanese society had outgrown this kind of learning; a reestablishment of Tokugawa education would destroy the independent, progressive spirit of Japanese youth and leave them unfit to survive the social struggles of their times.

The second school of thought was that advocated by early Meiji reformers and set forth in the preamble of the Education Act of 1872. Tokutomi called it "unbalanced" because it was preoccupied with utilitarian learning but indifferent to moral training. Its adherents were perceptive in recognizing the inadequacy of Confucian morals as the basis of education, and yet blind to the underlying social need for moral direction. They were content to base education solely on a practical, utilitarian philosophy that regarded training for a livelihood as the only object of education. To Tokutomi, this approach was tantamount to abandoning all hope for purposeful social progress. "The Meiji period," he lamented, "is an age of fault-finding, skepticism, and unbelief."[28] The spiritual tyranny of the Tokugawa period had been replaced by spiritual anarchy. Tokutomi considered Fukuzawa Yukichi a leading exponent of the unbalanced approach; in a recent essay Fukuzawa had argued that public attitudes (*kōgi yoron*) determine social morality and that merely to establish moral education would not suffice to change the moral climate. Tokutomi regarded this view as a policy of drift, a policy that ignored the possibility that an education in morality could in fact provide the basis for public attitudes.[29]

He considered a third school of thought, the "syncretic" or "eclectic" approach (*setchūshugi*), as closer to his own thinking, because its adherents recognized the need for a clear standard of moral values. By syncretism he meant the blend of matter and spirit through which the scientific ethos of the West could be synthesized with the moral values of the Orient. This was the view, he said, of "partially enlightened old people," and it was gaining adherents throughout the country, especially in government and education circles. (Already the educational policy established by the Act of 1872 was beginning to be modified: in 1881 the Ministry of Education had instructed elementary school teachers to stress training in the traditional moral values.) Tokutomi argued, however, that Western science and Eastern morals were fundamentally incompatible, and that the civilizations of the Orient and the West had contradictory characteristics that could not coexist or be successfully fused. One civilization was static and authoritarian; the other was progressive, inquisitive, and free. If Western utilitarian principles were taught alongside traditional Confucian morality, the result would be confusion, tension, and ultimately skepticism in the minds of schoolchildren.[30]

Rejecting the third school of thought, Tokutomi triumphantly proclaimed his own: Japanese education must be wholly Western. The material and spiritual aspects of Western society, he emphasized, were indivisible. It was folly to adopt techniques and institutions without the values that inspired them. Arguing in a fashion that was itself reminiscent of Confucian logic, Tokutomi said that morals and learning were "one path"; they were meant to assist and not to check one another. "Every society forms a code of ethics in accordance with its nature and customs." In Rome the code had stressed

military values, in Carthage commercial values. "We have imported Western techniques, politics, scholarship, etc., and we
hope now to build a Western society. Therefore we must also
import the Western code of ethics, which alone can coexist
with the progress of knowledge."[31] In addition to teaching the
practical aspects of Western culture, he said, the education of
Japanese youth must include instruction in the ethical values
that were the essence of Western social life. Tokutomi called
on youth to reject the traditional traits of the Japanese people,
traits that were the legacy of Japan's long feudal experience:
they should shun unprogressive and acquiescent characteristics, avoid social indifference, and overcome irrationality.
Youth should, rather, emulate the qualities found in the liberal, democratic societies of the West: they should develop progressive and innovative natures and become self-reliant, responsible, logical, and scientific.[32]

The ideas Tokutomi expressed in *Youth of the New Japan*
evinced a profound alienation from his country's traditions
and cultural heritage. Japan's past seemed to him devoid of
the ingredients necessary in modern society. Like Tokutomi,
most Japanese were convinced of the need for change and of
the validity of the Western example. The dispute was over the
extent of borrowing. Whereas most Japanese regarded as inevitable that Japanese institutions, techniques, and values would
have to be modified, he believed they had to be wholly displaced. He was impatient with compromises and halfway
measures in the process of Westernization.

III

Tokutomi's cultural alienation derived in part from—and
contributed to—the historical outlook set forth in his second
important work, *The Future Japan*. This ambitious book,
written in 1886 when he was twenty-three, was derivative of
Mill, the Manchester School, and especially Spencer. In it he
attempted to assess Japan's historical position and to foresee

the outcome of social change already under way in Japan.[33] He argued that there was a common pattern of social development in the world whose outlines were already clear in many Western countries, and that this pattern was beginning to emerge in Japan. He found support for his thoroughgoing Westernism in the belief that for Japan to advance she must inevitably become more like Western societies and, indeed, that Japan's progress could be measured by her acquired similarities to Western nations.

To trace the origin of this belief, we must first consider Herbert Spencer's theory of evolution in social structure, which provided an essential part of Tokutomi's world view and greatly influenced his thinking. He had read sections of *Principles of Sociology*, in which Spencer posited two fundamental, universal phases in the evolution of social structure.[34] The first Spencer called the "militant" phase, which was one from which no society had yet wholly escaped; the second he called the "industrial" phase, which was one toward which advanced societies were clearly evolving.

The "militant" society was a product of periods of endemic warfare. Only those societies best organized to protect themselves from external threat survived such periods.[35] To ensure unity against the threat of attack, coercive government was necessary and "compulsory cooperation" was demanded of the entire community. Economic and social relations were meticulously regulated. Unable to trust its neighbors, the militant society espoused a protectionist policy and became sufficient unto itself. It established rigid controls over commercial activities and subordinated life, liberty, and property of individuals to the principal end of preserving corporate life. Those individuals who did not bear arms were compelled to spend their lives supporting the combatants; personal initiative was further restricted by restraints on private association and on changes in occupation and residence. Regimentation thus extended to the entire community, which in time came to be organized into a rigid hierarchy of status; society had an army-like structure characterized by successive grades of subordination. As Spencer put it, "from the despot down to the slave, all are masters of those below and subjects of those above."[36] Members of this society, moreover, typically manifested distinctly militaristic character traits: physical courage, loyalty, obedience, and patriotism. Because of the society's low regard for the life, property, and freedom of its individuals, vengeance, cruelty, and selfish disregard of inferiors were frequent. Commerce was scorned, individual initiative discouraged, and the government relied on for all services.

Writing during the Pax Britannica, Spencer believed that the militant phase was evolving toward a second, entirely different, more advanced phase, which he called the "industrial" society.[37] He argued that warfare was becoming less frequent and that it no longer demanded the energies of entire populations. Conquests by militant states had created larger and larger social units within which warring had ceased, allowing the development of peaceful industrial arts. As a result social structure was gradually being transformed. The industrial society, Spencer admitted, existed nowhere in pure form, because all societies had still to defend themselves occasionally from external threats and therefore continued to exhibit some traits of militancy. But in several advanced societies—France, the United States, and especially England—the traits of the emergent type were sufficiently apparent for one to describe its ideal form.

The prime characteristic of an industrial society was the freedom it accorded its citizens; as the need for compulsory cooperation diminished, regimentation of the individual relaxed and arbitrary authority was replaced by representative government, whose sole function was to provide security for the life and property of its individuals. Once social and economic relations were no longer determined by status, society lost its former rigidity. Place of residence and occupation were determined by individual choice rather than by heredity. Nor was apportionment of wealth any longer determined on the artificial basis of status, but rather on the merit and value of the individual's service as determined by the market. With the establishment of peaceful relations among nations and with the spread of industrialism, economic autonomy disappeared; protectionism was replaced by free-trade policies: and divisions between nationalities weakened. In sharp contrast with the character traits of the militant society were those now produced by the industrial phase: humanity, beneficence, honesty, independence, individual initiative, self-reliance, and a more qualified patriotism.

In *The Future Japan,* Tokutomi used Spencer's concept of evolution in social structure to describe the nature of change under way in Japan. Believing that Japan was subject to the same kinds of forces that Spencer had described in Western nations, he pictured Meiji Japan as moving from an aristocratic, militant social structure toward a democratic, industrial society.[38]

Tokutomi described Japan's traditional social organization as a classic example of the militant type of society whose despotic government regimented all social and economic relations. "Schoolchildren in our country are astonished by stories they hear from their teachers about Sparta. . . . They do not realize that the Japan of their ancestors was an even more thoroughgoing militant society than Sparta. . . . In all ages there has never been and there never will be a society like that of our ancestors. . . . The country was a military camp; everyone was either a soldier or a laborer for soldiers."[39] The vast hierarchy of Japan's militant society, which had submerged the individual in status relations, had been demoralizing: it had produced a docile, passive people incapable of individual initiative; it had wasted individual talents by making occupations hereditary and by requiring subordinate classes to labor in support of an idle, unproductive aristocracy.

The militant society had fostered a wasteful, stagnant economy by suppressing foreign trade, discouraging private commercial association, and inhibiting division of labor by fragmenting the country into mutually antagonistic units.

Tokutomi believed (with Spencer) that the controlling factor in the struggle for survival among nations was no longer brute force but economic strength. Therefore the conditions that had evoked the militant society were disappearing. Though admitting that there still was abundant evidence of militarism in Europe, Tokutomi nonetheless believed that the "trend of the times" (*jisei*)* was toward a world in which peaceful commercial competition among industrial nations would prevail. Countries that did not follow this trend would be dominated by the industrial nations.

Believing that the militant and industrial societies were mutually exclusive and that elements of the two could not successfully coexist, he argued that Japan must be entirely transformed. Although traits of an industrial social order had begun to emerge since the Meiji Restoration, vestiges of the traditional society were everywhere present. Tokutomi saw Japan in his own day as a battleground of the old and the new elements and lamented that his countrymen, misunderstanding the trend of the times, were trying to fuse these elements. He particularly lamented that his "friends and allies" in the People's Rights Movement distorted the "true Anglo-Saxon liberalism" by frequently subordinating the people's welfare to national prestige.[40] Their support of military adventure

---

* The concept of "*jisei*" had been used in Rai Sanyō's *Nihon gaishi* (1829) (which Tokutomi's father had often read to him) to denote a trend in human affairs, generated by past events, by which the most able and virtuous of men might have their aspirations frustrated. See Beasley and Pulleyblank, p. 262. In Fukuzawa's writings, *jisei* was often used to refer to "the general state of public opinion or the 'spirit of the times,' [which] inevitably exerted a limiting and determining influence on the actions of great men." Blacker, pp. 93–94. Tokutomi, under Spencer's influence, used the concept (as R. P. Dore has pointed out) to denote "a kind of dynamic force impelling society along a road of inevitable progression from the military to the productive form of society." Dore, *Education*, pp. 309–10, n. 3.

overseas revived militant traits in society and thus impeded the growth of individual rights and of the institutions of an industrial society. Preoccupation with national honor while problems of the people's well-being went unsolved was another remnant of the old habit of mind typified by the Tokugawa aphorism that "a warrior glories in honorable poverty."[41] Tokutomi moreover decried the "rich country—strong army" slogan, which summed up the national goals of Japanese leaders. He regarded these twin goals as contradictory, for establishing a large army would impede social progress by keeping alive militant traits. He argued that the world was leaving behind the era of military power and parochial nationalism, and that Japan's best course lay in transforming herself into a great industrial democracy.

In a long section of *The Future Japan,* Tokutomi cited Japan's many natural assets for pursuing industrial development. None of these assets were cultural; they concerned instead the physical geography of the country. He pointed to favorable aspects of climate, soil, and topography, but gave special attention to Japan's geographical position: "Our land is small; clearly, then, we cannot by our size dominate other countries; but our location affords us the opportunity of becoming the center of Asian trade."[42] Japan, he continued, was ideally situated for trade with China, Australia, Russia, and America; and the building of a transisthmian canal promised further advantages.

Tokutomi's view of the future, based on the notion of a universal pattern of social development, left little room for cultural diversity or for the free play of the unique qualities of a people. For example he expressed distaste for Japanese arts and crafts because he regarded them as products of a decadent and wasteful society. "People regard it as a source of pride that the fine arts are advanced in our country. But is it something to boast of? How is it that a poor country such as ours has produced such elegant arts so disproportionate to the national wealth? Only through aristocratic patronage. And why did such patronage exist? Because of mass poverty."[43] A Japanese ought not to feel pride in Kutani ware, silk brocade, or the splendor of Nikkō, for they were the products of an idle, unprogressive social order. Japan's unique arts and crafts were the result of an unequal and artificial distribution of wealth; and because they were incompatible with an industrial society, they should have no part in Japan's future cultural development.

Implicit in his writing was a conviction that the path of social progress was essentially unilinear, that it was uniform for all people, that as Japan advanced she would become more like the industrial societies of the West, and that her progress could be measured by her acquired similarities to England, France, and the United States. In short, these more advanced nations offered Japan an image of her own future. It was this way of thinking that led to his cultural alienation.

IV

The Future Japan quickly went through four printings; and Tokutomi, emboldened by the success of his writings, decided to close his Kumamoto school and again seek out a career in journalism in Tokyo. In contrast with his first attempt six years earlier, he could now count on influential acquaintances and financial backing. Accompanied by his parents (his father had retired), his bride (the daughter of a former Kumamoto prefectural official), and several of his followers and associates from the school, he moved to the capital in late 1886.[44]

He began at once to carry out plans for establishing a magazine patterned after the liberal American weekly he had read for many years, Edward L. Godkin's *Nation*. He named his magazine *Kokumin no tomo,* subtitling it in English *The Nation's Friend,* and formed a small group called the *Min'yūsha* (Friends of the Nation) to help him publish the magazine. The group was composed of Tokutomi's associates from Kumamoto

and a few young Christians, some of whom had, with Tokutomi, been protégés of Niijima Jō at Dōshisha. In its first
years, the Min'yūsha was dominated by Tokutomi, and served
primarily as a vehicle for his ideas. In 1890 it extended its
activities to include the publication of a daily newspaper, *Kokumin shimbun*; and the group grew with the addition of
other talented young men, including the novelist Tokutomi
Roka (1868–1927, Sohō's younger brother), the novelist Kunikida Doppo (1871–1908), and the journalist Yamaji Aizan
(1864–1917)—all of whom gave the Min'yūsha a breadth lacking in its first years.[45]

Kokumin no tomo infused the Japanese intellectual world
with a fresh, vigorous style of reformism clearly intended to
appeal to the new generation. For its first issue, which appeared in February 1887, Tokutomi wrote an inaugural editorial that sounded the major themes of the magazine—youth
and Westernism. He stated that Japan had reached a critical
point in her history. The energy of the Restoration leaders
was spent, and the momentum generated by twenty years of
reform was abating; the zeal of an enlightened and progressive
new generation was needed to recharge the reform spirit and
complete the transformation of Japanese society. Tokutomi
saw everywhere about him discordant elements—a jumble of
new and old, civilized and uncivilized, Western and Oriental
—which to him were evidence of the unfinished work of reform. Some Japanese were thinking new thoughts but behaving in the old way; others were behaving in a new way but
thinking in the old; churches were prospering, but so were
temples; there were advocates of Western music and theatre,
but people still played the samisen and attended kabuki. What
Tokutomi sought for Japanese society was a Westernization
of *all* its parts, with an inner consistency and a harmony of
purpose.

"Meiji youth," whom Tokutomi likened to orphans because
they had not had parents qualified to rear them in the new

social values, now had the task of building in Japan a wholly Western society. Youthful energy was needed to eliminate the disparities and inequalities that persisted in Japanese life. The material benefits of civilization, which were enjoyed in Western democracies by the common people, were monopolized in Japan by the upper classes. Indeed, "the great majority of the people . . . are quite indifferent. They are unaware of reforms in dress, in diet, in architecture, and in social intercourse."[46]

Youth likewise had to assume the initiative in revolutionizing Japanese politics. The early issues of *Kokumin no tomo* carried a series of editorials entitled "Youth and Politics in the New Japan," which urged the new generation to reject Oriental political practice. The old politics, the editorials said, were no more relevant than the haphazard methods of Chinese physicians, whereas Western politics, like Western science, were based on precise investigation. Oriental politics resembled more the responses of a soldier, a pursuit of expedients and rough-and-ready action; Western politics resembled the tactics of an industrialist, determined by contract and geared to demand. "The world is changing from government by decree to government by contract. . . . Thus both our society and our politics are breaking out of the Oriental style and are adopting the Western style."[47] Japanese youth, the editorials counseled, should emulate Western politicians, should learn their qualities of reason, self-reliance, and individual responsibility.

Heiminshugi, as Tokutomi called his ideas, may be thought of as a 'democratic' philosophy. Although clearly not democratic in the twentieth-century sense of espousing universal suffrage or economic equality, heiminshugi was democratic in that it rejected the old forms of social stratification, hereditary status, and formal rank.[48] It opposed coercive rule by a closed elite and advocated limited government. It held high hopes for a parliamentary government that would function through rational deliberation and enlightened legislation, with responsible ministries and an impartial, law-abiding administration. The philosophy opposed wars and military expenditures and supported an emerging internationalism. Heiminshugi favored a policy of laissez-faire economics, viewing government involvement in commerce with suspicion and advocating freedom of trade as the best way to increase the nation's wealth and standard of living. It expected that with industrialization would come a more open and flexible society in which economic rewards would be commensurate with individual talent and effort. Socially, heiminshugi hoped for the replacement of the extended hierarchical family groups by independent households consisting only of parents and children. It hoped as well for the emancipation of women.* It stood, above all, for a social ethic that would liberate the individual from group control and cultivate self-support, self-expression, and self-responsibility.

Tokutomi's ideas evoked an enthusiastic response from his generation. *Kokumin no tomo* was an immediate success. The first issue sold out three printings; and the magazine soon attained a circulation of well over ten thousand—an extraordinary number for the time.[49] At first it was published monthly, but as its popularity soared it appeared fortnightly, then every ten days, and at last weekly. The young Kitamura Tōkoku, a member of a rival literary group not always friendly to the Min'yūsha and its views, admitted in 1893 that "the influence of *Kokumin no tomo,* which has a circulation of tens of thou-

---

* Disparity between the sexes was a frequent subject of *Kokumin no tomo* concern. Tokutomi wrote in his first editorial: "In human life there are many for whom we can feel compassion. We pity the poor, the ignorant, the blind, and the deaf; and we commiserate with widows and orphans; but we have not yet been able to feel compassion for our Japanese women. In themselves they combine all the characteristics of those with whom we ordinarily sympathize. Who is poorer than they? For even if they live in splendid houses they have not the right to own property. Who is ignorant in the way they are? What have they to occupy their minds? With their eyes they cannot see the happenings in society. With their ears they cannot hear of conditions in the world. They have husbands, but they cannot enjoy the same pleasures. . . . Their obligations do not extend beyond the kitchen. Their pleasures are limited to several yearly visits to the theatre."

sands, is felt throughout the nation. In the Meiji period no one else has produced such influential writing. One cannot disagree with this, no matter how much one opposes that group."[50] Although exaggerating its circulation, Kitamura's comment suggests the success of the magazine.

Tokutomi, as a result, emerged as a leading spokesman of the new generation. The novelist Masamune Hakuchō (1879–1962) relates that "progressive youth leaned toward Sohō. His writings were read and almost memorized—even in the countryside."[51] He adds that "the name 'Min'yūsha' aroused in the hearts of the young a feeling of newness and freshness. Perhaps in the early Meiji period Fukuzawa had had this power, but the Min'yūsha captivated those of us youth who in the Meiji twenties [1887–97] were consumed by a love of study and reading."[52] Masamune writes that *Kokumin no tomo* and *Kokumin shimbun* greatly intensified his desire to go to Tokyo.[53] Yamaji Aizan recalled that he was in the mountainous countryside of Echizen when he first read *Kokumin no tomo* and that the magazine had so dazzled him that he became blind to the scenery of the area. In 1889 Yamaji visited Tokutomi and he later became a member of the Min'yūsha.[54] Maruyama Masao, the intellectual historian, tells of the indelible impression Tokutomi's writings made on his father, Maruyama Kanji (1880–1955), one of Japan's leading journalists.[55] The father was so deeply inspired by Tokutomi's ideas that he determined to leave his native village, although he was the eldest son, and go to Tokyo to make a career for himself. "Even now I cannot forget my elation," Maruyama Kanji wrote in 1941, "when at the age of fifteen or sixteen I read *Education of Youth in Nineteenth Century Japan* and *The Future Japan*."[56] The novelist Futabatei Shimei, a year Tokutomi's junior, was captivated by his writings, and during the summer of 1887 visited his house several times seeking his opinions of political and social trends.[57] (The vision of a New Japan that the Min'yūsha described in the 1880's was still so compelling a half-century

later that the intellectual historian Ienaga Saburō, oppressed
by the climate of the Pacific War years, found solace poring
over old copies of Kokumin no tomo.)[58]

The reform ethic of the Min'yūsha had an important influence as well on the first generation of Japanese socialist
leaders. A History of Japanese Socialism, published in 1907,
which Kōtoku Shūsui (1871–1911) helped write, acknowledged
Kokumin no tomo as the first publication to devote extensive
attention to the problems of Japanese society.[59] Testimony to
the magazine's influence on early socialists was also given by
Sakai Toshihiko (1870–1933), a companion of Kōtoku in the
socialist movement after the turn of the century. Sakai recorded in his autobiography the admiration he and his fellow
students in middle school in the late 1880's had felt for Tokutomi and for Kokumin no tomo.[60] European socialist movements of the 1890's were reported in Kokumin no tomo by a
correspondent in Paris and Brussels. These reports attracted
attention and were important in the development of Japanese
socialist thought.

Several contemporary observers commented on the appeal
the Min'yūsha had for youth from the provinces, who, buoyed
by the promise of a new age, streamed into Tokyo seeking advanced education and opportunities for new careers.[61] Tokutomi expressed special confidence in wealthy peasant sons (such
as himself), who, he said, constituted the majority of youth
studying in Tokyo; he predicted they would be the leaders of
a transformed Japanese society. Now that legal barriers to their
advance had been removed, he said, gōnō were in a preferred
position: they were qualified financially for the franchise and
for elected office; they already comprised the majority of prefectural assembly members; and they would dominate the national diet when it convened. Yet nothing assured the new
status of gōnō quite so much, according to Tokutomi, as their
means to finance an advanced Western education for their
sons. The old aristocracy had, by its impoverishment, lost

sway over education; and the "country gentry" (*inaka shinshi*) would become the new bearers and interpreters of culture. They were the "new middle class," and their experience in guiding village affairs had developed in them the qualities of self-sufficiency and enterprise needed to carry into effect the institutions adopted from the West.[62]

We must be careful not to attribute too much of the success of *Kokumin no tomo* to Tokutomi's essays,* for he often solicited contributions from well-known writers outside of the Min'yūsha. During its eleven years (1887–98), *Kokumin no tomo* carried articles by many of the leading thinkers and writers of the time, such as Nakae Chōmin, Ueki Emori, Uchimura Kanzō, Ōnishi Hajime, Taguchi Ukichi, Yano Fumio, Shimada Saburō, Niijima Jō, and Uemura Masahisa. Many of the occasional contributors were older intermediary figures who were nonetheless sympathetic with the reformism of the young Min'yūsha writers.

In addition to social and political commentary, *Kokumin no tomo* offered literary essays, reviews, short stories, and translations. These contributed to the magazine's popularity and afforded it a special importance in the development of modern Japanese literature. Mori Ōgai (1862–1922), Futabatei Shimei, Yamada Bimyō (1868–1910), and many other leading young literary figures published some of their early works here. The influence of Western literary trends and forms pervaded *Kokumin no tomo*: there were translations of Hugo, Turgenev, Dostoevsky, and others.

v

Tokutomi's thought was dominated by a negative image of Japan's traditional culture and the character traits it had bred.

---

* One finds in many reminiscences the observation that Tokutomi's fresh writing style was as much responsible for his appeal as were the ideas he expressed. Masamune Hakuchō recalls, for example, "I was even more captivated by Sohō's style than by his ideas, for in his literary and poetic qualities he was no less gifted than his younger brother." See "Sohō to Roka" in Masamune, VI, 152.

He disowned the Japanese past, finding in it none of the ingredients essential to a modern nation. His view was of a world
divided into perpetually warring old and new elements; there
existed in his mind a radical cleavage between the static traditional society, and the dynamic new society toward which he
saw Japan evolving. Japan was about to undergo a total
change, making a clean break with the past; and the new Japan
would be a wholly Western society. "Oriental elements are
disappearing," he wrote, "and Western elements are emerging."[63]

One searches Tokutomi's early writings in vain for some
sense of Japanese individuality that might give a modern Japanese pride. But one finds only a shameful negative identity:
the existence of unique Japanese cultural characteristics is
admitted, but their value is rejected. Traditional political
methods, ideas, art forms, values, and ways of handling human
relations are criticized and contrasted with distinctive Western
characteristics. Tokutomi was confident of a universal process
of social evolution that would mold all nations along like lines;
and hence he rejected the idea of preserving a Japanese cultural identity.

Were it not for the unmistakable evidence of the appeal and
broad acceptance of his views among members of the new generation, we might dismiss Tokutomi's extremism as a personal
aberration. But despite his expressed alienation from the traditions of the society in which he lived, Tokutomi clearly was
not a lonely, despairing figure estranged from his contempo-
raries. On the contrary, his special significance for us lies in
the representative nature of his thought. How was it, then,
that such a sweeping repudiation of the cultural heritage
found such widespread acceptance and approval among young
Japanese?

In the first place, Tokutomi's Westernism was a medium
for declaring the increased importance of youth in society. In
repudiating the traditional culture he was not only dispatch-

ing the past; he was also asserting the independence of youth from the authority of the adult generation. As education in the 1870's and 1880's imparted to young Japanese a knowledge and appreciation of a new culture, the wisdom and skills of their elders, formed in a previous phase of social development, became increasingly irrelevant, outmoded, remote, and discredited. In the rapid evolution toward an industrial society, it was often the most recent graduates of the new schools who had the knowledge necessary for the new professions. An advanced Western education was the special asset of youth, for it opened new avenues of advancement in a society that placed high value on rising in the world; it provided new forms of self-expression; and it offered new values and institutions consonant with an industrial society. Since in many ways they were beneficiaries to the passing of traditional culture, youth were naturally receptive to Tokutomi's faith in Westernism.

Second, the new generation was responsive to Tokutomi's ideas because he provided a new orientation that accorded with the historical experience of youth. The rapid tempo of change in the early Meiji period had disrupted their sense of continuity with the past, creating the impression of a sharp break in historical development. Having grown up amidst this disruption, young Japanese now required a new historical outlook that would somehow relate their unique experience to the past and the future and so provide a perspective for understanding and evaluating the significance of their time. Tokutomi's writings, particularly *The Future Japan*, reflected a concern with questions that had been raised by the accelerated process of history: he sought above all to understand the nature of change, to show what kind of happenings determined others and why, to explain the direction in which history was moving, and to foresee the outcome of the change under way in Japan.

He argued that the revolutionary transformation of Japan during his lifetime was related to a pattern of historical development perceptible in the West. Using Spencer's concepts of evolution in social structure, Tokutomi explained the change under way in Meiji Japan as a transition from the militant, aristocratic phase of society to the industrial, democratic phase. He believed, with Spencer, that passage to a new social order was an irreversible process impelled by universal historical forces (which Tokutomi variously called *jisei, hitsuzen no ikioi, tenka no taisei, sekai no kiun*). Tokutomi saw this view of historical causation as explaining an essential paradox of the Meiji Restoration: how, he asked (and historians still echo his question), was one to understand a feudal aristocracy's carrying out a social revolution so sweeping that its own privileges were eliminated in the process? He could see "no ordinary cause-and-effect relations" at work in the process of the Restoration. The leaders of the Restoration had formulated no a priori plan to overturn feudal society—for such a revolution would destroy their own privileged position. Instead, he explained, they had been swept along by inexorable historical forces, led in spite of themselves from one reform to another, so that they had "unwittingly laid the groundwork for transforming the aristocratic, militant society in our country into a democratic, industrial society."[64]

Masamune Hakuchō recalled that Tokutomi's historical outlook, though "fanciful" in retrospect, had accorded in the 1880's and 1890's with the hopes and expectations of youth like himself. The view of Japan as progressing toward the type of society already emergent in the industrial West and the conviction that the characteristics of this society were utterly at odds with those of the pre-1868 militant society in Japan justified the prevailing cultural alienation of the new generation. Likewise Tokutomi's belief that the impetus for this advance was to be found in universal forces of historical change rather than in the particular trends of national history implied that the process could not be restrained by the Japanese past; youth therefore were not hopelessly committed to what had transpired in their own national history. This confidence that they were in step with the times and unfettered by past generations accounts in part, I think, for the optimism and independence of the new generation and for the initial success of Tokutomi as its spokesman.

Chapter Three

PROBLEMS OF JAPANESE IDENTITY

THE NEW GENERATION in Meiji Japan was not of one mind. Some were not so eager to accept ideas of the sort espoused by Tokutomi. But this was not because they lacked understanding of Western civilization, nor because they clung to a traditional outlook. They were, in fact, strongly attracted to the liberating elements of Western culture and committed to extensive borrowing from the West. Rather, these young Japanese held aloof from Tokutomi's ideas because they were openly troubled by the implications of his total Westernism.

Like the Min'yūsha adherents, they felt a sense of uprootedness from Japanese cultural traditions. Of the three young intellectuals whom we shall discuss in this chapter, all had attended new Western-oriented schools from a young age. All had been subject to the influence of Western teachers, from whom they had learned Western languages, political theory, philosophy, history, and literature. Two of them had come from families long interested in Western studies. All spoke frequently of building a "New Japan" and all detested the conservative label that Tokutomi and others pinned on them. But despite their liberal backgrounds, they chose to resist the headlong rush to Westernism that many of their peers were embracing under similar circumstances.

At a time when Western nations were exerting pressure on

Japan through extraterritorial privilege, these young Japanese were painfully conscious of the self-effacing nature of the trend toward Westernism. They argued that a strong national spirit was essential to self-defense in an age of imperialism, that weak-willed association with Westerners was dangerous as well as humiliating, and that national independence demanded the preservation of cultural autonomy. Their thinking was informed by studies of Western history, which taught that European states jealously preserved their individual cultural traditions and pride of nationality despite the apparent uniform trend toward industrialization and democratization. The craze in Japan for Western things, which Sansom describes as an "almost fanatical phase"[1] of popular sentiment in the 1870's and 1880's, reinforced the misgivings these young intellectuals had for the more sophisticated forms of Westernism. Even more than by the popular aping of Western manners and customs, the revulsion they felt for Westernism was provoked by their government's eager attempts to achieve early revision of the unequal treaties by accommodating to demands of the treaty powers that Japan adopt Western administrative, legal, and commercial practices. To accept cultural subservience to the West would destroy, they believed, that cohesive spirit which resulted from pride in a common heritage and which was a vital resource of the nation-state.

But though they suffered these misgivings, these young intellectuals and their followers could offer no clear-cut alternative to Westernism. They banded together and formed a group opposing the Westernization of Japanese society, but they were unable to achieve the kind of clear and united advocacy that characterized the Min'yūsha. They wished to preserve a distinct Japanese culture, but there was much disagreement among them over what of value was redeemable from their heritage. They shared a belief in the existence of a unique Japanese character formed by historical and environmental forces, and they argued that the strength and vitality of the nation depended upon its preservation and upon making all borrowings compatible with it; but there was considerable uncertainty among them in defining this character.

These young Japanese were (to borrow a phrase from Professor Commager[2]) in search of a usable past. They wanted somehow to restore nourishing ties with the cultural heritage from which they had been cut off. They sought to reevaluate Japanese tradition, to find something in their national past that they and the world could esteem and that need not be sacrificed in the course of modernization, something by virtue of which they could define their uniqueness and thus feel themselves the equals of Westerners.

Shiga Shigetaka (1863–1927), Miyake Setsurei (1860–1945), and Kuga Katsunan (1857–1907), all members of the new generation, were influential publicists who sought to refute the Westernizing theories of Tokutomi and others. The purpose of this chapter is to examine their upbringing and education and to understand the difficulties and dilemmas they encountered in developing their early ideas.

I

Curiously, one of the first challenges to Tokutomi's thought appeared in the early pages of his own *Kokumin no tomo*. Following the practice of the American magazine *Nation*, Tokutomi had established a column of "Special Correspondence" for which he solicited articles from writers outside of his own circle; and he invited Shiga Shigetaka to write for this column in the tenth issue of the journal.[3] Shiga had gained recognition with a published account of his travels through the South Pacific. In his treatise *Conditions in the South Seas* (*Nanyō jiji*), published in 1887, Shiga had emphasized the advantages of Japan's island position for her development as an industrial, trading nation like England; and perhaps Tokutomi expected an article of this viewpoint when he invited Shiga to contribute to the "Special Correspondence" column.

But Shiga chose to "put aside for the time any discussion of the expansion and encouragement of agriculture and industry and to turn instead to another program for securing the foundation of the nation—a policy that would cultivate esteem for Japan. In this essay, entitled "How Can Japan Be Made Japan?", he warned of the danger of thoroughgoing Westernization:

In Japan as it is today, with reform being advocated for every aspect of society, my fear is that, as these reforms are instituted, scorn will gradually develop for things that are uniquely Japanese. We shall see a tendency to cherish those countries that inspire the reformers, and to neglect our own heritage. . . . If reformers are the patriots they claim to be, why do they busy themselves only with imitating?[4]

Even as he wrote this article, Shiga was joining with other young intellectuals opposed to extreme Westernization to plan a magazine that came to be regarded as the rival of *Kokumin no tomo*. As the editor of this new magazine, *Nihonjin*, Shiga later wrote: "I enthusiastically urge the importation of Western ways, but I cannot agree with the argument that there is nothing of beauty, no special talent, nothing refined in Japanese civilization and that we must therefore imitate Western styles, uproot the whole of Western civilization and transplant it in Japanese soil."[5]

Shiga was born in 1863 in what is now Aichi Prefecture.[6] He was the eldest son of a scholarly, high-ranking Okazaki fief warrior, Shiga Jūshoku, who died while Shiga was still young. Despite the straitened circumstances in which he was left, Shiga received an education through the help of his father's friends. At the age of eleven the boy was sent to Tokyo and was enrolled in a private academy. Later he spent two years in the Tokyo University Preparatory School (Tōkyō Daigaku Yobimon), and in 1880 he entered Sapporo Agricultural School (Sapporo Nōgakkō) in Hokkaido. (Why he left the Preparatory School, which was known as a ladder to success in Meiji society, and made the long trek to the new school in Hokkaido is not clear, but one of his classmates later recalled that he had been lured by the location of the school. He had a lifelong love of hiking, exploring, and travel; he was restless, and Hokkaido was Japan's new frontier.)

Many of the older students at Sapporo, including Uchimura Kanzō and Nitobe Inazō, had become Christians, under the influence of Dr. William Clark, an American who had come to Japan in 1876 to take charge of the newly founded school. When Shiga enrolled, however, Clark had already returned to the United States. Shiga himself did not become a Christian; on the contrary, the austere spirit of the school rankled him. Though many of the students signed pledges not to smoke or drink, Shiga remained unreconstructed.

The school was strongly Western-oriented. English was used almost exclusively, and, as Shiga later wryly recalled, "Chinese learning was excluded, and . . . my knowledge of Japanese and Chinese literature was gained entirely outside the school."[7] But if the school left unsatisfied his desire for traditional studies, it nevertheless stimulated his interest in the natural sciences. After his graduation in 1884, he held for a short time a position as instructor of botany at the Nagano Prefectural Middle School. In December of the following year, still restless, he gained permission from the navy to accompany the warship *Tsukuba* on a training mission to the Korean straits. This was the first of Shiga's many trips abroad. In 1886 he was aboard the same ship on its ten-month cruise through the southern Pacific. Stops were made in the Carolines, Australia, New Zealand, Samoa, Fiji, and Hawaii.

Soon after he returned from the voyage, Shiga published *Conditions in the South Seas*, in which he sought to convey to his readers a sense of the importance of geographical environment to Japan's future. He lamented that "when reading books in our country, one finds many concerning Europe and America, but . . . only one or two regarding the history and geography of the southern Pacific."[8] Shiga was impressed by the perils as well as the potentialities for Japan in the South Pacific. He observed that "the white race" dominated these islands because the natives too often had no will to resist invaders or to preserve their own independence.[9] "If the colored races do not now exert themselves," he warned, "then ultimately the world will become the private possession of the white race."[10] Japan must rouse herself to her destiny, which was no less great in the Orient than England's was in the West. Shiga called for a policy to secure "the foundations of the nation by choosing a task that comports with her geographical position."[11] He urged the building of a New Japan that would be based on commerce.[12]

Shiga could, therefore, agree with Tokutomi that Japan's mission must be to develop herself as an industrial and trading nation. But the danger in naïve and weak-willed association with Westerners and their culture had also impressed Shiga during his voyage. Consequently, when invited by Tokutomi to write an article for the "Special Correspondence" column of *Kokumin no tomo*, he used the opportunity to condemn Westernism. Shiga wrote that natives in New Zealand, for instance, had become so enchanted with Western culture that they had lost the spirit and will to resist English domination. He concluded his article by urging "the cultivation of praise for the superlative natural beauty of Japan and the development of affection for the nation."[13]

We shall see that the influence of Japan's physical geography on her culture and national character increasingly preoccupied Shiga's thought. Amidst the great flux that had disrupted the Japan in which he had grown up, her geographical position as an island nation off the Asian continent and her "unparalleled natural beauty" had remained constant assets. They now were elements that might be used to bridge the gap between Japan's present and her past.

II

Another young Japanese who, despite his deep study of and admiration for Western civilization, could not accept the Westernizing theories of Tokutomi was Miyake Yūjirō. (He came to be known more often by his pen name, Miyake Setsurei.)[14] Miyake and Tokutomi are frequently compared because of their leading roles in Japanese journalism. Both were born on the eve of the Meiji Restoration, and both lived to see the Occupation of Japan following World War II. Both combined serious scholarly careers with popular journalism. Tokutomi was an astonishingly prolific historian and biographer; Miyake was untiring as a historian-philosopher. In many respects, however, they remained intellectual opponents throughout their long, parallel careers.

Miyake was born in Kanazawa in 1860, the third son of a samurai. Miyake's father, a former pupil of the famous Confucian scholar Koga Dōan in Edo, was physician for the chief minister of the *daimyō*. Medicine was the family profession on Miyake's mother's side as well; but whereas his father practiced the traditional Chinese methods, his mother's family was known for its progressive spirit, her two brothers having studied in Nagasaki under the German physician Siebold.

Miyake's early education was of the traditional type, emphasizing memorization of Confucian classics and long hours of calligraphy practice. When he was eleven he entered the French Academy in Kanazawa; later he attended the prefectural English school and then the Aichi English School in Nagoya. At the age of sixteen he entered Tokyo University Preparatory School (which Shiga entered soon after). Miyake recalled in his autobiography that at these schools there were mostly foreign instructors using foreign textbooks: "At Nagoya there were many American instructors; in the case of geography, for instance, we had to memorize the mountains, rivers, and cities of each state in the United States. . . . When I transferred to the school in Tokyo, there were even more foreigners, and they increasingly confused learning with the study of language."[15]

Consequently Miyake spent much of his time in the library of the nearby Confucian temple, Yushima Seidō. His primary interest at this time was in Oriental philosophy, and he was so engrossed that he allowed a change in the school system to pass by unnoticed. When he was called to account for failing to observe the new regulations, Miyake angrily withdrew from the school and returned to Kanazawa. Later he reentered the school; and after completing the preparatory course, he entered Tokyo University in 1879. He concentrated on philosophy (Indian and Chinese philosophy as well as Western and Japanese), and was already concerned with what was to become a lifelong preoccupation—an attempt to synthesize the precepts of Eastern and Western philosophy.

Many of Miyake's new teachers were foreigners, the most remarkable being the young American Ernest Fenollosa. Only twenty-five and fresh from Harvard, Fenollosa had arrived in August 1878 to hold the first chair in philosophy at Tokyo University. Miyake later recalled in his autobiography that the young teacher's enthusiasm and eloquence immediately attracted the attention of Japanese students.[16] Fenollosa, for his part, confided his regard for his intense young students to a former Harvard classmate in a letter written in 1880:

I found the University in remarkably fine condition, considering that the country had so lately emerged from what must be termed, at least relatively speaking, a state of profound ignorance. Some two hundred students were at work in the special elective courses, reading English books, and speaking and writing that language fluently. A finer set of young men, or more earnest workers and keener thinkers, cannot, I venture to say, be found in any university in the world.[17]

Using Francis Bowen's *Modern Philosophy* as a text, Fenollosa lectured on the development of Western thought from Descartes to Hegel. Miyake wrote that this introductory survey was "epoch-making" to Japanese ears.[18] Fenollosa who had formed a Spencer club at Harvard, devoted much of his teaching to this particular English philosopher. (Toyama Shōichi, who had studied in England and at the University of Michi-

gan, was another teacher who gave Miyake large doses of Spencerian sociology.)

It is difficult to determine the extent of Fenollosa's influence on Miyake—beyond introducing him to the study of
Western philosophy. He may have influenced Miyake's later
arguments for the preservation of Japan's unique artistic talents. For the most part, though, Miyake made light of lectures:
"I felt that knowledge was largely acquired in libraries."[19] On
his own, Miyake delved into the writings of Spencer, Hegel,
Guizot, Buckle, and Carlyle.

An essay Miyake published in 1883, the year of his graduation from Tokyo University—it may have been his senior thesis—deserves close attention here, for it reveals his struggle
with the problem of Japanese character. The essay was entitled
"Characteristics of the Japanese People" and was published
under a pseudonym in a prominent intellectual magazine.[20]
Miyake was seeking historical reasons for Japan's failure to
progress as swiftly as Western countries. Like Tokutomi, he
felt there were flaws in the traditional character of the people.
Some might boast of Japanese character traits, he said, but if
one dispassionately examined the characteristics of the Japanese people, one in fact found few that were excellent:

Our own countrymen—not to mention foreigners—have often
pointed out the Japanese people's lack of perseverance, their friv-
olousness, their content with small successes, and their constant
imitation. It has been said . . . that although Japanese appear better on the surface since the Restoration, they are in fact the same
people as before: people haughty toward those below and currying
toward those above, untutored and lecherous; people who find no
enjoyment in reading, who are lacking in perseverance, self-reliance, and imagination; people who break promises, who lack ca-
maraderie and are difficult to unite; people who lack inventive-
ness.[21]

Miyake conceded that such a view might be excessive, but insisted that much of it was true.

Unlike Tokutomi, however, Miyake was unwilling to urge

that Japanese simply look to Westerners, follow their example, and adopt their characteristics. Such a policy would but increase the Japanese humiliation; moreover, it ignored the process by which racial characteristics were formed. National character was a product of a people's environment. The past was not so easily escaped as some hoped; in fact:

If our people had from the very beginning lived in the Japanese islands and had received their stimuli wholly from the geography, climate, soil, and features of this land, then no matter how mean and ugly their characteristics it would be hopeless to try to change them. Fortunately, it is not difficult to show that this is not the case.[22]

Miyake's purpose was to show, first, that the Japanese were descendants of the Mongol race and, second, that the environment of Mongolia had shaped undesirable traits still recognizable in the Japanese. To prove the Japanese were descendants of the Mongols, he devoted sections of his essay to a detailed examination of similarities in legends, customs, language, and physique. Because the environment of Mongolia had been suited only to nomadism, it had discouraged collective enterprise, division of labor, and development of trade and manufactures. It had encouraged the mere imitation of advanced civilizations rather than the development of a native imagination or invention.

Japanese therefore were handicapped by characteristics acquired prior to their migration from the continent. Miyake implied, however, that the Japanese people, now living in a wholly different environment, might be able to overcome those vestigial characteristics and thus "increase [their] inventive nature, preserve qualities of sturdy honesty, and nurture the spirit of independence."[23] He suggested a reassessment of the national character in terms of its development since the Japanese people migrated to the islands.

Miyake knew that he would be criticized by those who clung to belief in the divine origin of the Japanese people:

Those people who have recently been investigating the origins of our civilization and discussing our customs and attitudes have generally been satisfied to investigate things merely within the Japanese archipelago. . . . They give attention only to immediate causes. . . . Perhaps they fear for the dignity of the Imperial Household, or fear being seen as unpatriotic, or believe that ancient happenings are vague and cannot be ascertained. What foolishness! The imperial dignity is affected by political movements. Occasionally pure academic theory may have a direct effect on popular political ideas, but today people are not misled by interpretations of the *Kojiki*, so one can rest at ease. . . . To be unaware of our ancient past is disgraceful blindness. . . . Without a mirror we cannot see our own ugliness.[24]

In subsequent essays, as we shall see, Miyake went on to search for characteristics, developed during the history of the Japanese in the archipelago, that could be deemed honorable and useful in the modern world.

A gifted student, Miyake had attracted the attention of his teacher Toyama, who helped him attain a position after graduation in the Compilation Bureau of Tokyo University. There he was charged with drawing up a history of Japanese Buddhism. But as a result of an administrative reorganization, his work came to be supervised by the Ministry of Education, and Miyake found that he lacked freedom for research. In 1887, dissatisfied with government policies, he resigned,[25] and in a short time he found positions lecturing in philosophy at the Tōkyō Semmon Gakkō (now Waseda University) and at the Tetsugakkan (now Tōyō University). At this time, Shiga Shigetaka was teaching at the Tōkyō Eigo Gakkō (Tokyo English School), having returned from his voyage to the southern Pacific.

A small group of teachers at these schools—Miyake and Shiga and eleven others, many of them also recent graduates of Sapporo Agricultural School or Tokyo University—discovered among themselves a common concern over what they felt was a spineless attitude on the part of their government toward the

Western powers. They were disturbed also by the prevailing adulation of Western culture among large numbers of Japanese. They joined together in early 1888 to form the Seikyōsha (Society for Political Education) and began fortnightly publication of the magazine *Nihonjin* (The Japanese), which quickly came to be recognized as the intellectual rival of *Kokumin no tomo*.[26] In contrast with the immediate wide acceptance of *Kokumin no tomo*, however, *Nihonjin* in these early days distributed no more than 500 or 600 copies. (Later its circulation is said to have reached several thousand.[27])

The Seikyōsha, moreover, did not start life with the unity of viewpoint that Tokutomi's Min'yūsha had enjoyed. Although all of its original members opposed extreme forms of Westernization, there was as yet little agreement among them concerning what they favored as alternatives. Because of the diversity of their views, the statement of purpose in the first issue of *Nihonjin*, which appeared April 3, 1888 (the anniversary of the Emperor Jimmu's passing), was expressed in quite general terms:

Japan's present age is one of beginnings. Although government is increasingly complicated, the most immediate and pressing problem before us is to determine the attitude of the Japanese people toward the present and the future. This will be reflected in a choice of religion, education, arts, politics, and system of production that is compatible with the ideas of the Japanese people and suitable to the environment of Japan.[28]

The articles that followed in this and succeeding issues of *Nihonjin* clarified the problem that concerned all members of the Seikyōsha. Inoue Enryō (1858–1919), who had graduated from Tokyo University in 1885 and had founded the Tetsugakkan, wrote in the first issue of his concern over the trend toward total Westernization of Japanese society: "Our people are no longer Japanese. The country is no longer Japan. . . . If we want Japan always to be Japan, we must preserve Japanese spirit and thought, Japanese customs and traditions."[29]

Inoue, already deeply involved in studies that were to make him one of modern Japan's outstanding Buddhist philosophers, felt that Buddhism was "chief among the important factors that make Japan Japan; maintaining and propagating Buddhism is the best way that the Japanese can be made Japanese and that the Japanese can be made independent." Few others in the group agreed with Inoue that Buddhism was the essential aspect of Japanese civilization that ought to be preserved.* After all, was it not also foreign in origin?

They were agreed, however, on the target of their criticism. Kunitomo Shigeaki (1861–1909), one of the original Seikyōsha members, called attention to two dangerous types of Westernization, or "foreign-worship"; the two differed in their origins but not in their inherently destructive results for Japan. One type was found in political behavior: he had in mind government leaders who acquiesced to foreign demands in negotiating revision of the unequal treaties. The second type, which Kunitomo identified with the Min'yūsha, was similarly acquiescent in its political theory: though intellectually more sophisticated than the first type, its adherents nonetheless

would have Japan forfeit her national character and destroy all elements of Japanese society. . . . Their essential belief is that Western civilization is the most advanced in the world and that if we want our country to follow the path to civilization, we must learn from Western countries. To them, moderate measures like those of the eclectic approach are inadequate, for there is no such thing as a unique national civilization. . . . In their theory there is "mankind" but not "nation," "world" but not "state."[30]

Although admitting that the Min'yūsha's argument had an exciting liberal appeal, Kunitomo called it unrealistic at a time when nations were struggling to preserve their existence.

---

* One member of the original Seikyōsha group who did agree with Inoue was Shimaji Mokurai (1838–1911). He was older than the others and was a Buddhist priest of the Nishi Honganji Shin sect. Shimaji provided initial funds for publication of *Nihonjin*, but he was not active in the Seikyōsha after its early days. See "Seikyōsha kaiko zadankai," *Nihon oyobi Nihonjin*, Apr. 1, 1938.

It could, in fact, be every bit as dangerous as political acquies-cence.

Tanabashi Ichirō,* another founder of the Seikyōsha, ex-pressed the need all felt for establishing "a national ideology." The values that had buttressed Tokugawa society had lost their cohesive power, and no satisfactory substitute had been found:

What *is* today's Japan? The old Japan has already collapsed, but the new Japan has not yet risen. What religion do we believe in? What moral and political principles do we favor? It is as if we were wandering in confusion through a deep fog, unable to find our way. Nothing is worse than doubt or blind acceptance.[31]

Japan had progressed materially, but she now lacked the bind-ing spirit that grew out of an adherence to common principles. "Without that," he concluded, "we are not a nation." His sense of the need for moral direction was much like Toku-tomi's, for as young men whose society was in the midst of sweeping change, they both felt the need for a standard of val-ues that would provide moral certitude. It was in their response to that need that the Min'yūsha and the Seikyōsha members differed.

III

The problem of how to state clear alternatives to Western-ism vexed those who wrote in the early issues of *Nihonjin*. In an intellectual history of the Meiji era written in 1897,[32] Taka-yama Chogyū (1871–1902) credited Seikyōsha members with prompting reflection on indiscriminate borrowing from the

---

* Tanabashi, whose mother was a distinguished educator, established a private middle school in 1889 and served as its principal for several decades. Like many of the other Seikyōsha founders, he was not a frequent contributor after the early issues of *Nihonjin*. For a brief biography of Tanabashi, see Fujiwara Ki-yozō, *Kyōiku shisō gakusetsu jimbutsu shi* (Tokyo, 1943–44), I, 544; III, 819–20. For Tanabashi's reminiscences about the founding of the Seikyōsha, see the fifti-eth anniversary issue: "Seikyōsha kaiko zadankai," *Nihon oyobi Nihonjin*, Apr. 1, 1938.

West, but he charged them with failing to provide any clear concept of the Japanese nationality that they sought to preserve.*

Shiga Shigetaka, who served as the first editor of *Nihonjin*, tried to clarify the objectives of the Seikyōsha. He sought something that Japanese could define as their uniqueness, something they could identify with and hold up with pride to the world. The words he frequently used to express this objective were *"kokusui hozon."* "Kokusui," a term that soon gained currency, he used as the equivalent of the English word "nationality." Thus the phrase meant "preservation of nationality" or "preservation of the national essence."

Knowing that great civilizations had always borrowed from others to strengthen themselves, Shiga did not oppose a certain amount of borrowing; but he felt it must be consonant with preserving the kokusui. History seemed to demonstrate that when a people lost its national character, its defeat and submission were inevitable. The Greeks, Shiga wrote, began their downfall when they became Africanized. The Romans imitated the Greeks, and thus opened the way to their own defeat. The Koreans fell under the domination of China by imitating Chinese civilization without assimilating it to their own conditions.[33]

Shiga denied being reactionary or even conservative. "I am a red-blooded and virile soul and will not yield an inch to another man in my delight for daring enterprises."[34] Again, he insisted: "I am not a conservative; no, I am rather a reformer." He refused to express support for Shinto, Buddhist, or Confucian ideas. Yet if he claimed to reject the old and the traditional, how did he define "kokusui"?

* Takayama had his own axe to grind. He argued that his ideas about Japanese nationality, which he referred to as *Nihonshugi* (Japanism), had superseded Seikyōsha ideas. In contrast to the Seikyōsha's definition of the Japanese nationality, Takayama's was narrow and explicit. His views will be dealt with in Chapter 9.

In the second issue of *Nihonjin* Shiga wrote an essay entitled "Declaration of Principles Held by *Nihonjin*":

The influence of all the environmental factors of Japan—her climate and her weather conditions, her temperature and humidity, the nature of her soil, the configuration of her land and water, her animal and plant life and her landscape, as well as the interaction of all these factors, the habits and customs, the experiences, the history and development of thousands of years—the totality of all these factors has gradually, imperceptibly, developed in the Japanese race inhabiting this environment a unique kokusui. This so-called kokusui germinated, grew, and developed through adaptation to the influence of all environmental factors; the kokusui has been transmitted within the Japanese race from antiquity, has been purified, refined, and preserved down to the present. If it grows, is nurtured and encouraged, and becomes a foundation and norm for the present and future evolution and betterment of the Japanese, the process will be no more than the proper application of the fundamental principle of biology.[35]

For Shiga, Japan's physical geography was the most important factor in the shaping of the Japanese nationality. He also argued that because the kokusui had developed organically, only innovation of a gradual kind was permissible.

But though Shiga had explained how the national essence was formed and how it grew, he still had not stated what it was. Convinced of Japan's uniqueness and certain of the factors that had produced it, he nevertheless seemed uncertain how actually to define the national character. At one point in his early *Nihonjin* articles he vaguely defined the national essence as an *"artistic sense"* (*bijutsuteki no kannen*). Western civilization, he said, was based on science and mathematics and was therefore dependent on analytical methods:

This analytical influence creeps into all phases of Western society; ... thus it is selfish, commercial, and mercenary. The result is destructive to morals and ethics. Japanese civilization is diametrically opposed to the West's. Its foundation is in harmony, which is the source of art. Art assembles and harmonizes analyzed elements. . . . We have the writings of Murasaki Shikibu, the pictures of the Kano school, ceramics, lacquerware, *sashimi*, and *kuchitori*. All of these have an artistic sense.[36]

This definition, however, appears to have left unsatisfied Shiga's own need for a clear, dynamic explanation of Japanese identity, for he did not explain it this way in later articles.

Because it was not clearly defined in its special meaning for the Japanese, the concept of kokusui was open to broad misinterpretation—there was considerable divergence even within the Seikyōsha itself. One member, Kikuchi Kumatarō (1864–1904), who had graduated from Sapporo Agricultural School in 1885, admitted the difficulties raised by such disparity:

It has been a fixed rule of our group that each person sign his name to his essay, and thus the views are clearly only his own. Kokusui-shugi is the cherished view of our group, but we have not yet set forth a manifesto: for one thing, this is an important problem and should not be decided hastily; for another, we hold varying points of view.[37]

Because the members had not explicitly defined their views, he continued, the word "kokusui" had been misinterpreted by people outside the group. Some outsiders were arguing that anything in the past history of the Japanese people that could be boasted of to foreigners was a part of the national essence. Others taunted the Seikyōsha as a "reactionary" group.

Kikuchi attempted his own definition: "Kokusui is a unique, commonly held national spirit. It is intangible emotions, ideas, and intentions. It is something that cannot be manifested by such material relics as the Great Buddha of Nara. . . . The kokusui, then, is a particular national spirit that cannot be copied in other countries."[38] England's kokusui, he suggested, was "the spirit of independence and self-government that binds her polity in cooperative unity." As for Japan, he believed that her kokusui was the people's feeling toward the Imperial Household. "Other than this there is no unique attribute that need be maintained and promoted, none that can stand between us and the world and protect the nation and bring it glory."

Prodded by growing criticism and misinterpretation of its aims, the Seikyōsha ultimately issued a manifesto:

We seek to overcome the current evils by admonishing the so-called Westernizers who see the superb beauty of another country and forget the excellence of their own. We differ from those who rashly believe that preservation of the kokusui means merely preservation of old things inherited from our ancestors and who mistakenly believe that we want to resist Western things and close the road to innovation and progress.[39]

Kokusui, the statement continued, had three attributes: first, it was an intangible spirit; second, it was the special property of one country; third, it could not be copied by another country.

Some of the members must have been aware of their dilemma. A mystic concept of a national essence could easily lead to thoroughgoing conservatism.[40] How could "kokusui" be defined if not empirically, by appeal to Japanese history and tradition? Change could easily be stigmatized as alien to the national essence; and it was painful for the Seikyōsha members to see their ideas championed by opponents of change. After all, the manifesto declared, "We members were largely brought up on Western literature and science; it is easier for us to read the novels of Scott than to read the Genji Monogatari."

Caught, then, in this dilemma—on one side the deeply felt need for a separate national identity that could be explicitly defined only in terms of the traditional Japan, on the other side their estrangement from much of Japan's past—the Seikyōsha could state only a vague resolution: "Even though we adopt the modern conveniences of the West, even though we make use of Western knowledge, none of us must forfeit the spirit of the Japanese." This "Japanese spirit" was still undefined, but the term concealed the dilemma while the manifesto

moved on quickly to conclude with an explanation of their
method: Japan should borrow, but she should assimilate the
borrowings and make them Japanese.

The ambiguity of the Seikyōsha's language, together with
the diverse views of its original membership, left the aims of
the group open to interpretation and, quite often, to misinterpretation. Miyake later complained that from the time "kokusui hozon" had first been used by *Nihonjin* writers in 1888 it
had been a catchword for conservatism; their effort to preserve
a sense of "national individuality" in the modern world was
distorted by traditionalists and made a pretext for opposition
to needed reform.[41] Several observers recorded that the Seikyōsha had many partisans among Confucianists, Buddhists,
Shintoists, and unreconstructed samurai.[42] Yamaji Aizan recalled that although "the conservatism of the late 1880's represented the development of national consciousness" and although "the leaders of the group had an understanding of
Western culture," their intentions were initially misunder-
stood, and "many backwoods priests and Confucianists were
delighted to plunge into the movement."[43] In hopes of ending
this misrepresentation of their ideas, *Nihonjin* writers began
replacing "kokusui hozon" (preservation of nationality) with
the more positive phrase "kokusui kenshō" (promotion of nationality).[44] To overcome the misunderstanding, however,
what was really needed was a clearer, more definite expression of Japanese identity.

IV

Nihonjin, then, came to be dominated by Miyake and Shiga.
At the same time another periodical, one with similar views,
was gaining prominence; its editor, Kuga Minoru (pen name
Katsunan), is the third important figure we must consider in
the context of problems of Japanese identity. An articulate
young editor, Kuga became a powerful ally of the Seikyōsha
and its cause. His newspaper, the *Tōkyō dempō*, joined with

Nihonjin in a determined effort to answer the Westernism of Tokutomi and others. Kuga's ties with Miyake and Shiga were so close that he can be considered an affiliate of the Seikyōsha group.

Kuga was born in the castle town of Hirosaki in northern Honshu in 1857.[45] His father was a Buddhist priest and a tea master for the lord of Hirosaki *han*. Kuga's family, like Miyake's, combined traditional scholarship with an early interest in the new learning. Kuga's grandfather, court physician for the lord, was known for his erudition. A cousin of Kuga's father pioneered the introduction of Western medicine to northern Japan and established the first school for Western studies in Hirosaki.

Kuga was educated at home until he was fourteen, receiving the traditional training of a samurai's son. Then he entered a local school, where he studied Chinese classics with a prominent Confucian scholar. At sixteen he entered Tōō Gijuku, the former fief school, which farsighted officials had converted to a school for Western studies. In 1874 Kuga entered the Miyagi Normal School in Sendai; but after spending nearly three years there, he withdrew angrily following a sharp disagreement with its director. From there, he went to Tokyo to study French and French law at the Shihōshō Hōgakkō, a law school later absorbed into Tokyo University.

In 1879, while Kuga was at the law school, some of his fellow students staged a demonstration in opposition to school policies. When the ringleaders were punished, Kuga, though he had not participated in the demonstration, came to their defense by criticizing the school's director. As a result Kuga was dismissed. He returned to his home in the far north to work for a time as an editor of an Aomori newspaper.

Returning to Tokyo in 1881, he found work as a translator in the Archives Bureau (later the Official Gazette Bureau) of the government. His most important translation, published in 1885, was of a treatise by Joseph de Maistre on the theory of sovereignty (*Shuken genron*). (His reading of Maistre and other conservative French philosophers had an important influence on his intellectual development.) Soon after Kuga had completed this project, his bureau chief, Aoki Teizō, was replaced; and Kuga resigned over dissatisfaction with government policies. With the help of other malcontents, Kuga became the editor of a newspaper that Aoki managed, the daily *Tōkyō shōgyō dempō* (Tokyo Commercial Telegraph). Kuga shortened the name to *Tōkyō dempō*; and under his guidance it appeared for the first time April 9, 1888, just six days after the first issue of *Nihonjin*.

In the first issue of the *Tōkyō dempō* Shiga wrote a congratulatory message for the newspaper and its new editor: "The *Tōkyō dempō* proclaims the same views as we do, holds the same principles, and thus seeks to determine ideas about Japan's future course. . . . There may occasionally be differences in means between the *Tōkyō dempō* and *Nihonjin*, but in their ultimate objectives they are united." From the start there was close rapport between the two publications. Their offices soon occupied the same building, and Kuga and his associates were thought of by others as part of the Seikyōsha group. (And for the purpose of this study, they may hereafter be considered as such.)

In an important series of editorials published in June 1888 and entitled "Crossroads in the Progress of Japanese Civilization," Kuga explained the issues uppermost in his mind. He pointed out that the standard used for adopting Western things had changed since the early days of the opening of the country. At that time it had been based on a simple spirit–matter formula: Western science was demonstrably superior and should be adopted, but Eastern morals remained valid and should be preserved. But Kuga asserted that relationships in society had never been so simple nor so easily separated as this formula had implied. To hope that contact with the West could be limited to "inanimate machines" was unrealistic:

As exposure to foreign ways gradually increases, spiritual influences are felt along with the material, practical ones. When not
only weapons, medical arts, railroads, and the telegraph are
adopted, but also laws and scholarly theories, diet, clothing, and
living habits, then it is impossible to exercise judgment as before
according to simple formulas. That is because along with these
things there always come values and tastes that clash with the customs of one's own country.[46]

Kuga argued that because of the change in the nature of borrowing there was a need for a new formula. "We are," he said,
"at a great crossroads that will determine the fate of Japanese
culture."[47]

He went on to identify two plausible alternatives currently
being espoused by Meiji youth. One view often suggested was
of Japan as a backward country with no choice but to follow in
the train of Western culture. This school of thought held that
an eclectic position was untenable because society was not a
"patchwork." Japan could not borrow only what she considered were the strong points of Western society, because there
was a certain uniting spirit that interrelated all things in any
culture and rendered futile any effort to select and adopt only
the best elements.

Kuga defended an opposing viewpoint. He argued that
there was no valid comparison between Japan and the West,
nor between Japanese culture and Western culture; the valid
comparisons were between Japan and France, Japan and England, etc. Although the West might seem monolithic to the
Japanese, in actuality the people of different European countries fiercely preserved their own separate nationalities.*
Westernizers, he claimed, were making a patchwork of Japa-

---

* Okakura Tenshin (1862–1913), a graduate of Tokyo University in 1880, had
made the same point in 1887 after returning from a trip to the West: "Where
is the essence of the West in the countries of Europe and America? All these
countries have different systems; what is right in one country is wrong in the
rest; religion, customs, morals—there is no common agreement on any of these.
Europe is discussed in a general way, and this sounds splendid; the question re-
mains, where in reality does what is called 'Europe' exist!" Kōsaka, p. 220.

nese society by indiscriminate borrowing from the different cultures within Western civilization. Japan could hope to have a unified and integrated culture, Kuga believed, only if she borrowed selectively and assimilated wisely. "To the degree that it does not damage the national character, we can adopt Western things." Japan should regard reason and practical use as the standards for adopting foreign culture.[48]

The issue of cultural borrowing was vital to the nation. Kuga set the problem foursquare in terms of Japan's defense:

If a nation wishes to stand among the great powers and preserve its national independence, it must strive always to foster nationalism [kokuminshugi].... Consider for a moment: if we were to sweep away thoughts of one's own country, its rights, glory, and welfare—which are the products of nationalism—what grounds would be left for love of country? If a nation lacks patriotism how can it hope to exist? Patriotism has its origin in the distinction between "we" and "they" which grows out of nationalism, and nationalism is the basic element in preserving and developing a unique culture. If the culture of one country is so influenced by another that it completely loses its own unique character, that country will surely lose its independent footing.[49]

It became a recurring argument of the Seikyōsha: that nations were conquered not by force alone, that cultural acquiescence was the first faltering step toward national decline.

The best defense for the Japanese, Kuga concluded, was "national self-knowledge."[50] What precisely was the nationality, the uniqueness of Japan that must be preserved? Kuga confessed that he "did not yet have a clear answer," but along with the young men in the Seikyōsha he had begun the search. For he and Shiga and Miyake and the rest were convinced of one thing: imitation was self-effacing, and in the heyday of imperialism it could also prove to be self-defeating.

Chapter Four

THE AGONY OF NATIONAL CONSCIOUSNESS

THE DIVERGENCE of ideas between the Seikyōsha and the Min'yūsha aroused widespread interest. Yokoi Tokio (Shōnan's son) observed in July 1888, "There have been many public controversies in recent times, . . . but the one that has attracted the widest attention and the one that most directly relates to the public welfare is the debate over the adoption of foreign culture and the preservation of national character —that is to say, the debate over Westernism and Japanism."[1]

The feeling between the two groups was one of intellectual rivalry and occasional outright hostility. Tokutomi later recalled in his autobiography, "Although I had friendly relations with Kuga, there were many among the *Nihon** group who considered me a contemptible fellow and a heretic." Yanagida Izumi, Miyake's biographer and associate, relates that Tokutomi and Miyake remained opponents until late in their long lives.[2]

One may well wonder what led a young Japanese to take one or the other side in this debate. What, for example, particularly motivated Seikyōsha members in their opposition to Westernism? Did some common factor underlie their intellectual conviction? Was there discernible in their early lives

---

* Tokutomi is referring to the newspaper *Nihon,* which Kuga established in 1889.

some significant common characteristic of social background, geographic origin, or schooling that could characterize them and explain their common opposition to the Westernism that so many of their peers embraced? None is readily apparent. Moreover, such questions are misleading because they give the impression of a sharp demarcation between the two groups, when, in fact, the groups were not so polarized as they and their adherents supposed. Despite their opposition, they shared a common framework of experiences and concerns; and we find that individual members of both groups were often inwardly divided over the very issues they were debating. "To be excited by the same dispute even on opposing sides," Marc Bloch reminds us, "is still to be alike. This common stamp, deriving from common age, is what makes a generation."[3]

The two groups were, in short, much closer than they were often thought to be. In fact, both sought to dissociate themselves from the extremes with which their ideas were often confused. Miyake, Kuga, and Shiga were at pains to distinguish their views from obdurate nationalism and xenophobia; and Tokutomi and other Min'yūsha writers tried to separate their ideas from the indiscriminate Westernism that characterized popular sentiment in the 1870's and 1880's. The Min'yūsha could sympathize with goals and motives of the Seikyōsha: Yokoi Tokio wrote that although he was an adherent of the Min'yūsha, and although he felt *Nihonjin* was losing the debate because its writers had failed to define "kokusui," he nevertheless was in sympathy with the search for a national mission. A journalist for the *Tōkyō keizai zasshi* took a similar position in a treatise published in the summer of 1888 comparing the ideas of the two groups: although he found the arguments of *Nihonjin* writers based too much on emotion, he added wistfully that all Japanese needed the kind of national pride sought by the Seikyōsha.[4] Yamaji Aizan, soon to join the Min'yūsha, said in a speech at Shizuoka in 1890 that although Westernization must be the goal of Japanese society, "our spirit has recently turned inward somewhat, and we see friendly reception for the idea of kokusui hozon. But this is simply a good omen that our pepole are progressing from a period of childlike imitation to a more discriminating stage. And I doubt that it will bring an end to our civilized progress."⁵

An essay discussing Seikyōsha ideas, written in 1890 by Uemura Masahisa (1857–1925), a leading Christian whose sympathies were doubtless with Tokutomi, illustrates the difficulty of the Min'yūsha position. He expressed, on the one hand, understanding of the Seikyōsha desire to preserve the cultural autonomy so necessary to Japanese self-confidence: "A Westerner abroad takes pride in his country and respects it; wherever he goes he wants to be known by his nationality. Not so with our countryman. When [a Japanese] comes in contact with foreigners, he is like a mouse emerging hesitantly on a bright morning. . . . Such pervasive deficiency in self-respect portends national decline." Uemura's essay expressed, on the other hand, his fear that the attempt to preserve cultural autonomy would obstruct national progress and deflect Japan from the path of civilized nations: "It is possible to construct a society in keeping with national character, but . . . the most advanced nations base themselves on the universal nature of man. When kokusui advocates speak about [preservation of] customs, arts, literature, religion, etc., they would seem to be violating this principle." Another reason Uemura distrusted the movement for cultural autonomy was that he felt Japan had no heritage that could rival the culture of the West. "Our country," he said, "does not possess a literature it can boast of before the world. In poetry and prose alike we have no one like Shakespeare or Goethe."⁶

There is evidence to suggest that many young Japanese were thus torn between the two groups. Sakai Toshihiko, subsequently a leader in the socialist movement, recorded in his autobiography that when he was in his late teens "*Kokumin no tomo* as a magazine of new ideas was 'must reading' for us students. Our admiration and affection for Tokutomi Sohō and the Min'yūsha was unbounded. . . . But when *Nihonjin* appeared as a rival to *Kokumin no tomo*, we also admired Miyake Setsurei."[7] Hasegawa Nyozekan (1875–   ), a writer who began his career as a disciple of Miyake and Kuga, agreed that young Japanese like himself usually read the arguments of both groups' publications.[8] There were, in fact, instances of shifting allegiance. Maruyama Kanji, inspired by Tokutomi's early writings to leave his village for a career in Tokyo, became a Seikyōsha partisan in the 1890's while a student at Tōkyō Semmon Gakkō, and later wrote for Seikyōsha periodicals.[9] Kojima Kazuo (1865–1952), who joined the staff of *Nihonjin* in 1888, admitted despite his enmity for Tokutomi that *The Future Japan* had made a deep impression on him and his generation.[10]

The source of this conflict of sympathies, which was of course the source of the debate between the two groups, lay in the historical predicament in which young Japanese found themselves. They were the first generation in Japan to feel in their early lives the full force of cultural change. They were drawn to Westernism for the new avenues it opened to advancement in a society that placed a high value on rising in the world. And they were indeed in many ways the prime beneficiaries of the cultural revolution; but as time passed, they also became its victims. Their identification with the traditions and values of Western culture, and the corresponding negative image of their own heritage, involved them in painful inner conflicts. They grew up in a period marked not only by extensive cultural borrowing from the West, but also by rapidly mounting national consciousness; and the coincidence of these conditions created a dilemma to which young intellectuals were particularly sensitive. Their experiences at once uprooted their cultural inheritance and implanted strong national loyalties. In their own minds they often reconciled these experiences by giving their Westernism a nationalist justification—that is, they stressed that by adopting Western ways the Japanese nation would gain strength and prestige. But in a time of intense competition among nation-states, cultural subservience to the West frequently seemed demeaning. Their self-esteem as a people was wounded by this repudiation of their nation's past achievements. How then could young Japanese give substance to the intense national consciousness they felt? How express pride and confidence in a nation so much of whose past seemed discredited? What of value existed in their heritage that could serve as a source of pride and identity for modern Japanese?

Meiji youth were caught in a confrontation of circumstances that intensified awareness of their heritage and at the same time disparaged it. It was in response to this common concern with escaping their historical predicament that the two groups emerged, and it was in their proposals for solution of the dilemma that they diverged.

I

The arguments of the Seikyōsha and the Min'yūsha grew out of the intense national consciousness of the times in which they lived. We may think of national consciousness as having two parts: 1) a feeling of shared experience and an empathy with one's countrymen;* and 2) an awareness of the distinctive character of one's country—its environment, history, and culture.† National consciousness increased sharply during the

---

* I have in mind Daniel Lerner's use of the term 'empathy': "High empathetic capacity is the predominant personal style only in modern society, which is distinctively industrial, urban, literate and *participant*. Traditional society is nonparticipant—it deploys people by kinship into communities isolated from each other and from a center; ... people's horizons are limited by locale and their decisions involve only other *known* people in known situations. Hence, there is no need for a transpersonal common doctrine formulated in terms of shared secondary symbols—a national ideology." (Italics in the original.) Daniel Lerner, *The Passing of Traditional Society* (Glencoe, Ill., 1958), p. 50.

† "National consciousness ... is the attachment of secondary symbols of nationality to primary items of information moving through channels of social communication, or through the mind of an individual. Not wit, but 'French

first two decades after the Restoration and had a strong effect on young intellectuals.

Born on the eve of the Meiji Restoration, the new generation grew up during a period when the new government was deliberately destroying regional feudal ties and constructing national allegiances in their place. The establishment of a unified national government and systems of universal education and conscription were designed, in part, to lift loyalties from the regional to the national level. In this task the government had much in its favor: Japan's racial and cultural homogeneity, the Imperial Court as a traditional unifying symbol, and the spread of literacy and channels of national communication prior to 1868. Without such advantages the Meiji leaders would have found nation-building much more difficult.

Modern communications, by overcoming local isolation, also contributed to the growth of national consciousness. Once initial obstacles had been surmounted, development of the railway, nonexistent in Japan before 1868, was swift: by 1890 over a thousand miles of railway had been laid.[11] Development of the telegraph was even more rapid: the number of messages sent and received by Japanese telegraphs increased from 19,448 in 1871 to 2,223,216 in 1880, by which time almost all of the major cities were linked by telegraph.[12] Postal services also expanded with dramatic suddenness in the first decades of the Meiji period.[13]

During the two decades after the Restoration, as these new channels of communication opened, Japanese society acquired new mobility—both physical and psychic.[14] Passenger traffic on the railways increased rapidly; by 1890 Shimbashi Station in Tokyo accommodated up to 10,000 passengers a day. Lafcadio Hearn, writing in 1895, found mobility one of the dis-

---

wit'; not thoroughness, but 'German thoroughness'; not ingenuity, but 'American ingenuity'; not meadows on mountainsides, but—as Petrarca was among the first to discover—Italian meadows on Italian mountainsides." Karl Deutsch, *Nationalism and Social Communication* (New York, 1953), p. 146.

tinguishing features of Japanese society: "Nothing is more characteristic of [Japanese] life than its extreme fluidity.... In their own country, the Japanese are the greatest travelers of any civilized people."[15] Yanagida Kunio, the historian of Japanese folkways, pointed out a striking increase during the Meiji period in marriages that united men and women who had grown up great distances apart.[16]

Moreover, Japanese who did not travel were increasingly able to participate vicariously in distant events. This new psychic mobility was made possible in great part by the development of modern postal service and by the emergence of newspapers and magazines as mediums of mass communication. In the period 1874–92 the number of postcards and letters in the mails increased by more than tenfold. In the same period the number of newspapers and magazines handled annually by the post office jumped from less than 3 million to over 50 million copies.[17]

Increased knowledge of Western countries further stimulated national consciousness. As Western civilization became an object of comparison for the Japanese, it tended to draw attention to the distinctive nature of their own culture. Young, educated Japanese were more likely than others to be sensitive to cultural differences. They studied subjects adopted from Western universities; they read Western texts; many of their teachers were Westerners. As we have already noted, Miyake's awareness of these cultural distinctions led him to devote what appears to have been his senior thesis at Tokyo University to the historical development of Japanese character traits.

Tokutomi's experience with Western education provides perhaps an even clearer example of its nurturant effect upon national consciousness. Dōshisha was, in effect, an outpost on the new cultural frontier, where the young Tokutomi, removed from the familistic environment of his childhood, acquired perspective on the cultural setting in which he had been reared. "Dōshisha," he later wrote, "was a completely

American school. There was no recess for national holidays. The Japanese flag was not flown. There were no banzais for the Emperor. Saturday was a holiday and Sunday was a day for hearing sermons." Under the sway of American missionaries in its early years, Dōshisha was not a school that instilled national pride in its students. He explained in his autobiography the resentment this experience caused him. "The first thing I resented was the attitude of the missionaries; I felt they were rude and arrogant. . . . The second thing was the persistently toadying attitude of some of the students toward the missionaries and their wives. . . . And then it was always 'America this and America that,' completely forgetting Japanese things. This I detested." In retrospect Tokutomi believed that this exposure to the missionaries and their culture during his mid-teens had aroused in him a strong "national spirit" (*kokuminteki seishin*).[18]

This belief, recorded many years after his own thinking had undergone radical change, cannot be accepted uncritically. After all, the unabashed Westernizing policies that he advocated soon after his departure from Dōshisha indicate that he himself, though deeply aware of "Japanese things," took no pride in them. Nonetheless, his early writings do show a marked antipathy for missionaries. What was involved here, we may conjecture, was Tokutomi's resentment of cultural subservience to the West and to Westerners, in spite of his conviction that it was necessary for national progress.

National consciousness created painful tensions in the minds of young people who, like Tokutomi, had discovered their nationality to be a cause for embarrassment. The Western culture to which they were attracted became an object of comparison reminding them of the failings of their own cultural heritage and leading them to repudiate the Japanese past. At the same time national consciousness also awakened a need for pride and self-esteem. Could cultural alienation and passionate commitment to the nation, the two conflicting dominant themes of Tokutomi's thought, be reconciled? Could a Japanese advocate thoroughgoing Westernization of his society without implicitly stigmatizing his countrymen in the process? These were questions to which Tokutomi, responding to the Seikyōsha's challenge, was compelled to address himself.

II

The Min'yūsha was as concerned with Japanese national character as was the Seikyōsha. *Kokumin no tomo* pointed out in 1889 that " 'Know thyself' is a maxim every individual and every nation should follow. A nation ought to know where it stands and where it is going. . . . If a nation knows itself—its strong points, its shortcomings, its goals, its means—then it will be able to act independently."[19] The Min'yūsha, moreover, never questioned its rival's claim that the Japanese possessed a distinctive national character. *Kokumin no tomo* affirmed it—but labeled it a cause for self-rebuke. Dealing directly with the matter, an editorial in 1888 admitted, "A nation has a kind of character, just as a person, family, village, or region has. . . . It arises partly from the peculiar nature of the race; it is partly the effect of natural environment; and it is partly the product of religion, society, politics, etc. It develops through all kinds of circumstances, through many ages; and to change this nature is not an easy task."[20]

Nonetheless the Min'yūsha members wanted to try. For them—as this editorial made clear—the Japanese nature tended to be concerned too much with ostentation and too little with practical achievement, with face-saving rather than with ends. *Kokumin no tomo* called attention to a favorite Japanese proverb that said the samurai preserved his pride despite poverty, picking his teeth even as he starved. The emphasis that the warrior's code placed on pride and honor accounted for the characteristic Japanese concern with ceremony and outward appearances. The editorial expressed admiration instead for the English nature of wholehearted commitment to goals, and concluded that the guiding principle of democratic (*heimin*) societies was concern for practical achievements.

In the 1880's, foreign visitors, including Ernest Fenollosa, alarmed at neglect of the traditional arts, began to urge preservation of the Japanese cultural heritage. *Kokumin no tomo* scorned this idea: "Why should we boast of our country as the home of unique arts and aesthetics, not recognizing what a great flaw their prominence reflects in our national character?" The Min'yūsha writers attributed the uniqueness of their country's arts to a characteristic concern for show and ostentation. In an article entitled "What Value Has Foreigners' Flattery?" *Kokumin no tomo* argued that "these foreigners regard Japan as the world's playground, a museum. . . . They pay their admission and enter because there are so many strange, weird things to see. . . . If our nation has become a spectacle, then we ought to be especially interested in the reform and progress that will make us a normal, civilized country."[21]

The image that many Western visitors had of Japan as an exotic showpiece reinforced the Min'yūsha's determination to be rid of the past. The impressions, for example, that Sir Edwin Arnold expressed in 1891 during a sojourn in Japan particularly irked Tokutomi. The poet told an audience of journalists, politicians, and officials that Japan

appears to me as close an approach to Lotus-land as I shall ever find. By many a pool of water-lilies in temple grounds and in fairy-like gardens, amid the beautiful rural scenery of Kama-kura or Nikko; under long avenues of majestic cryptomeria; in weird and dreamy Shinto shrines; on the white matting of the teahouses; in the bright bazaars; by your sleeping lakes, and under your stately mountains, I have felt farther removed than ever before from the flurry and vulgarity of our European life. . . . Yet what I find here more marvelous to me than Fuji-san, lovelier than the embroidered and gilded silks, precious beyond all the daintily carved ivories, more delicate than the Cloisonné enamels, is . . . that almost divine sweetness of disposition which, I frankly believe, places Japan in these respects higher than any other nation.... Retain, I beseech you, gentlemen, this national characteristic, which you did not import, and can never, alas, export.[22]

Arnold's remarks were not received with quite the divine sweetness of disposition that he expected; for as another Englishman who was present, Basil Hall Chamberlain, observed, "The educated Japanese have done with their past. They want to be somebody else and something else than what they have been and still partly are." Chamberlain recorded that the day after Arnold's address one newspaper acknowledged "the truth of Sir Edwin's description but [pointed] out that it conveyed, not praise, but condemnation of the heaviest sort. Art forsooth, scenery, sweetness of disposition! cries this editor. Why did not Sir Edwin praise us for huge industrial enterprises, for commercial talent, for wealth, political sagacity, powerful armaments? Of course it is because he could not honestly do so. He has gauged us at our true value, and tells us in effect that we are pretty weaklings."[23] Twenty-five years later, Tokutomi was still bitterly recalling Arnold's evaluation, which he said attributed to Japanese the characteristics of "birds and butterflies."[24]

For Tokutomi, the uniqueness of Japan's culture served as an argument for reform. Whatever the difficulties involved, national progress depended upon changing the Japanese character and eliminating cultural differences between Japan and the West. Hence national consciousness led to a desire that Japanese be more like Westerners.

National consciousness even produced a desire for "denationalization."* Taguchi Ukichi gave voice to this desire in

---

* Karl Deutsch emphasizes that national consciousness "may hasten denationalization instead of nationalistic development, unless this spotlighted nationality happens to be valued. If it is not valued, its discovery may simply be embarrassing, as Zionism was felt to be embarrassing by some Jewish groups in Western Europe.... Only if nationality is valued; if it is seen as a winning card in the social game for prestige, wealth, or whatever else may be the things culturally valued at that time and place; or if it fulfills a need in the personality structure which individuals have developed in that particular culture—or if

the first issue of *Kokumin no tomo*. In an article entitled "Of What Value Is the Nation?" he argued that love of country was "a foolish sentiment" that tended to foment groundless disputes. Nationality was an outmoded concept. Although warriors had once been willing to give up life and fortune for Sagami or Musashi, Japanese would no longer go into battle for their provinces; they were conscious, he said, of belonging to a larger community. On a larger scale, to halt national disputes, Taguchi advocated the establishment of a world government. A nation was itself but an amalgamation of different peoples; he cited European and American countries as good examples and noted that Japan had blood relationships with China and Korea. An Englishman living in Tokyo was, after all, just as much "a Tokyoite" as a Kagoshima man living in Tokyo. Taguchi argued that all men indeed shared a common humanity; national distinctions were artificial and meaningless, and nationality ought to be ignored. If national consciousness exposed embarrassing traits, here was a way to escape it.

Because Tokutomi acknowledged Taguchi's influence on his writings,[25] and also because Taguchi proved to be persistently critical of the Seikyōsha, we ought now to turn to an examination of his background and his thought.

III

Taguchi Ukichi was born in Edo in 1855. His great-grandfather was the famous Confucian scholar Satō Issai; his father was a Bakufu foot soldier who died when Taguchi was a child. Despite the straitened circumstances in which he was left, Taguchi received an education through the help of family and friends. He attended a primary school in Numazu, south of the capital; and following the Restoration, he studied medicine in

it is at least valued for lack of any more promising opportunities—only then does it seem probable that consciousness of nationality will strengthen its development." Karl Deutsch, *Nationalism and Social Communication* (New York, 1953), p. 152.

Tokyo. He abandoned his plans for a medical career in 1872, when the opportunity arose to enter a school of foreign studies established by the Ministry of Finance. After completing the two-year course, Taguchi rose rapidly in the Ministry. He also began to exploit his newly acquired knowledge of the West. In two important books he applied it to conditions in Japan: the first, *A Free Trade Policy for Japan* (1878), drew largely on the ideas of Adam Smith; the second, *A Short History of Japanese Civilization* (published serially between 1877 and 1883), was inspired by the writings of Buckle and Guizot. Achieving sudden recognition at a young age, Taguchi resigned from the Ministry of Finance in 1878; and the following year, with the backing of the financier Shibusawa Eiichi, he launched the *Tōkyō keizai zasshi*. This magazine became the vehicle for his many reformist ideas, and remained so until his death in 1905.

The Japanese who first advocated the adoption of Western culture appear, paradoxically, to have been among the first to show an interest in studying their national cultural past.[26] Fukuzawa's *Outline of Civilization* (1876) had decried the previous lack of historical interest in Japanese culture. Historians, he wrote, had written histories of Japanese government but no histories of Japan. Briefly comparing the civilizations of Japan and the West, Fukuzawa found the fundamental difference to be that an imbalance of power (*kenryoku no henchō*) had pervaded Japanese society throughout its history,* whereas in Western history an increasingly balanced distribution of power had developed. Although Fukuzawa frequently

---

* Citing this interpretation of Fukuzawa for corroboration, Professor Maruyama speaks of the prevalence in Japanese society of what he calls "the maintenance of equilibrium by the transfer of oppression": "By exercising arbitrary power on those who are below, people manage to transfer in a downward direction the sense of oppression that comes from above, thus preserving the balance of the whole.

"This phenomenon is one of the most important heritages that modern Japan received from feudal society. It has been aptly interpreted by Fukuzawa Yukichi as the result of 'attaching too great importance to power,' which, as he says, 'has been the rule in human intercourse in Japan since the beginning.'

mentioned the historical development of Japanese culture, he himself never wrote a history of it.

Taguchi, by virtue of his *Short History of Civilization in Japan* and two essays published in 1885 and 1886, was the first in the modern period to write a detailed history of Japanese culture.[27] His purpose was to show why Japanese civilization had developed differently from that of the West. Accepting the contention of Buckle and others of the positivist school that Western civilization had developed according to natural laws, he found the same laws applicable to Japan. Regardless of apparent differences in race and nationality, all men possessed a common humanity (*jinsei wa ichi nari*); hence all were subject to the same laws of social development.[28]

Taguchi distinguished between two types of civilization: aristocratic (*kizokuteki*) and democratic (*heiminteki*).[29] Although civilizations had flourished in East Asia's past, they had always bestowed benefits and happiness solely on the aristocracy. Because aristocratic civilizations depended on artificial social restrictions that stifled the free working of natural laws, culture had become deformed—ostentatious rather than utilitarian, designed to benefit the privileged few rather than the common people. Democratic civilizations such as those of the West, on the other hand, developed naturally in response to the needs of all the people. Without artificial restrictions, civilizations developed according to fixed laws, and cultural distinctions between democratic societies tended inevitably to disappear. Western civilization had progressed far beyond Japan's chiefly because it had undertaken to rid itself of these restrictions.

If the laws of social progress were now allowed to apply nat-

---

Fukuzawa continues as follows: '[The Japanese] make a clear distinction between the moral codes that apply to people above and to people below, and an equally clear distinction in the field of rights and duties. As a result every individual is in one capacity the victim of coercion, while in another capacity he metes out coercion to his fellow-men. . . . Today's joy compensates for yesterday's shame, and thus dissatisfaction is evened out. . . . Peter is robbed to pay Paul.' " See Maruyama Masao, *Thought and Behavior*, pp. 17–18.

urally to Japan, argued Taguchi, a civilization identical with the West's would appear. Indeed, among the lower classes in Japan, where there were relatively few social restrictions, Taguchi discovered customs similar to those of the West; dressing and eating habits bore particular resemblance.[30] The object of reform, then, was the elimination of arbitrary social restrictions. To take one example, Taguchi saw a standard of taste applicable to all human beings, a standard based on a natural desire for the useful and on innate emotional likes and dislikes common to all men.[31] According to this standard, Japanese dress and architecture ought to be discarded in favor of the dress and architecture of the West; music and literature should likewise be reformed. Japanese theatre must be purged of its "aristocratic vestiges": plays were still based on feudal ethics of loyalty and self-sacrifice; they still displayed "feudal-type paramours."

When *Nihonjin* first appeared, on April 3, 1888, Taguchi recognized the challenge its ideas offered to his own, and he composed a vigorous defense of his viewpoint for the next issue of the *Tōkyō keizai zasshi*. Entitled "Japan and the West," the essay contended that the adoption of Western things did not, as the Seikyōsha contended, stigmatize the Japanese. The national origin of a civilization was fortuitous. The object of reform was not to "Westernize" Japanese society, but rather to follow the path of universal progress:

We study physics, psychology, economics, and the other sciences not because the West discovered them, but because they are the universal truth. We seek to establish constitutional government in our country not because it is a Western form of government, but because it conforms with man's own nature. We pursue the use of railways, steamships, and all other conveniences not because they are used in the West, but because they are useful to all people.[32]

Japan must adopt Western practices because of their universal value and applicability, for only thus would Japan be the equal of Western countries. For Taguchi, the path of civilized progress was a unilinear one, unaffected by national, racial, or environmental distinctions.* Those who understood the law of progress, he said, knew that one country could not possess abilities unattainable by others. Arguing that progress in non-material things went hand in hand with material progress, Taguchi concluded that no aspect of Japanese culture could be superior to Western culture.

The publishers of *Kokumin no tomo*, increasingly worried by "the conservative trend in Japanese society," were overjoyed with Taguchi's essay: "We feel," the magazine commented, "as if we had encountered an old friend on an isolated mountain road."[33]

Taguchi, then, sought to erase the stigma attached to borrowing from the West. Social progress obeyed fixed laws (*shakai no tairi* or *kaika no ri*) that governed both material and spiritual growth, and civilization, properly understood, was the natural product of these laws. There ought to be no shame, no destruction of integrity, attached to following the path the West had followed, because that was the universal path of mankind. Thus, he implied, civilized men, regardless of their native place, not only used similar machines; they also thought and behaved in similar ways, ate the same kinds of food, wore the same kinds of clothing, lived in houses of similar architecture, and enjoyed the same kinds of art. As the laws of civilized progress continued to inhere, people would become more aware of their common humanity; national borders would have less significance; and war would become outmoded.

IV

For Taguchi and Tokutomi, national consciousness involved unfavorable comparisons between their own culture

---

* The novelist Mori Ōgai (1862–1922), who returned in 1888 from medical studies in Germany and who soon began publishing literary works in *Kokumin no tomo*, was thinking along similar lines. Mori, Katō Shūichi points out, "argued vigorously that there was but a single real medicine and that one

and the West's. As a result, they chose to identify themselves with what they considered were universal traits and values of man. Thus they sought both to ease the stigma attached to cultural borrowing and to justify the rejection of those particularistic claims of their own culture that caused them embarrassment.

Members of the Seikyōsha were subject to the same feelings. Shiga Shigetaka called the Min'yūsha's ideas exciting."[34] And Miyake's essay "Characteristics of the Japanese People" showed that he also shared the Min'yūsha's pained and critical attitude toward Japan's cultural heritage. Both Miyake and Shiga, moreover, had been attracted by Western liberalism during their student days—particularly by the natural rights theories of the left wing of the Jiyūtō (Liberal Party).[35] But the massive rejection of their own national past demanded by the Min'yūsha argument seemed to the members of the Seikyōsha only to compound the shame. Moreover, as Shiga's voyage through the South Seas had convinced him, a self-effacing association with Westerners might be dangerous. As Kuga Katsunan said:

Differences in wealth and ability among individuals are unavoidable; but despite these differences, no individual should scorn and demean himself. Our nationalist group believes that a nation, just as an individual, must have a feeling of pride in order to exist. There are differences in wealth and power among all countries. Compared to European countries Japan is weak, but . . . she ought not to be frightened into self-abasement. . . . National independence . . . always requires national pride; . . . without it a nation cannot exist.[36]

By pride Kuga meant not self-aggrandizement, but a sense of self-respect based on an awareness of Japan's distinctive characteristics.

Drawing added attention to the debate between the Sei-

could not speak of such things as 'Western' or 'traditional Japanese' medicines." See Katō, "Japanese Writers and Modernization" in Jansen, *Changing Attitudes*, p. 434.

kyōsha and the Min'yūsha, Kuga launched a new daily newspaper, *Nihon* (Japan),* on February 11, 1889. He had abandoned the *Tōkyō dempō*, which had encountered serious
financial difficulty; his failure in that venture had been due
partly to his lack of business experience, partly to insufficient
backing. For his new journal he gained impressive financial
support from influential conservative opponents of the government, such as Tani Kanjō, who had recently resigned as Minister of Commerce and Agriculture, and Asano Nagakoto, the
former lord of Hiroshima,[37] both of whom were older and
more conservative than Kuga. The staff of *Nihon*, however,
was composed mostly of young Japanese; at a dinner held to
celebrate the founding of the newspaper, an observer remarked
on "the large number of new faces present."[38]

Kuga often wrote of the high ideals he held for his profession. Although prior development of newspapers had coincided with a period of intense political strife that tended to
render them party organs, Kuga rejected this role for *Nihon*;
neither narrow party goals nor hope of private gain would determine the course of his newspaper:[39] "I am often asked the
strange question: 'What principles does *Nihon* stand for, and
what party do you belong to? And I answer: *Nihon* stands
for principles of Japanism, and I belong to no party. I am a
Japanese.' The inquiring person can never understand; evidently he has no conception of an independent newspaper."[40]
Kuga believed the independent journalist had the highest
calling of his day. Especially as Japan was about to put into
practice a constitutional system, the journalist ought to place
himself above all parochial interests and seek only the good of
the nation.

In the first issue of *Nihon*, Kuga explained the need he felt
for preserving an independent national identity. "Whether

* Although the newspaper is also referred to as "Nippon," which is an alternative reading of the characters in the title, I am inclined to regard "Nihon" as
the pronunciation preferred by Kuga and others who wrote for the newspaper.

for an individual or for a nation, in order to be at all self-reliant it is necessary to hold steadfast to one's special character [honryō]." He chose the name *Nihon* for his newspaper because he sought to preserve "the very existence of Japan." Japanese had become so frenzied in their pursuit of Western things they were in danger of becoming "naturalized Westerners"; Kuga's purpose in *Nihon* was to discover Japan's special province in the world.

Kuga, nevertheless, was at pains to dissociate himself from traditionalist views:

We recognize the excellence of Western civilization. We value the Western theories of rights, liberty, and equality; and we respect Western philosophy and morals. We have affection for some Western customs. Above all, we esteem Western science, economics, and industry. These, however, ought not to be adopted simply because they are Western; they ought to be adopted only if they can contribute to Japan's welfare. Thus we seek not to revive a narrow xenophobia, but rather to promote the national spirit in an atmosphere of brotherhood.[41]

He pointed out that traditionalist groups had already misconstrued the views of *Nihonjin* and "made the new words 'kokusui hozon' synonymous with reactionism."[42] Kuga feared similar distortion of his ideas so much that he even declared *Nihon* to be ideologically closer to views held by the Min'yūsha than to traditionalist views.[43]

Kuga began his effort to formulate a viable national identity by turning to the major national symbol—the Imperial Court. He published the first issue of his paper on the day the Meiji Emperor promulgated the new constitution. One unique characteristic of the Japanese nation was that Japan had "possessed an unbroken line of imperial rulers since its founding 2500 years ago." Today, he continued, Japan had acquired another special trait, "the establishment of a constitutional system through the harmonious cooperation of the Emperor and the people. . . . Where else in the world can one see this?" Constitutions earlier granted by rulers in the West had been promulgated only under duress. In Japan, he wrote, the historical relationship between Emperor and people was unsullied by strife or jealous competition for rights. Japanese advocates of people's rights who had drawn their theories from Western liberal doctrines had ignored this relationship. Because Japan had never known a revolutionary struggle against its imperial institution, Western liberalism was irrelevant, he said, and would never find root in Japan.

In a treatise entitled *Recent Constitutional Thought*, Kuga discussed the origins of Japan's constitution.[44] "Its source," he emphasized, ". . . is not in the drafts of foreign advisers; nor is it an imitation of Western constitutions."[45] The principles expressed had developed gradually in the twenty years since the Restoration: "The evolution of things joins past and present; there is always continuity. . . . People regard the Constitution as a new and unprecedented document; officials in the government imagine they have created an unprecedented political system. But looking at history one will discover that the seeds of a constitution had already sprouted twenty years ago."[46] Kuga traced the growth of an "unwritten constitution" through successive imperial edicts since the Restoration. The written constitution, moreover, confirmed the Imperial Court's traditional role as the source of Japan's unique culture:

The culture of European countries derived from the people; the culture of Japan derived from the Imperial Household. In Europe, culture arose from the cities and villages; in Japan, it arose from the leadership of the capital, which is to say the Imperial Court. A glance at history prior to the period of military rule is sufficient to show that ceremonies, religion, the family system, politics, agriculture, commerce, and crafts all emerged from the patronage or leadership of the Imperial Court.[47]

As two leading political writers with opposing views, Kuga and Taguchi were bound to clash. On the day *Nihon* first appeared, Mori Arinori, Minister of Education, was assassinated.

Mori had been a Christian sympathizer, and the assassin's motive was to punish him for purported slights in ritual during a recent visit to the great Shinto shrine at Ise. Kuga, who had previously called public attention to Mori's conduct at Ise, deplored the assassination and called it a "bad omen" for the constitution, which was promulgated the same day. He and Taguchi, however, became embroiled in controversy when the latter, in a *Tōkyō keizai zasshi* editorial, attributed the assassination to "religious bigotry."[48] Doubtless feeling that he might be subject to this same charge, Kuga retorted in *Nihon* that the Ise Shrine was not an ordinary Shinto shrine and that Mori's behavior therefore had not been solely a religious issue; as the temple built to honor the Emperor's ancestors, the Ise Shrine had special political significance.[49] The ceremonies performed there, he wrote, were out of reverence for the Imperial Household, not for Shinto deities; they were national political ceremonies, not religious services. The distinction was an important one for Kuga, who viewed the Imperial Household as a symbol of Japan's historical continuity, as a living reminder to Japanese of their own unique traditions, and hence as the foundation upon which national identity might be built.

Taguchi's ideas evidently had rankled Kuga for some time. He bitterly recalled the article "Of What Value Is the Nation?" which Taguchi had written two years earlier for the first issue of *Kokumin no tomo*. Kuga charged him with wholly ignoring the significance of Japan's unbroken line of rulers and the concept of nationality.

Kuga's arguments were directed not solely against Taguchi and the Min'yūsha, but against all Japanese who thought Western liberal ideas could be applied to Japan. What was needed, he wrote, was a Japanese definition of liberalism that would fit the nation's own historical experience. In an essay entitled "What About Liberalism?" published serially in January 1890, Kuga held that liberalism had not been introduced to Japan by Fukuzawa and his fellow reformers; nor was it based on abstract principles of inalienable rights or natural law. Japanese liberalism had emerged from the concrete experience of the Meiji Restoration, from the overthrow of feudalism and the awakening of the national spirit. The Restoration had brought about the abolition of the old aristocracy; it had initiated freedom of speech and vocation and had established universal conscription. Because Japanese liberalism had arisen from the struggle against hereditary privilege, it recognized individual talents and sought the freedom needed to develop them. Kuga argued also that Japanese liberalism had been conceived in opposition to foreign interference and because of a desire for political and cultural autonomy. A nation, like an individual, he concluded, had talents; and liberalism in Japan sought freedom for their development.[50]

Kuga argued that in the search for an estimable national image the claims of history could not be waived. He maintained in an editorial entitled "The Concept of Nationality" that theorists who underrated the importance of the nation "failed to grasp the historic, that is to say the organic, relationship between the nation and the individual."[51] History was the molder of a "national spirit" that united all Japanese, living and dead. A Japanese acted not as a member of a bloodless humanity governed by universal standards; he acted as a member of his own vibrant people, inspired by his nation's own particular spirit. Because of their unique histories, all nations had different characteristics. What was of value in one society might not be valuable when transplanted to the different setting of another society. The concept of "civilization" was also relative; society did not progress according to fixed laws or universal patterns. Progress varied with individual cultures; and in fact, Kuga concluded, "world civilization progresses through the competition of different cultures."

v

Kuga's logic was sound. Pride in a common past was essential to the formation of a nation-state. So long as a nation did not prize its history, it would be impossible to develop any proud sense of community; and that proud sense was needed as a binding and integrative force, enabling the people to act in concert and to deal with their domestic and international problems. Yet—and this was Kuga's dilemma—the very act of building the nation-state had involved disowning the past and adopting the techniques and institutions of an alien culture. Pride in the heritage did not well up spontaneously; it had to be worked at.[52] Confidence in the traditional culture had been undermined, and there was no ready consensus about what could be salvaged from the past that could inspire the sense of proud identity Kuga sought.

Tokutomi's position was no less perplexing. By focusing attention on the degrading effect that cultural subservience had on the Japanese national image, the Seikyōsha compelled its rival to reconcile Westernism with the need for a proud identity. The response of Tokutomi and others of similar persuasion was that civilization in the West represented the universal path of progress that all nations must follow, that the place of origin of civilization was fortuitous, and that accordingly there was nothing demeaning in Westernization. Such an argument freed Tokutomi from the necessity of choosing between his cultural loyalty to the West and his national loyalty to Japan. For a time, such a solution to the dilemma was possible; but events were gradually conspiring to make it untenable for Tokutomi. No issue in the 1880's served more to underscore the difficulties of Tokutomi's position than did the treaty revision controversy.

Chapter Five

TREATY REVISION AND SELF-DETERMINATION

DURING THE LATE 1880's, the increase of national consciousness was evident in the growing popular concern over the issue
of treaty revision. Imposed upon Japan by Western nations at
the end of the Tokugawa period, the unequal treaties symbol-
ized a deeply felt shame: their persistence was a painful reminder of the national impotence that renewed contact with
the West had exposed. Recovery of national independence and
international respect became a goal that the government leaders shared with a growing number of their countrymen.

During the decade 1885–95, successive efforts of the Meiji
government to revise the treaties provided one of the major
issues of public concern and became a focal point in the intellectual controversy over the problem of Westernization.
Treaty revision involved fundamental issues of cultural borrowing and therefore had special relevance for the debate between the Seikyōsha and the Min'yūsha. This chapter examines
the effects of two attempts at revision, the Inoue proposals of
1887 and the Ōkuma proposals of 1889, on the ideas of the
rival groups.

I

Under pressure from Western nations, the Tokugawa government had agreed to a system of leased territories in certain
Japanese ports. For the most part, foreign residence and trade

were limited to these areas, and travel of foreigners in the Japanese interior was restricted. The Bakufu had agreed also to a system of extraterritoriality that provided for consular jurisdiction over foreign residents. Finally, by commercial treaties negotiated in 1858 and 1866, Japanese tariffs were placed under international control.

For twenty-five years after the Restoration, revision of these treaties was the primary goal of Japanese foreign policy. The leaders of the government that came to power in 1868 attached such importance to this goal that it deeply influenced domestic events as well. To achieve revision they were prepared to conduct patient negotiations and make sweeping reforms. As early as 1871, the Iwakura mission, which included many of the ablest members of the government, left Japan to initiate discussion of treaty revision with the Western powers. In Washington they stated their purpose to President Grant:

> We expect and intend to reform and improve the Treaties so as to stand upon a similar footing with the most enlightened nations. ... The civilization and institutions of Japan are so different from those of other countries that we cannot expect to reach the desired end at once. It is our purpose to select from the various institutions prevailing among enlightened nations, such as are best suited to our present condition, and adopt them, in gradual reform and amendments of our policy and customs.[1]

Thus, from the very beginning, successful revision of the treaties implied the need to borrow extensively from the West.

Members of the Iwakura mission concluded that the elimination of extraterritoriality depended above all on legal reforms. After the mission's return, the government plunged beyond the modest reforms already begun, and committees were appointed to compile penal and civil codes. They took French law as a model and engaged a French jurist, Boissonade de Fontarbie, to advise in the compilation. A German legal expert, Hermann Roesler, was entrusted with drafting a commercial code.

Zeal for treaty revision elicited many bureaucratic efforts to reform Japanese customs. Government policy sought to modify traditional morality in order to avoid the criticism and moral disapproval of foreigners. Ordinances that forbade public nakedness and mixed bathing in public bathhouses explained that although "this is the general custom and is not so despised among ourselves, in foreign countries this is looked on with great contempt. You should therefore consider it a great shame."[2]

Government efforts to win foreigners' approval also included methods of artful persuasion. In 1883 the Rokumeikan, a gaudy Victorian hall, was opened in Tokyo for the purpose of entertaining foreign residents with cards, billiards, Western music, dances, and lavish balls. Prime Minister Itō gave a spectacular costume ball for foreign residents in which he appeared as a Venetian nobleman and the Foreign Minister appeared as a strolling musician.

On the strength of its progress in undertaking reforms, the government again determined to broach treaty revision to the powers. In 1881 Inoue Kaoru, the Foreign Minister, initiated discussions with Western diplomats in Japan. The British, whose interests were the most extensive, were the least amenable. Inoue persisted, and in 1886 a conference of foreign representatives was convened in Tokyo to give consideration to his draft of a revised treaty. In return for the abolition of consular jurisdiction, his proposals offered the establishment of mixed courts, whereby a certain number of foreign judges would sit on the Japanese bench. Inoue was further willing to make concessions on what the Japanese called "mixed residence" (naichi zakkyo), which would open the whole country for foreigners to reside, to own property, and to carry on trade in the interior. Finally, all of Japan's new legal codes would be determined "according to Western principles." With these terms as a basis for negotiation, agreement of the treaty powers appeared likely.

II

On the verge of success after many years of preparation, Inoue was unexpectedly confronted with intense domestic opposition. The most influential leader of the opposition was Tani Kanjō, Minister of Commerce and Agriculture. Tani was openly hostile to Inoue's plans, and after resigning his post in June 1887, he made a public attack on the proposals. Tani's ideas merit our attention because he was the original rallying figure for many of the young men who formed the Seikyōsha the following year. He also became the most generous financial backer of the newspaper *Nihon*.

Tani belonged to an earlier generation than the young men of the Seikyōsha; born in 1837, he had participated in the events leading up to the Meiji Restoration.[3] As a high-ranking samurai from Tosa on the island of Shikoku, he had played an important role in military training and campaigns during the closing years of the Tokugawa regime. After the Restoration, although sometimes discontent with government policies, he had remained in the new army. He had been commander of the forces at Kumamoto castle that had decisively repulsed the army of Saigō Takamori during the Satsuma Rebellion.

Tani's opposition to the Inoue draft treaty was not his first criticism of the Meiji government. Earlier in his career, he had voiced discontent with army pension regulations issued by the War Office in 1879. According to these regulations, which were modeled after the French system, benefits were to be paid to the widow and children of a deceased soldier but not to his parents as the traditional Japanese family system would have dictated. "The basic tenets of this country," wrote Tani in a petition to the government, "are loyalty and filial piety."[4] Despite the adoption of new institutions from the West, the fundamental validity of these traditional Confucian values was unchanged; they were the "proper path of mankind," and to discard them would violate Japan's "national ideology." Tani's views coincided with those of others who were then in conservative opposition to the government, including Motoda Eifu, Confucian lecturer to the Emperor, and Nishimura Shigeki, who had organized a society to promote traditional Confucian morals.

Tani resigned his army post in 1881, and along with three other dissenting generals submitted a memorial to the Emperor asking for the establishment of a constitution and a parliament. Unlike the liberal opponents of the government, these conservative generals envisioned a constitution bestowed by the Emperor and instituting direct imperial rule with the advice of an appointive assembly. To counter the influence of the liberal opposition, the generals formed the Moderate Party (Chūseitō) to promote their views.

Later that year, the oligarchy expelled its liberal wing led by Ōkuma Shigenobu and promised a constitution and a parliament. Concluding that his aims had been in good measure realized, Tani dissolved his party, and later accepted an appointment in the cabinet as Minister of Commerce and Agriculture. In his new position he made a tour of Europe that had an important effect on his ideas. The cultural differences among European nations and the spirit with which each maintained its own nationality impressed Tani. By contrast, he concluded from his observation of peoples in the colonies of European nations that weak-willed association with Westerners led to subjugation.

He returned to Japan just at the time Inoue was pressing his plan for treaty revision. His faith in traditional values buttressed by the conviction that their preservation was also a matter of practical defense, Tani argued against what he considered submission to humiliating demands of the treaty powers. Tani submitted his resignation along with a statement of his views.[5] Deference to the values of foreigners, he felt, implied the superiority of the society holding those values. Inoue's promise to codify the law in accordance with Western judicial principles was a case in point. Reforming Japanese laws to suit the wishes of foreign governments and appointing foreign judges to the Japanese courts would prolong "the disgrace we have endured for thirty years."[6] Tani concluded that an issue of such magnitude as treaty revision should await the decision of the parliament, which would be convening in 1890.

His dramatic resignation and his severe indictment of government policies made him a leader of growing opposition to the oligarchy.[7] Leaders of the old Liberal Party, such as Itagaki Taisuke, supported him. Despite strict government censorship, the views of Tani and Itagaki were printed and widely distributed.[8] For the first time since 1881 liberals and conservatives found themselves in agreement in a common stand against the government. One newspaper reported that Tani's declarations had won support among many in the bureaucracy and that as a result there were some who followed his example and resigned from the government.[9] Among them were Miyake, who left the Ministry of Education, and Kuga, who left the Official Gazette Bureau.

We do not know in any detail the part Miyake, Kuga, and Shiga played in the opposition to the Inoue treaty. We do know that many of the original members of the Seikyōsha, including Shiga and Miyake, were teaching in various schools in Tokyo. Through a group of young intellectuals called the Kenkonsha (Cosmos Club), which had joined forces with Tani in a movement to defeat Inoue's proposals, many of these kindred spirits found one another.

Students throughout the country were remarkably affected by the patriotic fervor of Tani's and Itagaki's views. A recent historian of the treaty revision effort writes that students and other young political activists (sōshi) around the age of twenty provided the essential support for the attack on Inoue's revision plans.[10] Students from schools in outlying areas as well as in Tokyo participated. In Iwate Prefecture, north of Tokyo, students became so aroused that the governor wrote to Prime Minister Itō requesting a special ordinance to control assembly and publication. Young people in many parts of the country took the lead in secretly circulating publications and petitions.

In the face of an increasingly active opposition, Inoue adjourned the conference of treaty power representatives on July 18, 1887; and in September he resigned his post as Foreign Minister to accept soon after the office of Minister of Commerce and Agriculture. Despite stringent government measures to suppress the opposition that had grown over the summer months, liberal and conservative opponents of the government united in demanding freedom of speech, reduction of the land tax, and conclusion of the treaties on a basis of equality with the Western powers. On December 25 the government issued an ordinance further restricting assembly and banning agitators from central Tokyo.[11]

III

Tokutomi believed that the unequal treaties had served a useful purpose.[12] Because so many domestic reforms were designed at least in part to support the treaty revision effort, he concluded that from the time of the Restoration foreign policy goals had been the controlling influence in reforming Japanese society and politics. Although "foreign" in name, foreign affairs had become the great motive force (*ichi dai undōki*) in domestic government. The administration of a country was ordinarily, he observed, based upon relations between the government and the people. In Japan, however, 7,000 foreign residents had outweighed the influence of the 38 million Japanese people in determining the recent course of the nation. The result had been fortunate for Japan; without the demands of foreign policy, the Restoration would not have led to significant reforms. To Tokutomi, the break with the past was clear: in all Japanese history there was no precedent for these reforms. Looking to the future, he expressed hope that the Japanese people would abandon their passive role in making over Japanese society.

Tokutomi feared that the opposition to the Inoue draft

might lead to hostility toward all borrowing from the West. He was particularly apprehensive about the spreading influence of Tani and those grouped about him. In editorials published in the autumn of 1887 he called attention to a trend toward a "conservative reaction" (*hoshuteki handō*).[13] The blame lay, he wrote, with the excesses of the government leaders. Their borrowing from the West, which he labeled "aristocratic radicalism," had emphasized only the superficial aspects of Western civilization and had attempted to "flatter our guests." "The people," he wrote, "have already tired of masked balls, horse races, and dances." In its treaty revision program the government had endangered the entire course of progressive reform. But the remedy offered by the opponents of the Inoue draft treaty was worse than the malady:

Let us reject aristocratic radicalism but not the spirit of progress. If you hate dancing and therefore social intercourse between men and women, if you hate luxuries and therefore free trade, if you hate foreign interference and therefore mixed residence, if you hate aristocratic social reform and therefore democratic social reform, if you hate damage to national pride and therefore entrance into the civilized world, . . . then feeling for Japan will grow and feeling for the world will wane, then the ideal of the state will flourish and the ideal of the people will wither, then the spirit of conservatism will appear and the spirit of progress will die, and our country will have lost its vital energy. . . . Stop treaty revision, but don't halt the progress of nineteenth-century Japan![14]

Because he regarded Tani as the leader of a "new conservative group" (*shin hoshutō*), Tokutomi singled out his views for criticism.[15] Tani's thesis, proclaimed during the anti-treaty movement, was that Japan ought to borrow selectively from the West but preserve her own traditional morals. How, Tokutomi exploded, could a country institute the Napoleonic Code and yet preserve Confucian morals? And how could one teach Macaulay alongside traditional (Tokutomi called them "grade school") morals? Tani failed, Tokutomi wrote, to understand the nature of social progress. A society was like "an intricate organism": all its parts—scholarship, commerce, arts, politics, and religion—were mutually bound and inseparable. "If we want to adopt a strong point," said Tokutomi, "then we must also take the many things that go along with it, including the spirit and principles that produced this strong point." Tani, he concluded, mistakenly regarded society as a patchwork made by piecing together the virtues of different civilizations.*

Events justified Tokutomi's fear that the treaty revision controversy in the summer and fall of 1887 would mobilize opposition to his ideas. Early in 1888, only a short while after he voiced his apprehension, the Seikyōsha was founded, *Nihonjin* began publication, and Kuga assumed editorship of the *Tōkyō dempō*. Tokutomi regarded the Seikyōsha members as additions to the "new conservative group," which he described as a motley gathering that would offer good material for a sociological study. He characterized the "new conservative group" as led by discontented generals and encompassing unreconstructed samurai, Confucianists, Shinto and Buddhist priests, Chinese-style doctors, young political toughs, and all others who wanted to destroy the progressive trend of Japanese society.[16]

Members of the Seikyōsha resented the conservative label that Tokutomi put on them. Although they had personal ties with Tani, Torio Koyata, and the other generals who had formed a conservative party in 1881, the style of thought of Kuga, Miyake, and Shiga was essentially new. Later, Kuga distinguished carefully between Torio's Confucian and Buddhist beliefs and the ideas held by Miyake, Shiga, and himself.[17] Eventually the Min'yūsha recognized the difference, too, but

---

* Kuga used the same analogy to argue against the type of reliance on the Western model advocated by Tokutomi. Westernizers, he said, were making a patchwork of Japanese society by not allowing it to grow organically; they were piecing together unrelated elements from France, Germany, and England. See Kuga's essay "Nihon bummei shimpo no kiro," *Tōkyō dempō*, June 9, 12, 13, 1888.

only after Kuga, Miyake, and Shiga had further developed their ideas.* Though Tokutomi continued to fret about the "new conservative group" ("If I had my way," he wrote, "there would be no conservative parties"), by June 1889, nearly two years after the controversy over the Inoue draft treaty, he had decided that the conservatives were no longer a threat to Japanese progress. He believed they had missed their opportunity to exercise influence by not joining ranks to form a single effective party.[18]

<h2 style="text-align:center">IV</h2>

Tokutomi's hopes for the future of Japanese domestic reform were based partly on the appointment of Ōkuma Shigenobu as Foreign Minister in February 1888. By appointing its liberal opponent, the government had succeeded in allaying public concern over treaty revision.

Ōkuma resolved to proceed in secrecy with individual powers rather than to call a joint conference as Inoue had. In this way he could avoid inflaming Japanese public opinion; and he hoped in addition that by negotiating agreements first with the less intransigent powers, he could increase the pressure on the others to agree. He succeeded in winning greater concessions than Inoue had, but he could not gain unconditional jurisdiction over foreigners. The Ōkuma draft treaty was se-

---

* Many years later Yamaji Aizan, who had been a member of the Min'yūsha, distinguished between the two styles of thought: "Whereas the conservatism that appeared in 1881 and 1882 was nothing more than a rebirth of Chinese learning, the conservatism of the late 1880's represented the development of national consciousness. Of course in the latter case many backwoods priests and Confucianists were delighted to plunge into the movement, but . . . the leaders of the group had an understanding of Western culture. They absorbed the spirit of European nationalist movements, and regarded the attempt to make Japan over into a Western state as a most dangerous tendency. They observed that Western powers, through their language, literature, and customs, strove to preserve their nationality. Ultimately they reversed the intellectual trend, and national spirit (which those who did not sympathize called conservative spirit) finally prevailed." Quoted from *Gendai Nihon kyōkai shiron* in Motoyama, "Tani Kanjō," p. 111.

cretly submitted to London in January 1889. Various legal codes scheduled for promulgation were enclosed, and Japan agreed to employ a number of naturalized foreign judges in her Supreme Court. The treaty also provided for opening the interior to foreign travel, trade, and residence. In return, extraterritoriality would end after five years, and tariff autonomy would be granted to Japan after twelve years. On the basis of this draft, Ōkuma concluded treaties with the United States, Germany, and Russia; and negotiations with England and France gave every sign of proceeding to conclusion.

Again events belied expectations. The *Times* of London learned the purport of the negotiations and in April 1889 printed a summary of the proposed treaty. Komura Jutarō, Chief of the Foreign Ministry's Translation Bureau and a Seikyōsha sympathizer, apparently informed Kuga of the *Times* article; and in late May *Nihon* carried a translation of it.[19] Once again controversy erupted.

Attitudes toward the problem of treaty revision revealed the extent of uncertainty and anxiety that Japanese felt in their relations with the Western world. The doubt and shame provoked by the treaties was brought on not so much by their limitations on national sovereignty as by their presumed implication that Japan's traditional society and its supporting values were incapable of meeting the foreign challenge.* The

---

* Helen Merrell Lynd's ideas on the relation of shame and identity seem to me quite relevant to an examination of Japanese attitudes: "Sudden experience of a violation of expectations, of incongruity between expectation and outcome, results in a shattering of trust in oneself, even in one's own body and skill and identity, and in the trusted boundaries or framework of the society and the world one has known.... We experience anxiety in becoming aware that we cannot trust our answers to the questions Who am I? Where do I belong?... Doubt replacing basic trust in the way of life of one's social group or in one's place in it can undermine the sense of one's own identity. Thus shame [is] an experience of violation of trust in oneself and in the world." Helen Merrell Lynd, *On Shame and the Search for Identity* (New York, 1961), pp. 46–47. Mrs. Lynd also suggests that commonly felt shame can bring about a particular closeness among members of a group. One can find in the treaty revision controversy considerable evidence to demonstrate that an important ingredient of the growing national consciousness was a shared feeling of shame.

provisions of both the Inoue and the Ōkuma draft treaties that evoked the most anxiety were those opening the country to foreign residence, travel, and commerce. "Mixed residence" evoked deep fears and revealed a gnawing sense of inferiority toward Westerners.

A young Japanese studying in Berlin wrote probably the most widely read polemic on mixed residence. Inoue Tetsu-jirō (1855–1944) had been among the first students graduated in philosophy from Tokyo University.[20] Like Miyake, who followed him in the same curriculum, Inoue had been a student of Fenollosa. Two years after graduation he had been appointed assistant professor of philosophy at the university. In 1884 he had gone to Germany for study, and he remained there six years before returning to his professorship.

Inoue's essay, written in 1889, expressed alarm at the possible opening of the interior to foreign residence and trade.[21] His fears were based on the conviction that Japanese could not survive competition with the superior races of Western countries. Depending heavily on Spencerian theory, Inoue argued that the inflexible principle of the survival of the fittest foredoomed his countrymen in any contact with Westerners.

"Japanese," he wrote, "are greatly inferior to Westerners in intelligence, financial power, physique, and all else."[22] The superiority of the Westerner was evident not only from his greater stature but also from his more highly developed cranium. The shape of the Westerner's head was indicative of a superior intellect. Japanese, he said, were not equal to Westerners in either intricate analysis or profound generalization. Westerners also had a self-assurance and a spirit of independence that Japanese lacked: "We stand before Westerners exposing our weak and inferior civilization; it is rare that we can hold our heads high and peer down on other races as they do."[23]

Inoue said the security of the nation required a candid admission of Japanese inferiority. Mixed residence would allow foreign capitalists to dominate Japanese commerce and to monopolize the most valuable land. He feared that unscrupulous foreigners would also gain control of the government and that Japan would lose its unity. Even should Westerners become Japanese citizens and obey Japanese laws, they could never be assimilated, for their social customs, language, religion, and political beliefs were too different. History showed Inoue that more than cultural unity would be lost; racial destruction was the inevitable result of close contact between superior and inferior races. Inferior races (*rettō jinshu*) were never able to assimilate superior (*yūshū*) ones. Inoue cited instances of population decline among natives of the Pacific islands inhabited by Westerners.

He held out hope that the Japanese would independently evolve until they became able to compete successfully with Westerners, but for many years they must avoid close contact with the superior races. Inoue believed that rather than offer mixed residence as a concession for abolition of extraterritoriality, Japan should be content with the existing treaties, which limited foreigners to the leased territories.

Inoue gave expression to fears that already tormented many Japanese. Miyake Setsurei later wrote that all Japanese, whether they admitted it or not, saw Westerners as a superior race and felt uneasy in their presence.[24] Social Darwinist views had gained wide currency, and Inoue's opposition to mixed residence seemed to many Japanese the logical application of these views.[25] Katō Hiroyuki, perhaps the best-known exponent of Darwinian theories in Japan, likewise believed that proposals for mixed residence were premature.* Japanese civilization had not evolved enough to compete successfully with the

---

* Herbert Spencer wrote in confidence to Kaneko Kentarō in August 1892 that "the Japanese policy should, I think, be that of *keeping Americans and Europeans as much as possible at arm's length.* In presence of the more powerful races your position is one of chronic danger, and you should take every precaution to give as little foothold as possible to foreigners.

"It seems to me that the only forms of intercourse which you may with advantage permit are those which are indispensable for the exchange of commodities.... There should be, not only a prohibition of foreign persons to hold property in land, but also a refusal to give them leases, and a permission only to reside as annual tenants.... Respecting the intermarriage of foreigners and

West's.[26] Shiga Shigetaka's first-hand observation of the harmful effects on the South Sea natives of living with the white races led him, in *Conditions in the South Seas*, to warn against mixed residence. (Shiga feared that Japanese would suffer from competition with Chinese as well as with Westerners.[27] Chinese, too, would come in large numbers, he warned, and with their greater capacity for enduring physical hardship they would be able to compete successfully with lower-class Japanese). Nishimura Shigeki, a guardian of Japan's traditional morals, wrote:

> In resources, in intellect, in agriculture, in industry, in commerce, and in ambition for fame and profit our countrymen do not measure up to Westerners. If we permit mixed residence and allow foreigners to purchase land at will, agriculture, industry, and commerce will all gradually fall into their grasp. Most of our land will become the property of foreigners. In the end we will become employees and tenant farmers.[28]

Those who favored the Ōkuma draft treaty sought to relieve these fears of mixed residence. Shimada Saburō, editor of the Yokohama *Mainichi* and a member of Ōkuma's Progressive Party, argued that because Japanese had developed preventive medicine and had had previous experience with strong drink they would not be subject to the racial destruction that South Sea islanders had suffered.[29] Admitting that Japan's civilization was not equal to the West's, he argued that the Japanese were sufficiently advanced to profit from the stimulus of contact with Westerners.

Taguchi Ukichi, a stout proponent of the Ōkuma treaty, scoffed at Inoue's view. After the latter's return from Berlin, Taguchi expressed mock surprise that Inoue had emerged

---

Japanese, . . . it should be positively forbidden. . . . There is abundant proof, alike furnished by the intermarriages of human races and by the interbreeding of animals, that when the varieties mingled diverge beyond a certain slight degree *the result is inevitably a bad one* in the long run." (Italics in the original.) The letter, made public after Spencer's death, is contained in David Duncan, *Life and Letters of Herbert Spencer* (New York, 1908), II, 14–18.

safely from "mixed residence" with Westerners![30] Taguchi based his support of mixed residence on his belief in the common humanity of all men. Westerners had already stimulated Japanese progress, and Japan would continue to benefit from them just as she had from the Koreans and the Chinese who had come earlier in her history. Japanese had welcomed those early immigrants because they had come from a more advanced culture than Japan's: "Then why should we now object to the influx of foreigners, to mixed residence, intermarriage, and naturalization? In time they will become our beloved and faithful fellow countrymen."[31] Taguchi argued that mixed residence would stimulate trade and economic development. He took pleasure in twitting the opponents of mixed residence by saying that they themselves were actually "foreigners." In a speech in September 1889, he said he had consulted genealogy records and had discovered that Shiga, Tani, and Miyake were all descendants of immigrants from China and Korea.[32]

Tokutomi also supported the Ōkuma proposals. His argument, like Taguchi's and Shimada's, was based primarily on the economic advantage that Japan could expect to derive from opening the interior. An influx of foreign capital would lower the interest rate; it would also contribute to the development of new land and new industry. Japan could become the "entrepôt of Asia."[33]

A historian of the treaty movement has pointed out that although Tokutomi favored conclusion of the Ōkuma treaty, emphasizing that it was better than the existing treaties, and despite his personal ties with Ōkuma's Progressive Party, he did not actively participate in support of the draft treaty.[34] In assessing public support of the treaty, Kuga characterized *Kokumin no tomo* as tepid.[35] Tokutomi conceded his dislike for the provision that foreign judges be appointed to the Japanese bench, but as a small, weak country Japan could do little about such demands from the stronger powers.[36] In this admission we can begin to perceive the reasons why he gave only lukewarm support to the Ōkuma proposals. The problem of treaty revision plagued Tokutomi during these years because it confronted him with the perplexing reality of power politics. The nations of the West, whose civilization Tokutomi commended as a model for his countrymen, stood as obstructions to Japan's independence. To the extent that Western nations appeared to be adversaries, emulation of their culture could be discredited as subservience and even treachery. Moreover, how could he espouse independence as a worthy quality for individuals and countenance something less for the people as a whole? Was not self-reliance as praiseworthy for a nation as for an individual? Cultural deference to the West, even though justified as essential to national progress, could prove destructive if it undermined national pride and confidence. Tokutomi began to find his cultural alienation, on the one hand, and his passionate commitment to the nation, on the other, difficult to reconcile; they created a tension in his thought that became increasingly apparent. Faced with this dilemma and surely aware that arguments for national independence had special appeal to youthful self-assertiveness, Tokutomi, considering himself spokesman for the new generation, was forced to treat the problem of treaty revision gingerly.

v

Tokutomi's optimism that the "new conservative group" would soon dissolve proved unjustified. Following *Nihon's* disclosure of the treaty's provisions as carried by the London *Times*, opposition appeared in many parts of the country; petitions, public meetings, and ad hoc committees were organized. And although members of the old Liberal Party were active in the opposition, those Tokutomi called the "new conservatives" were again the most active.[37]

By all accounts Kuga's editorials in *Nihon* gave leadership to the anti-treaty movement. Throughout the summer and fall months of 1889, Kuga was engaged in editorial debates with Yano Fumio, the literate and respected editor of the *Yūbin Hōchi* newspaper and a close associate of Ōkuma. Their arguments drew wide attention because the *Yūbin Hōchi* was regarded as a mouthpiece for Ōkuma's own views. The tone of Yano's defense was pragmatic.[38] The Ōkuma treaty represented a great improvement over existing treaties, he wrote, and was the best that could be negotiated with the Western powers. Moreover, mixed residence was an appropriate concession because it was common practice in all the advanced countries of Europe.

Kuga denounced the Ōkuma draft because it obstructed Japan's pursuit of an estimable national identity. To accept a revised treaty on anything less than a basis of equality would renew the shame caused by the existing treaties. He regarded treaty revision as an opportunity to recover national pride as well as national sovereignty: "Now that Japan is emerging in the world for the first time, her present and future status will be determined by treaty revision. If we tolerate interference, we shall be classed with Turkey and Egypt."[39] The revision of legal codes and the appointment of foreign judges to the Supreme Court represented foreign interference. Kuga believed that a continuation of the system of leased territories in the treaty ports, which was a restriction on the area of sovereignty, was preferable to allowing restrictions on the function of sovereignty, which would be the effect of conceding to the powers the right to interfere with Japan's legislative and judicial affairs. If the powers refused to negotiate equal treaties with Japan, Kuga advocated abrogation of the existing treaties. The European nations were too divided, he felt, to undertake armed reprisal.[40]

Kuga paid especial attention to the provision for mixed residence. He did not, however, base his argument on the fear that the Japanese could not compete with Westerners; to have done so would have been to forfeit his hope for national pride. His reservations, in effect, derived rather from the fear that mixed residence might further impede the development of a national identity. So long as the Japanese remained uncertain of their own abilities and indifferent to their own cultural inheritance, mixed residence would only add to the existing social and moral disruption.[41] "This issue," he concluded, disagreeing with the arguments of Taguchi and Tokutomi, "cannot be settled in terms of economics or universal brotherhood, but must be judged on the basis of the special strategic needs of our own country."[42]

Reflecting several years later on the views he had expressed at the time of the Ōkuma treaty controversy, Kuga observed that he had not sufficiently emphasized the importance of the mental attitude (seishinteki soshiki) of the people.[43] Foreign judges, he concluded, were a minor matter; mixed residence was of only secondary importance. Self-determination was not merely the principle of maintaining a nation's political sovereignty; it was also a people's determining their own values and goals. "If one discards his own special talents and falls under the influence of another, then he loses his 'self' [ware]. When one loses his 'self' because of contact with others, it is not association; it is subservience."

Kuga felt that his countrymen were not sufficiently aware of the different forms that competition between nations could take. International struggles were decided not only by armed and economic competition but also by psychological (shinriteki) rivalry: religion, philosophy, language, arts, scholarship, and literature could be weapons of combat between nations. In short, equality among nations existed only when each maintained its own cultural identity: "How can we make Japan equal with the world powers? Only by striving to make the world know the reason Japan is Japan [tada Nihon no Nihon taru yuen o sekai ni shirashimen to tsutomuru nomi]."[44] If the Japanese regained their political sovereignty but not their own proud identity, their nation would nonetheless be doomed.

Ōkuma was beset by more than a hostile segment of public opinion: divisions in the cabinet also seriously weakened his chances of success. Prime Minister Itō and Inoue Kaoru, now Minister of Commerce and Agriculture, worried lest success strengthen Ōkuma's party in the impending diet session.[45] Many cabinet members joined them in opposing the draft treaty. The issue was resolved by a terrorist's bomb. On October 18, 1889, a member of the Fukuoka Genyōsha, a semisecret nationalist society, threw a bomb into Ōkuma's carriage as it left the Foreign Ministry. Seriously wounded, Ōkuma resigned, and his treaty revision efforts came to an end.[46] The treaties already signed by German, Russian, and American diplomats were shelved, and negotiations with France and England were suspended.

The Seikyōsha was elated. A writer for *Nihonjin* believed that nothing since the Restoration had so enlivened the national spirit as the controversy over the Ōkuma treaty.[47] His group had been awaiting the opportunity to expose the damage done to the nation by "foreign-worship." The treaty revision issue, he said, had at last put Westernizers on the defensive.

Tokutomi's reticence about an issue that was causing such agitation among young people of the time surely cost him the support of many in the new generation. As we shall see, shortly after the Ōkuma controversy Tokutomi began to complain of the desertion of youth from his cause.

Agitation over the treaties had given the Seikyōsha an opportunity to dramatize its efforts to formulate a Japanese identity. Yet the controversy did not contribute positively to the formulation of that identity; rather, it laid bare the doubt and uncertainty that many Japanese felt about their place in the world. The treaty revision controversy demonstrated the want of an identity.

Chapter Six

IN SEARCH OF MORAL SURETY

THE SELF-DOUBT tormenting many young Japanese was particularly evident in their search for an ethical foundation for the new era. Should they adopt the values toward which their Western education inclined them—values that transcended their cultural heritage? Or should they seek to preserve and revitalize the inherited values of their own culture?

The experience of growing up in the first decades after the Meiji Restoration had created in the minds of the new generation a radical cleavage between old and new values. During their childhood they had received traditional, Confucian-oriented training at home and in private academies. The remainder of their formal education, however, had been in the new schools, which had presented a vision of values beyond those of their own culture. Confidence in traditional values was undermined not only by the new education but also by the fact that traditional values were closely identified with the discredited Tokugawa social order. On the other hand, the attempt to live according to new values—values not absorbed in childhood as part of the natural order of things, but learned later in life as part of a self-conscious search for appropriate new forms of behavior—often created deep anxieties. Many in the new generation, as a result, felt torn between the familiar, comfortable values of their childhood and the new, liberating values of their later education.

Tokutomi's experience at Dōshisha serves as an example of the psychic conflict that often resulted from adoption of the new values and repression of the old. Under the influence of Niijima Jō, Tokutomi became convinced that the adoption of Christian ethics was essential for Japan's civilized progress. This intellectual conviction, however, caused him great emotional strain, for Tokutomi himself never felt totally committed to Christian dogma. As a student he underwent a serious emotional crisis because of his failure to achieve a wholehearted faith. When, in 1878, he accepted baptism, he had been converted more by the warmth and compassion of Niijima's personality than by the appeal of the Gospel. "I was a follower more of Mr. Niijima," he wrote, "than of Christ." In his autobiography there are frequent references to the mental turmoil he suffered during this period and to the concern of his teachers over his state of melancholia: "During 1878 and 1879 I was afflicted by a mental sickness [nōbyō] that was then widespread among students. One of the chief reasons for my affliction was that whereas I had faith in Mr. Niijima and, through him, faith in Christianity, as time passed I was seized with doubts. . . . I did not feel the intimacy with Christ that is the backbone of Christianity. . . . I was tormented by conflicting emotions." Tokutomi obeyed the school's rule that students pray every evening, "but no matter how much I prayed, my heart drew away from God. Nor was this what was often called spiritual backsliding. I felt no particular temptations; in matters of smoking, drink, and other things I followed the path of Christianity and did not feel oppressed. Rather it was because I felt difficulties in being an orthodox Christian."[1] We do not know from Tokutomi's account precisely how he overcame his personal crisis; we do know that after he left Dōshisha he wrote to Niijima renouncing his baptism.[2]

Throughout their modern history, Japanese have struggled with the issues of old and new, Japanese and Western, traditional and modern values. After the turn of the century, development of an orthodox philosophy of the Japanese state tended increasingly to inhibit discussion of the problem. Often it was internalized and lay hidden in men's minds, dividing them and creating tensions and frustration. But in the period we are dealing with here, the orthodoxy had not yet crystallized, and debate could therefore be conducted overtly; in this way tensions and frustrations generated by divided minds were given some relief.

I

During the early 1890's several events intensified public concern with the problem of values. Preparation for the enactment of Japan's first civil code raised the issue. The draft code completed in 1890 contained provisions that provoked acrimonious controversy between those who wanted to legitimize the traditional family structure and those who believed that Western family patterns were essential for a modern industrial state.*

The greatest outcry over the problem of values was caused by the Imperial Rescript on Education issued in October 1890. The Rescript was a product of conservative efforts, centering in the Imperial Household Ministry, to reassert traditional values in education.[3] Such efforts had been gaining momentum for over a decade. The Emperor Meiji, after touring schools in the provinces during the summer of 1878, had concluded that Westernization of education had gone too far and that Confucian ethics should again be emphasized in the schools. A memorandum accordingly sent to elementary school teachers by the Ministry of Education in 1881 had stressed the importance of traditional moral values: "Loyalty to the Imperial House, love of country, filial piety toward

---

* Professor Tōyama, in one of the best essays about the controversy over the proposed civil code, writes that although the debate was primarily between two groups of lawyers, the ideas of the Seikyōsha lent support to the opponents of the draft code. See Tōyama, pp. 273–83.

parents, respect for superiors, faith in friends, charity toward inferiors, and respect for oneself constitute the Great Path of human morality. The teacher must himself be a model of these virtues in his daily life, and must endeavor to stimulate his pupils along the path of virtue."[4]

During the 1880's the Ministry of Education had exercised increased supervision of moral instruction, first by prohibiting the use of translations of foreign morals texts and later by publishing its own traditionally oriented ones. By 1890 the Elementary School Regulations listed the objectives of education, in order, as: moral training, the development of a distinctive national polity, and the cultivation of skills and knowledge.[5] The priority given to moral and patriotic training represented a significant modification of the utilitarian spirit that had prevailed in education during the 1870's.

The Imperial Rescript on Education, which was issued shortly before the convening of the First Diet in 1890 and which remained until 1945 the fundamental statement of official educational aims, was a brief document setting forth the ethical principles upon which the new constitutional order was to be founded.* In stressing traditional ideals of social harmony and loyalty to the Throne, the Rescript implicitly sought to counter moral values and liberal political ideals introduced from the West. But because it was general in tone, attempting to achieve a compromise among the conflicting opinions of its drafters, the Rescript was subject to varying

---

* The Rescript read as follows: "Our Imperial Ancestors have founded our Empire on a basis broad and everlasting.... Our Subjects ever united in loyalty and filial piety have from generation to generation illustrated the beauty thereof. This is the glory of the fundamental character of Our Empire, and herein also lies the source of Our Education. Ye, Our Subjects, be filial to your parents, affectionate to your brothers and sisters; as husbands and wives be harmonious; as friends, true.... Pursue learning and cultivate arts, and thereby develop intellectual faculties and perfect moral powers; furthermore, advance public good and promote common interests; always respect the Constitution and observe the laws; should emergency arise, offer yourselves courageously to the State; and thus guard and maintain the prosperity of Our Imperial Throne coeval with heaven and earth." Quoted in Passin, p. 151.

interpretations. Much of its language had a traditional ring, and yet there were some passages that sounded new, such as those that urged respect for law and for the constitution. Japanese at the time were by no means agreed upon the precise intent of the Rescript, and it became the focal point of much of the controversy over values in the early 1890's.

II

Historians have frequently observed the advantage to which government in modern Japan put traditional moral sanctions in order to serve the purposes of the state. Ideals of loyalty and obligation, solidarity, and duty to superiors, which had deep roots in the family ethics and in the feudal experience of Japanese, gave support to the political myths of imperial divinity and the family state. These traditional ideals helped to justify and glorify the personal sacrifice and prodigious effort demanded by rapid industrialization. The reasons, however, why receptivity to old values persisted despite economic and social change have been less often considered. Mass media, military training, and education were to become effective means of inculcating these values in the twentieth century; but indoctrination alone does not adequately explain the tenacity of old values, for even prior to the period of effective government thought control there was evidence of deep yearning among a great many Japanese to preserve and revitalize traditional values.

As Thomas Smith suggests, old values in Japan retained their emotional power well into the twentieth century partly because of the dual nature of Japanese society. Despite the growth of industry, which fostered attitudes destructive to tradition in urban areas, extraordinary continuities in the mode of Japanese farming helped to perpetuate old values in the countryside. In contrast with developments in other countries, industry did not break up the peasant village in Japan, nor did it disrupt the traditional pattern of farming with the family as the basic unit of labor. Thus values of obedience and solidarity remained vital in the peasant family and village. Since the number of persons employed in agriculture remained stable, accounting for over 50 per cent of the population as late as 1930, "the countryside remained a vast and populous hinterland of conservatism."[6]

In the period we are studying, however, old values also held a strong appeal for many young Japanese who had left the countryside in their youth and who were exposed to the new values and attitudes of the city and the new schools. What was the nature of their commitment to the old values? In part it may have been a lingering emotional attachment to the familiar, comfortable ways of their childhood and early youth; in part it may have stemmed from a conviction that traditional values were not doomed, that they could be preserved in some modified form. Their commitment may also have stemmed from a belief that Western values were unsuited to a people of different history, that values so far transcending the experience of ordinary Japanese would prove disruptive to the integration of society that was required if the Japanese were to act in concert and deal effectively with their domestic and international problems.

In part, too, the commitment arose from the psychological need for national pride and identity. Building a powerful industrial nation required supplanting much of Japanese tradition. To compensate for their loss, many Japanese were groping for something in their national past that they could retain with pride as uniquely Japanese. Most of the borrowings necessary for industrialization were scientific in nature, "empirically demonstrable, hence ultimately irresistible."[7] In questions of social conduct and moral codes, however, judgments could not be empirically determined. Choice was still possible. If alien ethics could be rejected and indigenous ethics made viable in an industrialized Japan, then self-respect and identity might seem possible.

Kuga Katsunan spoke from this point of view. He embraced traditional values not, as his ancestors had, from confidence in their universal validity, but because he believed them to be psychologically necessary to the nation. Preservation of traditional morals and customs could perform a binding integrative function and help to achieve the cultural identity upon which Japanese nationalism could be built. A proud sense of community was essential to an effective nation-state, and Kuga therefore tried to foster respect for traditional Japanese feelings about the state, the community, and the family. During the New Year's season of 1892, for example, he expressed regret over the deterioration of social customs. He remarked on a disposition, especially among upper classes, to scorn Japan's traditional New Year's customs and ceremonies: "I am not concerned today about deficiencies of law, but about decline of customs. . . . Laws have had little effect in preventing friction among classes, divisiveness in neighborhood groups, quarrels among political parties, or dissolution of the Diet. If you seek the cause [of discord], it is that laws have needlessly increased while customs have gradually dissolved." He claimed no transcendental derivation for the morals and customs he sought to preserve. Instead the justification was quite practical: "I regard social customs as necessary for national unity [*kokuminteki itchi*], and I regard them as a fundamental element of national independence."[8]

Above all, Kuga stressed reverence for the Imperial Household as the focus of all the loyalties for the Japanese people. For this reason, he abhorred both sides of the controversy that arose in 1892 over a Tokyo University professor's objective historical treatment of Shinto. Kume Kunitake, in an essay first published in 1891 and then reprinted and given wide circulation the following year in a historical magazine edited by Taguchi Ukichi, described Shinto as the "survival of a primitive form of worship."[9] He traced the origins of great court ceremonies, of the Imperial Regalia, and of the shrine to imperial ancestors at Ise to Oriental patterns of primitive worship that had existed in prehistoric Japan. Some months later, after Shintoists called the essay sacrilegious and Kume was forced to resign his university position, Taguchi composed a vigorous defense for freedom of historical research.[10] Kuga's viewpoint differed from the stands taken by the Shintoists and by Kume and Taguchi. He dealt with the controversy wholly in terms of his concern for national identity. Without discussing the merits of Kume's argument, Kuga wrote that by involving the Imperial Household in public controversy Kume had run the risk of weakening the cohesive power of the Imperial Family as a historic symbol of national unity. "It is our moral obligation," Kuga said, "to refrain from making a public problem of anything that relates to the Imperial Household, lest such publicity produce an unexpected result —lest what began as an academic dispute result in jeopardy to the security of the nation. People like Mr. Kume are aware of their status as scholars, but they tend to forget their obligations as subjects."[11]

What Kuga feared most was social disintegration, which he linked with the rapid undermining of the traditional cultural heritage and the corresponding widespread uncertainty about values and norms. The loss of an "unshakable moral authority"* in Japanese society was a frequent subject of his editorials and essays, for he considered his goals of Japanese unity and independence unattainable so long as the ethical void persisted. He found moral values lacking among all groups and

---

* Yamaji Aizan, who joined the Min'yūsha in 1892, recalled years later the factors that had produced the "conservative reaction" his group had confronted: "Although part of the conservative trend of the time was produced by a simple yearning for the past, a further inquiry into its origins revealed more concrete causes. Foremost was the fact that the new Western learning did not satisfy the people, for although they disliked Confucian cosmology they did want an unshakable authority as the source of all morals. This need is always latent in the human heart; and of course the theorists of rights, the positivists, and the skeptics were unable to satisfy this need." Quoted from *Gendai Nihon kyōkai shiron* in Motoyama, "Tani Kanjō," p. 91.

classes, but he held the members of the most influential professions most responsible. Scholars, journalists, and above all
politicians and the new entrepreneurs were Kuga's culprits;
they set the example that others were following.[12]

Kuga acknowledged that the source of moral disruption was
deeper than individual failings. The overthrow of the feudal
system and the rapid introduction of Western science and institutions had done much to undermine traditional codes.[13]
Kuga emphasized that he had no wish to revive obsolete moral
codes of the Tokugawa period; his concern, rather, was with
preserving belief in the fundamental moral nature of man.
Because Japanese had found no satisfactory substitute for the
old codes, their belief in man's moral nature had weakened.
Many Japanese, he said, relied on Western law to regulate social conduct; but for Kuga, laws were negative, punishing but
not rewarding, curbing but not directing man's conduct. Faith
in Western liberal theory was even more dangerous. If pressed
to define progress, Kuga said he would call it the lessening of
selfishness; but so-called Japanese progressives argued for the
pursuit of self-interest as the source of progress and the basic
principle of liberalism.[14] "What *are* morals?" Kuga asked. "I
am not preaching the Way of Mencius and Confucius to politicians. . . . I am speaking of morals as a kind of fidelity. No
matter how many talented men we have, there will always be
some, lacking fidelity, who will mislead the nation."[15] Fidelity
to what? Kuga's response was always "national spirit."

Nor did Kuga oppose the adoption of foreign institutions.
He expressed confidence that Japan, because of the unique
character of her people, could assimilate successfully from
other countries. She could assimilate from the West just as
she had done in centuries past from China. Kuga, however,
stressed the danger in the present historical situation. Before
the new could be assimilated, and while men's minds remained divided, Japanese national spirit might be done in
by the aggressive challenge of other nations. Borrowing, there-

fore, must be kept in perspective; and care must especially be taken to strengthen Japan's own national spirit.[16]

The great value of the Imperial Rescript, according to Kuga, was that it sought to unite men's minds and to preserve the source of the Japanese spirit. "Filial piety, brotherly affection, marital harmony, and the loyalty of all to the Imperial Throne," he said, referring to provisions of the Rescript, "are Japan's distinctive national ethics. They are the historic customs of the Japanese people, the basic elements that support her society."[17] These moral relations, which united the Japanese and their sovereign in social harmony, were the products of Japan's 2,500-year history. Fearful of the destructive effect that rationalist thought might have on these ethics, Kuga emphasized: "They cannot be deduced by academic reason [*gakuri*], but [only] by the emotions [*kanjō*]" of Japanese.[18] History and national character gave the only possible legitimacy.

Because of the many interpretations given the Imperial Rescript after its proclamation, the Ministry of Education asked Inoue Tetsujirō, who had become professor of philosophy at Tokyo University after his return from Berlin, to write a commentary clarifying the meaning of the Rescript. Inoue attempted the kind of explanation that Kuga rejected.[19] He declared in the preface to his essay that his purpose was to explain the rational basis of loyalty and filial piety. These morals had always been justified intuitively; Inoue said they must now be explained inductively—in the style of Western academic theory—if they were to win people's hearts. Thus, in his interpretation, traditional morals were given utilitarian sanctions. Filial piety, for example, depended not solely on the physical relationship that led naturally to love for parents but also on the realization that "inevitably everyone grows old and weak. If there is no one to love and look after you, it will be a most miserable condition. Therefore, if you want your children to feel filial tenderness for you in the future, you must set the example. . . . If you do not, you cannot expect anyone to take care of you." Inoue sought similarly to rationalize the concept of loyalty. One was loyal to a ruler not because it was the natural obligation of a subject but because "if subjects do not follow the commands of their ruler, they will diminish national unity and do damage to policies that are intended to maintain their own well-being. Thus if subjects recklessly violate the ruler's authority, they may bring misfortune upon themselves."[20]

Inoue expressed the yearning of many Japanese to find some way to preserve and revitalize the familiar values of their childhood. But we could scarcely find a better example than Inoue's essay itself of the extent to which traditional—once axiomatic—ethics had been undermined. During the Tokugawa period, society had been regarded as an embodiment of the natural order: the principles that controlled the universe were at once the principles governing all aspects of human conduct. Ethics, then, derived from the prevailing perception of the natural world and, as a consequence, possessed powerful, transcendental sanction. But when the introduction of Western science broke up the Confucian world-view and undermined belief in a natural social order, trust in the old values began to weaken. The former assuredness was no longer possible. Many Japanese (to borrow Joseph Levenson's categories), though still emotionally tied to old values, were nevertheless intellectually alienated. By justifying these values in terms of the new rationalist thought, Inoue hoped to reunite emotional attachment and intellectual conviction. His undisguised utilitarianism, however, grated on Japanese sensibilities, and he was attacked from many quarters. Speaking to a philosophical society in 1895, Miyake criticized the moral obtuseness of Inoue's commentary; he could see no progress made by justifying morals in terms of "hackneyed self-interest."[21] For Miyake and Kuga, the morals in the Rescript were products of the nation's history and not intellectual choice.

Another essay that Inoue Tetsujirō wrote in this period

stirred further acrimonious controversy and drew increased attention to the problem of values. In 1893, Inoue (who was characterized by Lafcadio Hearn as "a fine, lean, keen, soft-spoken, persistent champion of Japanese national conservatism, and a good honest hater of sham Christianity")[22] published *The Clash Between Religion and Education,* in which he argued that Christian precepts of individualism, universal brotherhood, and denial of the Emperor's divinity were incompatible with the spirit of the Rescript.[23] Christians at once retorted,* and, in the words of one observer, "there was not a newspaper or magazine that did not print reports of the controversy."[24] In an intellectual history of the Meiji period, Takayama Chogyū saw this not merely as a controversy between Inoue and the Christians but as a confrontation of nationalism and Westernism.[25]

Kuga treated the controversy in terms of his concern for preserving national identity.[26] In a series of editorials entitled "Religion and Education," he drew a sharp distinction between moral philosophy (*rinri gaku*) and moral education (*tokuiku*). For Kuga, moral philosophy was concerned with universal aspects of man's behavior and with abstract ideals and pure ethics. He stressed, however, that history and circumstances of time and place intruded upon ethical absolutes, shaping them to the special nature of a people. In a period of intense competition among nations, the preservation of a people's particular morals was essential, because they provided the sense of unity that was a critical part of national defense. The function of moral education was to cultivate the particular ethics—or, as he sometimes said, "the common sentiments" (*futsūteki kansō*)—of the Japanese. Whatever influenced the "spiritual attitude" of the people should be reconciled with the need to preserve these ethics. The Japanese should not

---

* The most detailed and perhaps most bitter retort was a series of articles in *Kokumin no tomo* during March, May, and June 1893 by Takahashi Gorō, a leading Christian scholar.

necessarily proscribe Christianity; they should assimilate it as they had Buddhism. As an abstract ethical system, shorn of its foreign customs and ties, Christianity need not be considered alien ethics in conflict with moral education.

III

A basic cause of the conflict between the Seikyōsha and the Min'yūsha on the subject of old and new values was the split in their attitudes toward social progress. Was progress compatible with diversity of social structures? This question was especially perplexing for Japan as the first non-Western nation to modernize. Japanese in the late nineteenth century lacked the evidence sociologists now have to support the belief that industrial development is compatible with diverse social structures.*

As we have seen, the Min'yūsha members believed there was a social structure and value system common to Western nations that Japan must adopt to support her own industrial development. Tokutomi adhered to a Spencerian theory of social evolution that posited stages through which all progressing societies must pass. The barbarous, militant, and autocratic phase of society must eventually be superseded by an

---

* The issue is not resolved today. Reinhard Bendix argues against the views, still held, that "societies will resemble each other increasingly, as they become 'fully industrialized,' " and that "economically backward societies will become like the economically advanced countries—if they industrialize successfully." Bendix feels that "these views, conditional as they are on 'full industrialization,' have little warrant. The industrial societies of today retain aspects of their traditional social structure that have been combined with economic development in various ways. . . . The idea of tradition and modernity as mutually exclusive is simply false. The most general experience is that modern, industrial societies retain their several, divergent traditions. . . . Accordingly, our concept of development must encompass not only the products and by-products of industrialization, but also the various amalgams of tradition and modernity which make all developments 'partial.' " Reinhard Bendix, *Nation-Building and Citizenship: Studies of Our Changing Social Order* (New York, 1964), pp. 8–9. For an example of a contrary view, see John W. Bennett, "Japanese Economic Growth: Background for Social Change," in Dore, *Social Change*, pp. 411–53. Bennett and others believe that the functional necessities of an industrial society are such that in the long run diversity of social and cultural forms among industrial nations is bound to disappear.

industrial, pacific, and democratic phase.* His belief in the universality of evolutionary stages supported his conviction that Japan would increasingly resemble advanced Western nations as she progressed. Thus Japan's traditional social practices and values seemed archaic to the degree they differed from the Western pattern.

Kokumin no tomo expressed belief that Japan had developed far toward becoming a Western, democratic (*heimin*) society, for the Meiji Restoration had overturned the feudal system, dissolved the aristocracy, and abolished the restrictions of a class system. Nonetheless, social relations remained bound to old "aristocratic" patterns. Japanese, said an editorial entitled "Democratic Morals," did not yet understand or practice the ethics of a democratic society.[27] Social structure in aristocratic society stressed vertical relations of dependence— of child on parents, servant on master, pupil on teacher. "The weakness of aristocratic morals is their disregard of the 'self' [*onore*]." The individual in Japan had not yet been cut free from the chains of social obligation. Japan, the editorial concluded, must adopt the horizontal ethics of a democratic society, in which relations were between individuals or between the individual and society. Democratic ethics encouraged the individual to rely on his own efforts, knowledge, and skills, rather than on the joint effort of his group.

The Min'yūsha devoted itself to the reform of education and of the family system, believing that these two important

---

* Richard Hofstadter has succinctly summed up Spencer's view of social evolution: "The very process of social consolidation brought about by struggles and conquest eliminates the necessity for continued conflict. Society then passes from its barbarous or militant phase into an industrial phase.... There emerges the industrial type of society, a regime of contract rather than status, which unlike the older form is pacific, respectful of the individual, more heterogeneous and plastic, more inclined to abandon economic autonomy in favor of industrial co-operation with other states. Natural selection now works to produce a completely different individual character. Industrial society requires security for life, liberty, and property; the character type most consonant with this society is accordingly peaceful, independent, kindly, and honest." Richard Hofstadter, *Social Darwinism in American Thought* (Boston, 1955), revised ed., p. 42.

socializing agents must inculcate the new values essential to Japan's progress. Tokutomi was apprehensive over signs that the Ministry of Education was reintroducing traditional ethical principles in the primary school curriculum. Early in 1890, even prior to promulgation of the Imperial Rescript on Education, *Kokumin no tomo* began to express alarm. An editorial in June 1890 observed regretfully that primary school children in rural areas made a habit of bowing—to their schoolmaster, to the policeman, to the tax collector, and to anyone on the street who had the appearance of an official.[28] This submissive respect was indicative of the kind of education they were receiving. A nation's character was to a great extent the result of the training children received at this impressionable age. Today's kowtowing pupils, said *Kokumin no tomo*, would be tomorrow's kowtowing citizens. The editorial criticized teachers for submitting to the Ministry of Education; they were breeding hypocrisy by teaching what they did not believe. "Despite the great faults of Confucianism, it was practiced in the past because people truly believed in it. Today, people do not believe in it, but they still try to practice it."[29] Teachers should stress universal principles consonant with the new democratic age, principles that would command belief: truthfulness, hard work, persistence, independence, self-respect, and sincerity.

The proclamation of the Rescript, however, added the Emperor's authority to that of the Ministry of Education in sanctioning the conservative direction in education. *Kokumin no tomo* was plainly hard pressed to interpret the Rescript favorably. On the other hand, rejecting its validity would have been tantamount to questioning imperial wisdom, which Tokutomi was unwilling to do. (Although expressions of reverence for the Emperor were relatively sparse in Tokutomi's writings, there was nonetheless a marked reluctance to criticize the imperial institution. His reluctance was particularly noteworthy in view of his condemnation of traditional Japan, which was otherwise so thoroughgoing.) *Kokumin no tomo* took what it hoped would be an inoffensive position: it assured its readers that the Rescript effected no change in the policy of education.[30] The magazine attacked the view of a Tokyo University professor that the Rescript was intended to revive Confucianism. *Kokumin no tomo* defended the Rescript as much too broad in its meaning to be limited to Confucianism, Buddhism, Shintoism, or Christianity; rather, the Rescript proclaimed morals common in Japan since ancient times. This argument was an incongruous one for the Min'yūsha members to make, for as a matter of general policy it was Japan's ancient morals that they themselves wanted to replace.

Though not forceful in their initial reaction to the Rescript, the Min'yūsha members continued to express resistance to the conservative trend in education. In *Kokumin shimbun* for April 7, 1893, Tokutomi described a third-grade ethics class he had observed at the primary school in Atami, a sea resort south of Tokyo. He stressed the stultifying effect the teacher had had on the minds of his pupils:

"Why," the teacher asked, must we be loyal to the Emperor?" A pupil stood up: "The Emperor—" he began; but he stopped, tittering, unable to conclude. "Don't laugh!" the teacher scolded, and spoke deliberately: "Because we are indebted to the Emperor. Class," the teacher asked again, "why are we indebted?" The pupils stared in puzzled silence. "It is thanks to the Emperor," said the teacher, "that you come here and return home safely." To be sure the lesson was learned, the teacher continued: "To whom are we indebted that burglars don't enter our houses and that we have all come to school without meeting bullies?" A girl promptly spoke up: "The policeman." The teacher thought dejectedly for a time. "Of course that is true, but the policeman is ultimately the Emperor's." . . . The innocent girl did not understand the teacher's purpose and only stared in mystified silence.

The teacher allowed Tokutomi to ask a question:

"Class, we often hear of doing good and bad. What is doing good?" A bright youngster jumped up from the corner: "Practicing loyalty and filial piety!" I was startled by the overly sophisticated response. Seeing my astonishment, the teacher said: "Say what you think without using difficult words." At once from the girls' side a voice could be heard: "Not being a thief."[31]

The first reply to his question was a "manufactured" one, Tokutomi observed, and the second presumed that "outside of laws there were no morals." He deplored the "formalism" and "parrot-like repetition" that characterized ethics classes. Inoue Tetsujirō and others of his stripe, he concluded, would have been pleased to observe this class.

Kokumin no tomo emphasized the critical role of education in instilling a guiding spirit throughout the nation. "Spiritual anarchy" (*seishinteki museifushugi*) plagued Japanese because the character of their education was inconsonant with their new institutions. Confucian-style education would destroy the free institutions that Japan had only recently established: the constitution, the Diet, and local self-government. "What anguish it is," the editorial concluded, "to say and do what is not in one's heart."[32]

The other socializing agent the Min'yūsha sought to reform was the Japanese family system. Growth of national consciousness and the impact of Western culture had made the Japanese aware of the unique nature of their traditional family patterns. Except for the imperial institution, the Min'yūsha could not have attacked any part of traditional society to which Japanese felt a deeper emotional attachment. Even those who would reform the system found it difficult to practice their proposals within their own families.*

---

* Fukuzawa, for example, brought his daughters up in the strictest orthodoxy. See Blacker, pp. 157–58. Mori Arinori, author of the reformist *Essay on Wives* (and, later, Minister of Education), insisted that his own marriage be in the form of a contract (Fukuzawa was a witness) to demonstrate the equality of the partnership. But he later dissolved the marriage, remarking that his wife had become "peculiar and flighty" as a result of the new relationship, and that "to attempt a marriage like that with an uneducated Japanese woman was my mistake." See Nagai Michio, "Mori Arinori."

The Min'yūsha members believed strongly that the creation of a wholly democratic society depended upon reform of the family system. In September 1892 Tokutomi began publishing the *Katei zasshi* (Home Magazine) to help disseminate new family ethics.[33] And a *Kokumin no tomo* editorial of June 1893 entitled "Family Tyranny" offered a fierce denunciation of the traditional Japanese family system, which it condemned as "a breeding ground of . . . servility, double-dealing, mistrust, hypocrisy, jealousy, alienation, and treachery."[34]

Kokumin no tomo found family tyranny most oppressive in its effects upon young people. The weight of family obligation bore heavily on ambitious young men, preventing them from achieving individuality and from succeeding in the world. The burden of having to support parents, brothers, sisters, and collateral relatives encumbered young family heads. Japanese society forced young men, from a sense of obligation rather than from spontaneous inclination, to care for relatives of the extended family who were frequently capable of self-support. "Society regards it as proper that the lazy, idle, and shiftless should suck the blood of their relatives. If the diligent, self-controlled, and thrifty hesitate to support their relatives, then people say they are heartless, frivolous, cruel, and unprincipled." Rather than face ostracism, young men sacrificed their spirit and ambition on the altar of family obligation. And this burden continued inexorably from generation to generation: "It is the fault of the family system that youth must sacrifice themselves for today's elders, who once sacrificed themselves for their own elders. . . . Today's elderly take out the bitterness of their past on our young people. Thus if we do not change . . . to a system of individualism, we shall never be able to overcome the evils of family tyranny."

Kokumin no tomo urged the adoption of five measures to reform the family system. First, in order to foster self-reliance, property should belong not to families, but to individuals. Second, the practice of early retirements should be abandoned; parents still capable of self-support should not retire into leisurely dependence on their children. Third, parents and their married children should live separately; when the generations lived together, the family's welfare was gained at the expense of the individual's. Fourth, because early marriage endangered self-reliance, young men should marry only if they could support themselves. Fifth, relations with distant relatives should be limited, so as to avoid "unnatural relationships of obligation [*giri*]."

In a series of *Nihon* editorials, Kuga defended the existing family system on several grounds.[35] He felt *Kokumin no tomo* had not described the prevailing practices. Among both the rich and poor, for example, parents and married children often lived separately and possessed separate property. When parents and married children lived together, economic convenience rather than the compulsion of an oppressive "system" made them do so. Moreover, there existed effective moral restraints to deter the abuses *Kokumin no tomo* deplored. Brothers, sisters, and relatives dependent on the family head experienced uncomfortable feelings of debt (*on*) and shame (*jikuji*) which they sought to avoid. Cultivation of moral sanctions through education was the proper way to prevent the occasional abuses that *Kokumin no tomo* deplored. There were only isolated instances, said Kuga, of parents retiring early to live supported by their children's efforts. Parents wanted to further their sons' success, not obstruct it. Kuga believed furthermore that when parents were unable to care for themselves, a young man could not be satisfied to put them in a poorhouse so that he could rise in the world unencumbered. The cold, self-seeking ways of Western individualism were not worthy to replace the harmony and warmth of the existing Japanese family relations.

IV

In the early 1890's a pessimistic tone began to appear in *Kokumin no tomo*, reflecting, I believe, a rapid decline in re-

ceptivity to Min'yūsha ideas. At the time of its founding in
1887, the Min'yūsha had had an optimistic faith in the capacity
of the new generation to complete the transformation of Japanese society. But the hopes raised by the pace of change in the
two decades following 1868 were still unfulfilled. Society now
seemed sluggish, less tractable and less receptive to reform than
the Min'yūsha had foreseen.* A settled class system with new
vested interests had developed, and the range of possible experimentation had begun to narrow. Tokutomi and his associates now expressed doubt that young men would accomplish
their mission.

Realization that it was easier to adopt a new institution—a
cabinet system or a constitution—than to reform entrenched
patterns of behavior produced frustration which, as we have
seen, the Min'yūsha members vented on the family system.
Their confidence in the new generation had weakened, and
they blamed "family tyranny" for preventing ambitious young
people from rising in the world to perform the great tasks Tokutomi had set for them. We do not know whether social mobility was actually declining in the early 1890's; but it is
apparent that because young people seemed increasingly frustrated in their hopes for remaking society there was, especially
in the minds of Min'yūsha members, at least a psychological
reduction of mobility.

In the next chapter we shall consider two of the causes for
the changed climate of opinion in Japan that adversely affected receptivity to Min'yūsha ideas; they need only be mentioned here. First, the inauspicious beginning of constitutional

---

* Opponents of radical social change won a significant victory when the Diet
voted in 1892 to postpone the enactment of a civil code. Widespread opposition
to the draft code had caused the government to adopt a cautious approach.
The civil code eventually promulgated in 1898 gave greater regard to Japanese
custom than the 1890 draft had. The 1890 draft had allowed, for example, for
the deposition of unsuitable family heads; the 1898 code deleted this provision,
regarding it as an undue threat to the traditional family structure. Professor
Ishii writes that custom was given particular regard in the provisions that dealt
with relatives and succession. Ishii Ryosuke, *Japanese Legislation in the Meiji
Era*, translated by William J. Chambliss (Tokyo, 1958), pp. 590–91.

government produced disillusionment with Western-inspired reform efforts. Second, in the early 1890's Japan began to feel international tensions more acutely than at any time since the Restoration. The intrusion of foreign affairs tended to evoke latent nationalist sentiment. Increasingly, Japanese considered domestic reform movements to be destructive of national unity.

Kokumin no tomo emphasized that the treaty revision controversy had been a significant cause for the decline in receptivity to its views. It recalled that in 1886 a leading newspaper, the *Mainichi shimbun*, had held a contest for essays on mixed residence.[36] Of 127 essays submitted from throughout Japan, all but fifteen had favored mixed residence. By 1891, however, only a few outspoken Japanese like Taguchi Ukichi publicly supported opening the country to foreign residence, travel, and trade. Kokumin no tomo believed that opposition to the Inoue and Ōkuma proposals in 1887 and 1889 had transformed admiration of Westerners into fear and resentment. As a consequence, Westernizing zeal had waned.

Perhaps the most significant source of Tokutomi's pessimism was the realization that opposition to his ideas came increasingly from members of his own generation. He had hitherto been regarded as a leader of Meiji youth, but by May 1891 he was admitting that young men were deserting to the "conservative group."[37] Youth by their nature, he said, should be expected to ally themselves with progressive movements; instead they had not only submitted to the conservative cause, they had even become its leaders.

What had caused the change in attitudes among young Japanese? Tokutomi laid much of the blame on the progressives themselves. He repeated his belief that Fukuzawa's ideas had failed to give young people the moral direction they sought. For a time, Christianity had filled this spiritual need by attracting confused and searching youths into youth groups and by offering them a moral standard for the new age. Unsophisticated missionaries, however, had tried to introduce a lifeless dogma that would have stifled the youthful spirit by controlling every aspect of conduct and inquiry.

The political parties, too, had lost their attraction. Itagaki's Liberal Party, Tokutomi said, by resorting to methods of political violence, had forfeited its intellectual appeal to youth. Ōkuma's group had matured, and youth no longer constituted the core of his Progressive Party. As Ōkuma aged he relegated young men to disciple roles and emphasized seniority. "The leaders of the Progressive Party understand the need for order in a group, but they have forgotten the need to capture the unsettled human heart [fuchitsujo no jinshin]."

In contrast with the progressives, who failed to respond to the needs of young Japanese, the conservatives succeeded by appealing to their idealism. Youth, Tokutomi said, "swarmed to the conservative banner," attracted by its ideals of patriotism, loyalty, and honor. The conservative appeal, he implied, was also largely an emotional one that offered ample latitude for youthful self-assertiveness. Unlike other groups, the conservatives had few rules and little organization to stifle the initiative and spirit of youth. "In their eyes," he wrote, "it is not conservatism."

Another cause of Tokutomi's despair in the early 1890's was what he called "middle-class depravity."[38] By "middle class" he referred primarily to the rural landlords, whom he described as the most important beneficiaries of the Restoration.* Hitherto Tokutomi had believed that their experience in establish-

---

* Tokutomi wrote of the rural landlord class: "Country gentlemen (inaka shinshi) comprise the largest single element of our middle class. Indeed they are the middle class! . . . Good fortune, riding on the wings of a revolution (kakumei), fell into its lap. Who, after all, were the beneficiaries of the 'liberation' of the people? The samurai lost power and the rural middle class gained it (seiryoku). The so-called autonomous local governments have fallen into its hands; so has the power to elect provincial assemblies, and now a national parliament. In the twenty years since the Revolution, this class has been given so much political power, it can scarcely hold it in its two hands." Quoted in Smith, "Landlords' Sons," p. 98.

ing rural industry had nurtured an independent and enterprising spirit that would make them a sturdy social base for the democratic, industrial society he envisioned. By 1892, however, he was disillusioned. The new economic and political power of landlords was bringing them to the towns and cities, where they succumbed to habits and excesses of easy living; citified, they lost the spartan simplicity and the characteristics of thrift and hard work they had developed in the countryside. Unless this "middle class" overcame its depravity, concluded Tokutomi, Japan's future would be bleak.

Controversy surrounding the Rescript on Education gave the Min'yūsha members further evidence of the diminishing receptivity to their views. We have already seen *Kokumin no tomo*'s incongruous response to the proclamation: the Min'yūsha was unwilling to reject the validity of the Rescript, unwilling to argue that ethical values proclaimed by the Emperor were no longer valid and useful. Thus when Inoue Tetsujirō and others effectively invoked the Rescript to arouse anti-Christian sentiment, Tokutomi and his associates, in attempting to justify their ideas in terms of the Rescript, seemed to be accepting new limits on their thought. A *Kokumin no tomo* editorial of October 1892 complained of the cunning use many writers were making of the Rescript to attack their enemies. The Rescript had put the Min'yūsha on the defensive.

The same *Kokumin no tomo* editorial sought to show that the democratic, individualist philosophy of the Min'yūsha was compatible with the Rescript's principles.[39] To support its position, the editorial quoted the least explicit section of the Rescript: "Bear yourselves in modesty and moderation, and extend your benevolence to all; pursue learning and cultivate arts, and thereby develop intellectual faculties and perfect moral powers." The Min'yūsha could embrace this dictum as "the great and primary object of individualism." Moreover, the editorial emphasized that individualism was an essential part of patriotism, for "self-love is truly the source of love of country. . . . In a democratic society we need not worry about the lack of patriotism but about its superabundance. The only real patriot in an absolutist monarchy is the ruler, and in an aristocracy the only real patriots are the aristocrats. But in a democratic society, all the people regard the nation as 'ours.' " Finally, *Kokumin no tomo* insisted that Christianity was not destructive of loyalty and filial piety. If it were, how could monarchy and family have remained established institutions in the West?

The Min'yūsha's attempt to reconcile values that it had hitherto claimed were incompatible revealed a weakening commitment to its original ideas. Tokutomi's Westernism had been supported by his conviction that the path of social advance discernible in the history of the more advanced Western nations represented a fixed pattern of universal development that all progressing nations must follow. In his mind, therefore, Westernization and the sweeping rejection of the Japanese cultural heritage had had strong nationalist motivation. But by the early 1890's Tokutomi was beginning to feel tensions between his national and cultural loyalties; he and other Westernizers, by their ambivalent reaction to the Imperial Rescript, showed themselves hard pressed to reconcile patriotism with cultural alienation, nationalism with Westernism. In the climate of opinion that was developing after the issuance of the Rescript, national loyalty came increasingly to be identified with adherence to traditional cultural values; social reform was regarded with suspicion.

Tokutomi began to seek historical reasons for the frustration of his hopes. In 1893 he wrote a long essay in *Kokumin no tomo* (which derived largely from a biography he had just completed on the Restoration hero, Yoshida Shōin) in which he sought to explain the origin of the conservative movement that was emerging. He found its roots in a fundamental but neglected aspect of the Meiji Restoration.[40] Tokutomi believed that the great reforms carried out in the twenty years after 1868 had misled observers into interpreting the revolution itself as basically progressive in its aims. He argued that the Japanese experience had been fundamentally different from the French Revolution, for during the Tokugawa period there had been no mass disaffection, no reformist sentiment motivated by mass social discontent. On the contrary, owing partly to the system of local rule, which had made the government responsive to local needs, and partly to the Confucian emphasis on the welfare of the people as the proper standard of politics, the great mass of the people had been content with Tokugawa rule.

Tokutomi concluded, then, that the Meiji Restoration had been a reactionary "spiritual revolution" (*seishinteki kakumei*) rather than a progressive social movement. The Tokugawas had built their system on the inviolable loyalty of retainer to lord, but this precept had contained "a dangerous element that could tear apart the feudal system, and even Ieyasu, as great as he was, never foresaw it." Rationalist writers had pressed the concept of loyalty to its logical conclusion and had found the Emperor to be the highest lord of all. To this rationalism had been added the religious fervor of Shinto and the self-interest of talented men dissatisfied with the hereditary system. The goal of all these elements had been a revolution to reestablish the old system of direct imperial rule.

The impact of Western civilization, however, had taken the revolution in an unexpected direction, giving it progressive characteristics previously lacking. Tokutomi did not explain why Japan in the throes of a reactionary movement had been receptive to the progressive Western influence. He did emphasize the fortuitous nature of the impact: Japan had fallen into "a swift current of world affairs that carried her into an unexpected harbor." For twenty years after 1868, the progressive influence of the West had overshadowed the fundamental, reactionary goals of the Restoration. Only in recent years had reactionary goals reemerged. Opposition to mixed residence, the *kokusui* movement, the new conservatives, the Confucian revival, Germanism, statism, the anti-Christian movement— all could be traced to the basic nature of the Restoration.

Events of the early 1890's had awakened Tokutomi to the restraining influence of Japan's past. He attributed the great progress achieved after the Restoration to fortuitous influences that now appeared spent. The Western impact had not been sufficient to uproot old values and traditional patterns of behavior. This reluctant recognition of the inescapable influence of the Japanese past ultimately set in motion profound changes in Tokutomi's thought.

Chapter Seven

THE QUEST FOR A NATIONAL MISSION

I

THE PROMULGATION of the new constitution on February 11, 1889, and the convocation of the First Diet on November 25, 1890, came after many years of groping for a suitable political framework. The movement for some form of representative national assembly began late in the Tokugawa period when the fall of the Bakufu appeared imminent. After the Restoration, men excluded from power in the new government joined in the People's Rights Movement, organizing parties and invoking Western liberal theory in support of a campaign for representative government. Finally, in 1881, an imperial rescript announced the government's decision to convene a national assembly in 1890.

Government leaders regarded the Diet as a safety valve for political and social unrest and as a means of building national unity. Moreover, like many other reforms, the decision to introduce a representative system was in part designed to support the treaty revision effort: a popular assembly would demonstrate to the Western powers Japan's progress in reforming her political and legal structure.[1] Of greatest concern to us here is that many Japanese themselves came to regard the constitution and the Diet as a measure of their national progress and development; they saw these institutions as a means of recovering national pride and even of demonstrating Japan's equality with Western nations. A leading politician wrote that at the time the constitution was promulgated "certain European people ridiculed the idea of Japan's adopting constitutional government saying that . . . [it] is not suitable for an Asiatic nation, and is only adapted to the cool-headed people of Northern Europe; even the Southern European nations have failed in establishing constitutional government. How can an Asiatic nation accomplish what Southern European nations have found impossible?"* If despite these odds the Japanese could succeed with parliamentary institutions, they could prove to the world and to themselves that their capacity for representative government was equal to the Westerners'. The Japanese had invested their self-confidence in the outcome of the Diet. Failure would tend to increase the self-doubt that many Japanese had expressed during the controversy over mixed residence.

From the time the Diet opened in 1890, the success of constitutional government was endangered by hostile relations between the oligarchy and the parties, and by their divergent views of the Diet's function. Determined to establish the principle of cabinet responsibility to the Diet, the parties used their budgetary power to try to disrupt government programs. The oligarchy countered by claiming to represent the whole nation rather than any one faction.

The writings of Seikyōsha members indicate that the initial results of the parliamentary experiment depressed many Japanese. Miyake wrote that the First Diet had destroyed the expectations raised during the long years of preparation for constitutional government; the result had been "only secretiveness among ministers and factionalism among Diet members,

---

* As late as 1899, Itō Hirobumi still felt that "if there is one mistake in the progress and direction of constitutional government, there will be those who question the suitability of constitutional government for the Orient." I have drawn both quotations from Akita, "Meiji Constitution."

only estrangement and corruption."[2] Kuga concluded that just as revision of the treaties could not of itself ensure Japanese independence, so the mere establishment of a constitutional form of government was not sufficient to attain his other cherished goal—the unity of the Japanese people. Everyone, he said, had harbored inordinate and unreasonable hopes for the constitutional system. It had not had "the slightest success" in unifying the country.[3] This goal could be achieved only by means of a binding ideology, a cause higher than party.

The Min'yūsha, which had been even more enthusiastic than its rival about the proposed constitutional system, was also disappointed with the results. Shortly before the Diet opened, *Kokumin no tomo* had described it as the greatest achievement of two decades of reform. Historians would remember 1890 as a "great turning point" when representative government had transformed the spirit of Japanese society.[4] Once the outcome of the First Diet was clear, however, *Kokumin no tomo* reluctantly admitted that its hopes had been excessive; the millennium had not arrived. People had been "too optimistic" in expecting the "statesmanship of Pitt and the eloquence of Burke" in Japan's first attempt at parliamentary government.[5] Success would come only with experience and, above all, perseverance.

After 1890 *Kokumin no tomo* editorials increasingly stressed the importance of national self-respect, for Tokutomi and his associates feared that, lacking confidence in their own abilities, Japanese would lose heart for reform. Yet what cause was there for Japanese pride and assurance? This question, the source of much spiritual torment, presented the Min'yūsha members with a dilemma to which they had no wholly convincing solution. They urged national self-confidence but at the same time repudiated the only possible basis for such self-confidence— the worth of Japan's traditional culture. In making self-confidence dependent on Japan's achieving the civilizing values and institutions of the West, they left unanswered the questions that most needed answering if Japanese were to believe in themselves. If, as the Min'yūsha insisted, Japanese were equal in ability to Westerners, why had they not independently produced a society and a culture equal to those of Western countries? Was there nothing of intrinsic value in the Japanese past?

A *Kokumin no tomo* editorial of May 23, 1891, entitled "Great Nations" revealed the predicament.[6] The writer deplored Japan's self-doubt but offered no remedy for it; he urged self-assurance but offered scant grounds for it. The editorial lamented the sway that "prophets of gloom" held over Japanese society; fear of mixed residence, Christianity, and any close association with Westerners was a sign of self-effacement. Western nations, in contrast, had a confidence worthy of Japanese emulation:

If someone stood on London Bridge and shouted that England's independence was in danger, that England was on the verge of destruction, how would Englishmen treat him? They might consider him insane and put him in a mental institution. Or they might consider him good material for *Punch*. That would be all. No one would take him seriously, because the English have complete confidence in their country's independence. The reason the English are a great nation is not only that they are a great people, but that they believe they are a great people.

Fortunately, according to *Kokumin no tomo,* there were signs that Japan was catching up with the West: national wealth had increased five or six times in two decades, population was increasing more rapidly than in most European countries, and most Japanese were now getting an education comparable to that received by Europeans. In short, Japan was gradually rising in the civilized world: "If one impartially compares our country with European countries, we are above Spain and abreast of Italy." Advancement in this hierarchy of great nations depended on diligence, frugality, independent spirit, public spirit, self-respect, and a belief in progress, God's will, and the sanctity of labor. These were the universal values of civilized nations; to acquire them would bring pride. The Min'yūsha could find no worth in the particularistic values and achievements of Japanese culture: "Our country can never be preserved by . . . the Tosa School of painters, or by the architecture of the Hōryūji or the Shōsōin, or by sculpture, or by the celebrated capitals Nara and Kyoto."

II

At the root of Japanese self-doubt lay the belief that as societies progressed naturally they adopted like habits, institutions, and values. Thus Japan's progress could be measured in terms of her acquired similarities to advanced Western nations. During the 1870's and 1880's the belief that the course of Western civilization represented the universal path of man's progress was so pervasive that the term *bummei* (civilization) was often used as a synonym for *seiyō bummei* (Western civilization). Discouragement over the seeming failure of the parliamentary experiment owed much to this view, for the Japanese regarded representative government as a fundamental attribute of civilized nations. If, by contrast, progress could be shown to be compatible with diversity of habits, institutions, and values, there would be grounds for Japanese confidence. To accomplish this task, Seikyōsha members had to change their countrymen's concept of what "civilization" was.

One manifestation of the dominant belief in the superiority of Western civilization was extreme revulsion from an Asian identity. Progress, in this view, required discarding traditional Asian institutions, customs, and patterns of social behavior in favor of their Western counterparts. We find a good example of this attitude in the impression Itagaki Taisuke recorded in 1883 after a trip to Europe. He expressed resignation that Westerners would always regard Japan as "Asian": "Consider, for example, a primitive [*yaban*] country. Some of its people are intelligent, but because the majority are not, the country is inevitably called primitive. In the same way, no matter how far Japan progresses, no matter how enlightened she becomes, just because the great majority of people in other Asian countries are ignorant and primitive, the whole of Asia is considered primitive."[7] Itagaki concluded that Westerners' association of Japan with other Asian countries was jeopardizing the treaty revision movement.

Fukuzawa gives us an even clearer example of this attitude. In an 1885 editorial entitled "Escape from Asia" (*Datsu-A ron*),[8] he exulted over the progress made in adopting Western civilization, but argued that this progress was not in itself sufficient to win the favor of Western countries:

Not only have we escaped the old habits of Japan, but we have devised a new strategy concerning Asian countries; its fundamental idea is "escape from Asia." . . . Today China and Korea are no help at all to our country. On the contrary, because our three countries are adjacent we are sometimes regarded as the same in the eyes of civilized Western peoples. Appraisals of China and Korea are applied to our country, . . . and indirectly this greatly impedes our foreign policy. It is really a great misfortune for our country. It follows that in making our present plans we have not time to await the development of neighboring countries and join them in reviving Asia. Rather, we should escape from them and join the company of Western civilized nations. Although China and Korea are our neighbors, this fact should make no difference in our relations with them. We should deal with them as Westerners do. If we keep bad company, we cannot avoid a bad name. In my heart I favor breaking off with the bad company of East Asia.*

---

* Fukuzawa would have been pleased with the recent assessment of an American scholar: "Japan today cannot be considered an Asiatic or East Asian culture. Deep now, after a hundred years, deep in Japanese culture are ideas, values, ways of handling human relations which ultimately, historically go back to the western traditions, to Greece and to Israel. . . . Japan now participates in the tradition of western culture." Robert Bellah, "Values and Social Change in Modern Japan," *Ajia bunka kenkyū*, 3 (1962), 55. David Riesman and many others have pointed out, though, that the Japanese themselves are less convinced. "Whether in humility or in submerged pride, the Japanese tend ethnocentrically to think of themselves as alone in the world. . . . Japanese ethnocentrism is related to the uneasy perplexity of the Japanese intellectual as to what league he plays in. Is his an island that by accident is not located on the English

Tokutomi shared the prevailing attitude toward Asia. In his writings, as we have seen, "Oriental-style" was an epithet synonymous with decadent, sterile, passive, unscientific.

To combat this widely felt preference for Western over Asian values, Kuga and Miyake formulated the concept of *sekai no bummei* (world civilization). They pointed out that the culture of a nation was not the product of a few of its members, but the "result of the cooperation of influences of every type." Similarly, world civilization could fully develop only if nations with different cultures exercised their influence and contributed their special talents. "Since it is the mission of every nation [*kokumin tenshoku*]," Kuga wrote, "to exercise its influence on world civilization, it follows that in order to fulfill this mission, each nation must strive to preserve and develop its own unique influence and abilities. This is the first concept of our nationalist group, and all other concepts derive from it."[9] If a nation neglected to develop the unique characteristics that history and environment had bestowed on it, it failed to make its potential unique contribution to world civilization.

The best explanation of the Seikyōsha position was a treatise Miyake wrote in the spring of 1891, *Shin-zen-bi Nihonjin* (The Japanese: Truth, Goodness, and Beauty), in which his purpose was "to bring the Japanese to know themselves and to fulfill their mission of contributing to the process of world civilization."[10] He said in the preface that he also hoped to dispel the gloom his countrymen felt over the outcome of the First Diet.[11]

Miyake believed that the progress of civilization was the product of competition; he argued in Spencerian fashion that man had progressed first through individual competition and then through competition between increasingly large social units. Through this competitive process, the competing units

---

Channel and happens to be in Asia, uncomfortably close to a lot of 'backward' people?" David Riesman, "Japanese Intellectuals—and Americans," *American Scholar*, XXXIV, 1 (1964–65), 63.

or groups improved their abilities and contributed to the advance of world civilization. World civilization thus attained higher stages, proceeding in telic fashion toward the ultimate perfection of man. Miyake defined civilization's final goal as the attainment of truth, goodness, and beauty.

Perception of these absolutes, however, was always limited by perspectives of time and place. Just as one had to look from many different positions to determine the actual shape of a mountain, so truth, goodness, and beauty had to be measured from different vantage points, by different methods, and by different criteria. The testing of various viewpoints by competition was essential in determining the absolutes.

In the present age, said Miyake, the unit of social competition was the nation-state. World civilization was now advancing because of competition between nations with different cultures. The culture of Western nations, Miyake admitted, was at the highest stage civilization had yet reached; but concepts of value besides those of Western culture were necessary if world civilization was to progress to an even higher stage.

Japanese therefore had an obligation to preserve and develop their distinctive talents and values in order to supplement the contributions of Western culture. This emphasis on Japan's unique qualities was of course a necessary part of self-defense, but it was more than that. Cultural nationalism was an honorable and progressive pursuit. Miyake emphasized this fundamental point in his preface: "To exert oneself on behalf of one's country is to work on behalf of the world. Promoting the special nature of a people contributes to the evolution of mankind. Defense of the homeland and love of mankind are not at all contradictory." By this deft stroke Miyake made cultural nationalism both a moral obligation (*gimu*) and a progressive cause; he elevated his countrymen's sentimental attachment to Japanese culture and gave it intellectual justification.

Miyake believed that the greatest obstacle to fulfillment of the Japanese mission was the sense of shame and inferiority that most Japanese felt toward Westerners. A significant cause of these feelings, he wrote, was the greater physical stature of Westerners, which he attributed to a more demanding physical environment during their early historical development. In the present age, however, the important factor in international competition was not physical strength but intellect. During the controversy over mixed residence, Inoue Tetsujirō had said that the larger skulls and more prominent foreheads of Westerners indicated their superior intelligence. Miyake dismissed this belief by remarking that Ainu and elephants also had large heads!

It was not much harder to answer the argument that the superiority of Western civilization was proof of a superior intellect. (Inoue Tetsujirō had said that Japanese lacked the Western capacity for profound generalization and precise reasoning.) Miyake argued that comparisons in terms of knowledge or achievement between peoples in vastly different historical circumstances could give no indication of their relative intellectual ability. The Japanese schoolboy knew more about the shape of the world than Socrates had known, but that did not make the schoolboy more intelligent than Socrates. Bismarck had ruled a greater empire than Pericles, but that did not prove Bismarck a better, more intelligent statesman. The undeniable superiority of much in Western civilization was not in itself proof that the Westerner possessed a superior intellect.

Miyake urged Japanese to summon confidence from their racial identity as Mongoloids. He said that Japanese could take as much pride in the origins of "Mongoloid civilization" along the Yellow River as Westerners took in their origins. He compared the Hsia, Shang, and Chou periods to the great age of Greece; he compared the Duke of Chou to Pericles, Confucius to Socrates, China in the Ch'in and Han periods to the Roman Empire, and the spread of Confucianism to the emergence of Christianity. In sum, the development of the

West during the ancient and medieval periods had in no way been superior to Mongoloid development. The Japanese were among the most talented members of the Mongoloid peoples; they had every reason to take pride in the early accomplishments of their race.

Miyake argued that during the modern period Western civilization had developed beyond Mongoloid civilization for reasons of geography and timing. Europe had been favored by a network of rivers that facilitated trade and development. The rugged Chinese terrain, on the other hand, penetrated by only three or four rivers, had not permitted such rapid development. Moreover, because European civilization had begun its development a thousand years later, it had benefited from the achievements of the older Arabian, Indo-Egyptian, and Mongoloid civilizations.

Japanese had reason to be proud not only of their racial identity but of their national identity as well. How many people in Western history could match the political acumen of Tokugawa Ieyasu, the generalship of Toyotomi Hideyoshi, the skilled cartography of Inō Chūkei,* or the literary art of Murasaki Shikibu? These and many other Japanese had demonstrated talents that "could not easily be surpassed by Westerners." Their accomplishments proved that Japanese had abilities useful in the development of world civilization.

Having established grounds for Japanese self-confidence, Miyake sought next to explain Japan's special historical and geographical role in the pursuit of truth, goodness, and beauty. The pursuit of truth (shin) required the study, sorting, and analysis of material drawn from many different experiences and circumstances. The Japanese had had considerable experience in this regard. They had imported ideas from India and China and subjected them to searching examination, re-

---

* Inō Chūkei (1745–1818) used rude instruments to survey the Japanese islands and constructed maps that were the basis of all subsequent Japanese maps of Japan in the nineteenth century.

finement, and development; they were now doing the same
with Western ideas. Whereas other peoples, such as the Chinese, who had had longer contact with the West, remained
oblivious to new ideas, the Japanese had shown a decided
talent for investigation.

In particular, Japanese had a mission to apply their scholarly
ability to a study of the history, society, and culture of Far
Eastern countries. Western scholarship—Spencerian sociology,
for example—had not dealt adequately with East Asia. Miyake
urged that Japanese scholars and scholarly expeditions be sent
to points of interest throughout East Asia, and that museums
and libraries be established in Japan to support their research.
He believed Japan's own history and society offered new material for profitable study; among other things, her development in relative isolation should make it possible to discern
certain cause-and-effect relations more clearly than would be
possible with other countries. By directing their investigative
talents toward the study of East Asia, Japanese could help
develop new scholarly theories and preserve an independent
tradition of scholarship.

Japan must also contribute to progress toward the second
ideal, goodness (zen), by taking positive steps to support justice and right in international affairs. In order to make her
definition of justice felt in the world, Japan must become
strong enough to meet Western nations on an equal basis.
Once strong, Japan could protect weaker nations in East Asia
against Western imperialism. In contrast to Tokutomi, who
argued that a nation should maintain arms only for defense,
Miyake believed military power necessary in order to assume
a forthright stance in international affairs. Japan was weaker
than European countries because she had isolated herself
during the Tokugawa period from the stimulating effects of
national competition. Miyake called for a deliberate, long-
range plan for building up Japan's national strength to Western levels. (He criticized the government, however, for in-

creasing the land tax to support a rapid increase in armaments. He felt that first priority should go to improving the people's livelihood.)

The third mission of the Japanese was to preserve and develop their unique conception of beauty (*bi*), with its emphasis on the delicate and the exquisite. He was not opposed to studying and experimenting with other styles, the solemn and magnificent styles of the West, for example; but he stressed that borrowing should be judicious. Japanese should reflect on whether the "solid style" that was characteristic of Western architecture was appropriate for the Japanese climate. The availability and cost of materials should also be carefully considered. The criteria for adopting Western mediums of painting, sculpture, and music should be their ability to communicate the feelings of Japanese artists to Japanese audiences.

Loss of cultural autonomy, moreover, was demeaning. Social customs, for example, ought not to be discarded readily; they had evolved during the nation's history according to the nature of the people. In this connection, he questioned the suitability of Western dress for the "bent posture" of Japanese. (Seikyōsha and Min'yūsha members attached symbolic importance to their different styles of dress; pictures of the groups generally show Seikyōsha members dressed in kimonos and Min'yūsha members in Western suits.) Miyake argued that Japanese who wore ill-fitting foreign clothes invited Westerners' derision. Westerners might laugh openly at the pigtail and robe of a Chinese, but inwardly they respected his independence; they might openly praise a Japanese for his Western clothing, but inwardly they mocked his unseemly imitation.

Miyake's treatise attempted to supplant Japanese shame and doubt with a world view calling for national pride and confidence. His concept of world civilization, with its corollary of national mission, rejected the prevailing belief in uniform social development. National progress did not require that Japanese society become wholly Westernized, for national progress was compatible with cultural diversity. Indeed, cultural diversity was an indispensable condition of human progress. World civilization evolved through competition among diverse national talents fostered by different historical experiences and environments. Preserving and developing Japan's unique characteristics was not a mere reactionary enterprise; it was an exciting, progressive activity, undertaken in the service of mankind. Because Japan's past was the source of their distinctive talents, Japanese should esteem it rather than repudiate it. The same was true of Japan's identity with Mongol Asia.

According to observers, *Shin-zen-bi Nihonjin* was widely read. Taguchi's *Tōkyō keizai zasshi* said the essay had been very influential, that it had quickly gone through a number of printings, and that Miyake no longer could be dismissed as a mere conservative.[12] Professor Yanagida, Miyake's biographer, writes that the treatise made a particularly deep impression on young people.[13] Maruyama Kanji, who became a Seikyōsha adherent at about the time the essay was published, later recalled its important role in inspiring confidence in national abilities and pride in the national past.[14] *Kokumin no tomo,* though it withheld approval of the substance of Miyake's argument, expressed agreement with its spirit: Japanese must respect themselves if they expected respect from others.[15] The magazine cautioned, however, against arrogance and self-aggrandizement.

III

Determined to overcome what they believed was a debilitating preoccupation with Western culture, Seikyōsha members sought practical ways of developing a Japanese mission in world affairs. In May 1891, the month Miyake's treatise was published, they took the lead in forming a group called the Oriental Society (*Tōhō kyōkai*), which they hoped would be instrumental in diverting Japan's primary attention from the

West to her immediate surroundings in the Pacific and East Asia. The Society published a monthly magazine, the *Oriental Society Report* (*Tōhō kyōkai hōkoku*), which contained material on the geography, economics, diplomacy, and history of East Asian countries. In addition, the founders expressed their intention of sending study expeditions to various parts of Asia and establishing a library and a museum for the study of Asian culture. The immediate object of the Society was to provide reference material for Japanese emigration, shipping, foreign trade, government, and scholarship. Ultimately, however, the Society's purpose, as the *Report* described it, was to help Japan fulfill her mission of guiding the less developed countries of East Asia, protecting them from Western powers, and contributing to world civilization.[16]

The founders of the Oriental Society believed that Japan's national identity must be defined in terms of her historical ties with East Asia. "The Japanese people must study their own things," said the first issue of the *Report*, "and in order to do this they must also investigate the cultures of neighboring countries."[17] Since the Restoration, the Japanese had so busied themselves in amassing knowledge of the West—much of it of little value—that they had neglected their own country and neighboring countries with whose destiny Japan's was most closely linked. As a consequence, Japanese scholars were dependent for knowledge of Japan itself on the research of Fenollosa, Chamberlain, and other foreigners.

Japan's national identity was also a matter of her geographical position, which bound her to the Pacific islands and the Asian continent: "Japan's most important problem is deciding where her destiny lies. Europe and America are not areas where Japanese now can compete, owing to our geographical position and our inadequate strength. East Asia is the place for Japanese progress."[18]

Not content with trying to redirect Japanese scholarly attention toward East Asia, certain Seikyōsha members actively tried to expand Japanese influence in that area. Inspired by their own developing concept of national mission, they managed to stir up a lively interest in the islands of the southern Pacific—an enthusiasm described in the early 1890's as "South Sea fever" (*nanshin netsu*).[19] In 1886 Sugiura Jūgō, one of the original founders of the Seikyōsha, suggested that the traditionally outcast Eta class establish a colony in the South Pacific.[20] Since the Restoration the Eta had gained legal equality with other Japanese, but old attitudes toward them persisted. The best way they could improve their lot, wrote Sugiura, was by settling in a new land. He suggested that 90,000 able-bodied Eta be sent with their families to the Philippines to establish a Japanese colony. By leading a revolt of the oppressed natives against their Spanish masters, the Eta would improve their own livelihood, escape old stigmas, and bring new glory to Japan.

Shiga's *Conditions in the South Seas,* published in 1887, warned that Japan's interests were endangered by "white domination" of the Pacific islands.[21] He urged Japanese to compete for the benefits of this area through emigration, colonization, and foreign trade. In 1890 he wrote in *Nihonjin*:

Every year on the anniversary of Emperor Jimmu's accession, February 11, and on the anniversary of his passing, April 3, ... we should ceremonially increase the territory of the Japanese Empire, even if it be only in small measure. Our naval vessels should on each of those days sail to a still unclaimed island, occupy it, and hoist the Rising Sun. If there is not an island, rocks and stones will do. Some will say this is child's play. It is not. Not only would such a program have direct value as practical experience for our navy, but it would excite an expeditionary spirit in the demoralized Japanese race.[22]

One of the most passionate advocates of Japanese participation in Pacific affairs was Fukumoto Nichinan (1857–1921). Fukumoto, a friend and former schoolmate of Kuga's, traveled to the Philippines in 1890 hoping to develop a colonization scheme. When he returned to Japan the following year, he helped found the Oriental Society, contributed articles dealing with the southern Pacific to *Nihonjin,* and joined the staff of *Nihon.* In 1892 Fukumoto wrote a series of eighteen articles for *Nihon,* which the newspaper subsequently published in book form under the title *Political Discourse on the Open Country.*[23] He complained that the oligarchy and the Diet were concerned only with negative and defensive measures such as treaty revision, domestic reform, and coastal defenses; over thirty years had passed since the arrival of Perry, and still the full meaning of "open country" had not been realized. Foreigners had opened up Japan to foreign trade, but the Japanese, for their part, had not extended their influence abroad since the Tokugawa government adopted an isolationist policy in the early seventeenth century. Although he acknowledged that conventional opinion might scorn his arguments as those of a "mere student" (*shosei ron*), Fukumoto was convinced that the Japanese could best begin to achieve national unity and a sense of purpose by undertaking a mission of colonization and trade in the southern Pacific.

Shortly after writing *Shin-zen-bi Nihonjin,* Miyake, along with several other civilians known for their enthusiastic support for Japanese involvement in Pacific affairs, was permitted aboard a navy drill ship on a training mission in the southern Pacific. He embarked in September 1891 on a six-month tour to Guam, New Britain, Australia, New Caledonia, New Guinea, the Philippines, and Hong Kong.[24] Years later he related that the ship had searched in vain for a tiny island marked "unclaimed" on the English sea map, hoping to acquire it for Japan. "At that time," he wrote later, "the desire for colonies, especially in the South Pacific, was strong. . . . We felt Japan had to acquire territory."[25]

In June 1891, when the government, invoking one of its press laws, suspended publication of *Nihonjin* for its criticism

of the oligarchs, Miyake and Shiga responded by launching
a new magazine, *Ajia* (Asia), which they published during
Nihonjin's suspension. Its name was symbolic of their effort
to redirect Japan's primary interest toward her Asian environment and culture. Although none of their many plans for ex-
panding Japanese influence in the southern Pacific found immediate fulfillment, they did succeed in making Asia more
prominent in Japanese thinking. One indication of their success was the growing membership of the Oriental Society,
whose membership lists for the early 1890's reveal the names
of many prominent politicians, scholars, and journalists.

IV

In 1894 the Seikyōsha's campaign to promote national pride
and unity was graced by the publication of Shiga's *Japanese
Scenery (Nihon fūkei ron)*, a book widely read even today for
its prideful description of Japan's unique natural beauty.[26]
Shiga's book sought to cultivate the profound affection for
natural environment already implanted by traditional culture. But he hoped, in addition, to invest this attitude with
new authority by expressing it in terms of botany, geology,
meteorology, and the other new sciences. Proclaiming Japan's
natural beauty unique among the countries of the world,
Shiga carefully dressed this traditional claim in a new garb
appropriate to the enlightened era.

In separate sections Shiga examined four essential reasons
for the beauty of Japan. First, owing to their geographical
position, Japanese experienced unusual diversity of climate
that provided favorable periods of growth and development
for an extraordinary variety of plant and animal life. Second,
as an island country situated at the conjunction of wind and
sea currents, Japan had a great amount of precipitation that
produced a luxuriant soil and a verdant countryside. Third,
the many volcanoes and the igneous rock gave Japan unusual

mountain peaks and ranges. Finally, the severity of erosion produced unusual rock formations.

Shiga's purpose was to arouse national pride in Japan's "elegant, beautiful, and powerful" environment. Though he made occasional references to the Asian continent, his main concern was comparisons with Western countries. How could the English boast of their green and pleasant hills when they had no impressive volcanic peaks? How could their autumn compare to Japan's when they lacked Japan's many varieties of maple and the paulownia tree that gave Japanese mountainsides their fiery autumn colors? How could England's spring beauty rival Japan's when she did not have Japan's abundance of plum and cherry blossoms? Japanese artists and novelists should emphasize features of the native environment that were characteristic of Japan and not of Western countries.

Volcanoes, he said, were the primary reason for Japan's superlative beauty. Praised by Japanese and foreigners alike, Fuji was the measure for all other great mountains.[27] A major theme of Shiga's book was the encouragement of mountain climbing as a way of promoting awareness of national scenery. He devoted separate sections to descriptions of important mountain peaks, how they could be reached, what preparations were necessary, etc. According to Yanagida Kunio, it was during the Meiji period that mountain climbing gained popularity; formerly an expression of religious faith, it now became a sport, a chance for travel and adventure.[28]

Shiga's book is said to have been "one of the most widely read books among students" in the latter half of the Meiji period.[29] Within eight years of its publication it had gone through fourteen printings.[30] Yoshino Sakuzō, only sixteen at the time *Japanese Scenery* appeared, recalled many years later how Shiga's writing had aroused strong patriotic feelings in him and his middle school companions.[31] Affection for the Japanese countryside and pride in its distinctive beauty were important elements in a developing national identity. Here were aspects of their heritage that few Japanese would reject.*

Nevertheless, there were some who found the beauties of the Japanese landscape insufficient grounds for asserting Japan's equality with the West. *Kokumin no tomo* regarded Shiga's type of argument as foolish; the natural beauty of Japan was not of itself able to create the needed confidence and pride, for "our country can never be preserved by Mount Fuji or Lake Biwa."[32] And Natsume Sōseki later echoed that it was "frivolous" to boast of Mount Fuji at a time when Japan obviously owed so much to her borrowings from the West.[33]

Such questioning persisted, as did extensive borrowing from the West, but gradually the Seikyōsha view gained ground. In explaining the sources of Japanese uniqueness, each of the three leading Seikyōsha writers placed his emphasis somewhat differently: Kuga stressed the shared moral values and social customs that history had shaped to the Japanese nature; Miyake agreed but also emphasized Japan's distinctive cultural achievements; Shiga sought to cultivate affection for the Japanese environment. The Seikyōsha writers had no desire to close Japan to foreign influences, no wish to isolate Japan spiritually from the rest of the world. They all stressed, however, that because the progress of man depended upon cultural diversity and competition, Japan had a mission—a moral obligation—to develop her distinctive national characteristics in order to contribute to world civilization.

---

* As Professor Riesman recently observed, Japanese intellectuals generally feel no desire to reject nature: "Was there conceivable in Japan an anti-Fuji cult? We could find none. Obviously Japanese intellectuals reject many aspects of their culture all the time, as in the common rejection of what is dubbed 'monopoly capitalism' or 'feudal remnants.' ... But nature in general and Mount Fuji in particular are not rejected." David Riesman, "Japanese Intellectuals—and Americans," *American Scholar*, XXXIV, 1 (1964–65), 65.

Chapter Eight

WAR AND SELF-DISCOVERY

THE EARLY 1890's saw the development of an important trend that greatly favored the Seikyōsha's effort to turn Japanese concern toward Asian affairs. For nearly a generation, foreign affairs had been quiescent and crises had been few. The challenge of the West had become more economic and social than military; and the prime aim of Japanese foreign policy had become treaty revision, which depended more on domestic reform than on diplomatic negotiation. The crises of 1887 and 1889 sparked by treaty revision proposals had been almost entirely domestic in their origin and significance. Among Japanese, the treaties had created a sense more of shame and frustration than of danger and insecurity.

In the early 1890's, however, the Japanese began to feel international tensions more acutely than they had at any time since the Restoration. The Far East was becoming the center of rivalries among several of the European powers. In 1891 Inagaki Manjirō, a frequent contributor to *Nihon*, wrote a widely discussed book entitled *Eastern Policy* (*Tōhō saku*), in which he warned that the intensification of European rivalries in the Orient would inevitably involve Japan and affect her future. The announcement in February 1891 of Russia's intention to construct the Trans-Siberian Railway, which would stretch from Europe to Vladivostok, caused deep apprehension: as Kuga recalled three years later, this announcement, coinciding with signs of a hardening Chinese attitude toward Korea, marked "the beginning of our Far Eastern problem."[1] Japanese alarm over Russia's intentions was evident in an incident three months after the Trans-Siberian Railway announcement. The Czarevitch, after attending a ceremony to mark the beginning of the railway's construction, traveled to Japan for a state visit. While sight-seeing outside Kyoto he was wounded in an attempt upon his life by a young Japanese. News of the event aroused extraordinary turmoil and a fear that Russia might seize the incident as a pretext for war. "One need only look at the newspapers of the time," Miyake wrote years later, "to see that many people thought the nation was on the verge of ruin."[2] The menace of Russia's emerging power in the Far East also aggravated the problem of Japan's relations with Korea, which the oligarchs had long held in abeyance. Moreover, the political chaos and Chinese ascendancy in Korea jeopardized Japan's growing economic interest there.

The growing national concern over foreign events heightened the tensions in Tokutomi's thought. We have seen the despair that Tokutomi and his associates already felt over the frustration of their hopes; by 1893 they were seeking ways to overcome their disappointment. During 1894 and 1895, several important events caused a profound change in the thinking of Tokutomi and other Min'yūsha members. The emergence of a united opposition to the oligarchs' foreign policy, the signing of a revised treaty with Great Britain that heralded the end of extraterritoriality, the stirring victory in the war with China, and the forced retrocession of the Liaotung Peninsula impelled the Min'yūsha toward a celebration of Japanese identity; and the debate between the Min'yūsha and the Seikyōsha drew to a close. The purpose of this chapter will be to explain the change these events brought about in Min'yūsha thought.

I

Tokutomi's reformism had thrived in the mid-1880's on optimism bred by the rapid and sweeping change that followed the Restoration. The trend of events in the early 1890's, however, frustrated his hopes and undermined the basic premises of his thought. By 1893, receptivity to Westernizing proposals had decreased, and fewer Japanese were inclined to follow Tokutomi's lead. The mixed residence controversy had aroused Japan's mistrust of Western countries, a mistrust that increased as foreign affairs began to intrude upon Japan with greater force in the early 1890's. In a climate of opinion that was increasingly concerned over the imperialist motives of the Western treaty powers, Westernism could be—and frequently was—construed as submissive and treacherous. The Imperial Rescript on Education became a powerful weapon in the hands of Japanese opposed to Westernization; they used it to impugn the loyalty of reformers who sought to supplant traditional values. The Min'yūsha members were increasingly at pains to defend their views and to declare their patriotism. Moreover, Western-oriented reformism suffered when the Diet failed to fulfill the expectations many Japanese had for it. Frequent dissolutions of the lower house frustrated hopes for a responsible cabinet system. Another setback was the Diet's rejection in 1892 of a draft civil code that would have adopted important aspects of Western family patterns. Expectations that Japanese society could be remade in the Western image increasingly seemed premature—if not quixotic. Tokutomi had also become disillusioned with the rural landed class, which he had expected to serve as the social base for a reformed society; and he was disheartened by the defection of youth, who he had hoped would act as a vanguard for the reform movement.

Despite these many disappointments, and despite the loss to

his position as a leader of public opinion, Tokutomi might still have clung to his principles. But, as we have seen, his despair led him instead to conclude in an essay on the Meiji Restoration that Japan lacked the liberal tradition necessary for social reform modeled after Western countries. Tokutomi reluctantly admitted that the influence of Japan's past prevented her from becoming a wholly Western nation.

Forced at last to acknowledge the weight of the Japanese past, Tokutomi and other Min'yūsha members were now groping for a means of reconciling that past with their own continuing need for pride and a sense of national equality. If Japan could not become truly "civilized" (that is, Western), then how could she consider herself the equal of Western nations? What of Japan's own past could offer pride to modern Japanese? These were difficult questions for the Min'yūsha members, whose alienation from Japanese history and whose admiration for Western culture had been extreme.

An editorial in *Kokumin no tomo* in late 1893 demonstrated their predicament. Entitled "Japan's Talent for Assimilation," it revealed the Min'yūsha members to be torn between their intellectual commitment to the West and their growing desire to make peace with the Japanese past.[3] Their dilemma caused them frustration and bitterness that they this time vented on the West. The editorial said that Westerners' praise of Japan for her swift adoption of Western civilization was unflattering and condescending: "They regard us as only a step above Fiji or Hawaii." They praised Japan only because they were accustomed to comparing her to Siam and Annam. "They observe only the developments of the thirty years since the opening of the country. They do not know of our twenty-five-hundred-year history. They do not know that for twenty-five hundred years our society, people, culture, and resources have developed splendid national qualities. . . . They do not know that we have the talent to assimilate the virtues of Western civilization and to put them to our own use." Japanese who

opposed mixed residence, said the editorial, likewise un-
derestimated the remarkable ability Japan had developed
throughout her history for assimilating foreign culture.

What were the "splendid national qualities"? The Min'-
yūsha had no answer; stress on Japan's talent for assimilation
was an attempt to evade their dilemma—to satisfy their need
for pride in the Japanese past without deserting their lingering commitment to Westernization. In this way Min'yūsha
members hoped to find value in their own history even as they
rejected it; they could extol Japanese abilities and still urge
the adoption of Western culture. But assimilation implies
more than use; it implies the conversion of what is used into
the substance of the user. Because they had no clear idea of
what the special nature of Japan was, they could not explain
how or to what purpose Japan should convert foreign culture.

Nonetheless, the fact that the Min'yūsha members had begun to emphasize "assimilation" rather than "adoption" of
Western culture made it clear that they were groping for a Japanese identity. For example, an editorial in *Kokumin no tomo*
in June 1893 entitled "Japan's National Dignity" complained
that despite Japan's great progress in adopting civilized institutions and in developing her national strength, she had not
received the respect due her from the rest of the world.⁴ There
was as much bitterness as regret in the *Kokumin no tomo* la-
ment that "the most progressive, developed, civilized, intelligent, and powerful nation in the Orient still cannot escape the
scorn of white people." The editorial observed that in terms
of respect there was a hierarchy among nations. In the first
rank were strong, civilized (*bummei ryoku*) countries like
America. In the second were countries like Russia, which,
though lacking civilization, nevertheless commanded respect
because of their barbarian strength (*yaban ryoku*) and lust for
conquest. Finally, at the bottom, were countries like Egypt and
Korea, which lacked both civilization and barbarian strength.
What was Japan's position in the hierarchy? Once, as the

"Sparta of the Orient," she had been securely in the second rank. During the latter part of the sixteenth century, her expansionist appetite and military might had exacted meek obedience from Korea and the Ming Dynasty, as well as from Portuguese and Dutch traders. But the long period of peaceful seclusion that had followed allowed this barbarian strength to atrophy, and Perry's arrival in 1853 revealed that Japan had fallen to the lowest rank.

New values, ones that were at once respected by the world and discernible in the Japanese past, were finding their way into Min'yūsha ideas. Emphasis on military power and territorial expansion was a significant departure from earlier Min'-yūsha ideas; it presaged a new standard that measured national progress not solely in terms of conformity to a universal process of civilization but in terms of a nation's individual strength as well. The editorial pointed out that since the Restoration Japan had been developing her military power while going about the business of adopting "civilized" institutions and techniques. Why then did Westerners still relegate Japan to the third rank?

The Min'yūsha writers attributed Japan's failure to impress the West to her own "lack of dignity." Japanese, unlike Westerners, were irrational, high-strung, and lacking in presence of mind. The turmoil and confusion among the people at the time of the attempted assassination of the Russian Czarevitch was characteristic of their impulsive nature. "At no time since the Restoration," said the editorial, "has our loss of dignity been so great. It is unbearable to think how the Russians' scorn for us must have increased as a result of that incident." A second cause for Japan's failure to gain respect was her submissive attitude toward Westerners. Japanese needed more confidence and self-esteem. Finally, the great number of Japanese prostitutes in foreign countries and the low social position of Japanese emigrant workers, particularly in North America, reflected unfavorably on all Japanese at home and abroad.

II

The search for a pride-giving national identity gained momentum from Tokutomi's active participation in a popular movement that erupted during 1893–94 in opposition to the government's foreign policy. The strength of the movement was in large measure a product of accumulated frustrations created by the oligarchy's oppressive measures against the Diet. So long as the oligarchy continued to move cautiously in governing Japan's relations with other countries, the issue of foreign policy could be effectively exploited to embarrass the oligarchs and to unite their opponents in and outside of the Diet.

Leaders of the opposition movement adopted a new tactic for use in advocating a strong foreign policy. They demanded that until the powers agreed to a revision based on equality, the government should strictly enforce the existing treaties. "Strict enforcement," which became a slogan of the movement, was advocated for the regulations governing foreign travel outside the leased territories, regulations frequently winked at by Japanese officials. Likewise, the often neglected regulations forbidding foreign ownership of dwellings outside the leased territories should be rigorously enforced. Foreigners guilty of violating Japanese laws should be treated sternly.[5] The leaders of the strict enforcement movement argued that by creating such hardships for foreign residents Japan could induce the powers to renegotiate the treaties.

What most concerns us here is that the movement brought the Seikyōsha and the Min'yūsha, for the first time, into close cooperation. A confederation of groups from both inside and outside the Diet was formed to lead the movement. Kuga's *Nihon* took the lead in shaping public opinion, as it had at the time of the Ōkuma proposals. Kuga was also active in gathering support for the movement from other journals—including *Kokumin shimbun*. In this way the newspapers of the

Seikyōsha and the Min'yūsha came to work closely together.[6]

Opposition to the oligarchy and frustration over the continuing treaty problem were so great that they reconciled bitter enemies. In his autobiography Tokutomi recalled that he had considered Kuga's *Nihon* the chief rival of his own *Kokumin shimbun*. The newspapers had held opposing principles and had competed for readers among the same groups—primarily students, political activists, and intellectuals.* Now, for the first time since 1888, when the two groups had taken their opposing stands, Tokutomi found himself on friendly terms with many in the Seikyōsha group. During early 1894, he frequently visited the offices of *Nihon* to consult with Kuga about publicity for the strict enforcement movement. When the government suspended publication of *Kokumin shimbun* for a short period, Kuga invited Tokutomi to publish an essay in *Nihon*.[7]

Reading the *Kokumin no tomo* editorials of early 1894, one can scarcely miss the desperate eagerness with which the Min'yūsha seized the strict enforcement issue as a means of regaining contact with national sentiment. The goals of the movement, revision of the treaties on an equal basis and the establishment of an independent foreign policy, were ones with which Tokutomi could readily agree. And although he knew that there were many in the movement whose opinions were at odds with those he had expressed, his own ideas were shifting, and he was in a mood to gloss over differences of viewpoint. He expressed elation over the reconciliation of Seikyōsha nationalism and Min'yūsha progressivism that the strict enforcement movement had accomplished.[8] Historians, he said, would look back after a century to see the uniting of

---

* Professor Yanagida, Kuga's biographer, believes that *Nihon* had overtaken *Kokumin shimbun* in daily circulation by the time of the Sino-Japanese War. In his autobiography Tokutomi wrote that the two newspapers were about even in circulation prior to the war—each had a daily circulation of somewhere between five and ten thousand. Conversation with Professor Yanigida. See also Yanagida, "Kuga Katsunan," p. 167; Tokutomi Iichirō, *Jiden*, pp. 288, 301–2.

these principles as "a watershed [*bunsuirei*] in the nation's thought." The two groups had been in conflict all these years, Tokutomi explained, only because "bigoted conservatives" had obscured the true nature of nationalism, preventing him from understanding the fundamental agreement in the views of the Seikyōsha and the Min'yūsha. He now spoke of the common ground between nationalism and his individualist philosophy: "National spirit refers to the individuality [*dokuji ikko*] of a nation. And does not the individuality of a nation presuppose the individuality of each citizen in that nation? Liberalism is the belief that a nation achieves independence only by establishing individual independence as its foundation. Witness how patriotism abounds in the nations of the free and independent Anglo-Saxon people!" In attempting to harmonize the views of the two groups, Tokutomi ignored the fundamental point at issue: the Seikyōsha's contention that national spirit depended on an allegiance to the traditional Japanese essence. He did so not because he was unaware of the contradiction, but because he had not yet found roots in Japan's past.

III

Under the pressures of internal turmoil and intense domestic opposition to their existing foreign policy, the oligarchs began to adopt a more emphatic, self-assertive attitude toward treaty negotiations with the Western powers. In April 1894 Foreign Minister Mutsu Munemitsu informed the British Minister that the Japanese would not "go on maintaining indefinitely a system of relations with foreign Powers which they considered to be no longer compatible with the progress and changed institutions of the country."[9]

Other powers had been willing for many years to renegotiate the treaties on a basis favorable to Japan; but Britain, whose economic interests in Japan were the most extensive, had been intransigent. By mid-1894, however, in return for a favorable commercial treaty, the British Government had agreed to a provision that would terminate extraterritoriality as soon as Japan's new civil code was enacted; and a new treaty to that effect was signed on July 16. Similar treaties with other powers followed.* With the most offensive aspect of the unequal treaty system thus removed, the Japanese had made a significant step toward regaining their national pride.

But there was scarcely time to enjoy this victory before a more dramatic event supervened. Little more than two weeks after the signing of the treaty with Britain, Japan declared war on China and embarked upon her first great foreign adventure in three centuries.

In the month preceding the outbreak of war, the anticipation of national accomplishments had spurred Tokutomi toward the identity he had been seeking. In early June 1894, as intrigue and chaotic politics in Korea led to increasingly tense relations between China and Japan, Tokutomi made a decisive departure from his old ideas. In an editorial entitled "Japan's Expansionist Nature" he argued that expansionism had been an innate property of the Japanese since they had migrated to their island homeland.[10] The Tokugawa rulers had suppressed this tendency but, Tokutomi believed, Japan was now on the threshold of a new period of great national expansion. This inherent characteristic had already, since the opening of the country, begun to reassert itself in individual Japanese: peasants who had hitherto known few places outside their villages had migrated to Hawaii and North America; fishermen lacking even rudimentary navigational instruments now plied the Pacific; pearl divers ventured as far as the South Pole. Other characteristics that in Tokutomi's view favored expansion were their extremely high rate of population growth and their unusual adaptability to diverse climates.

---

* The new treaties provided that foreign merchants be permitted to trade in the interior, but the question of foreign ownership of property was left to future Japanese legislation. Japan regained full control over her own tariff in 1911.

A year earlier, deploring the low rank Japan occupied in the eyes of Western nations, *Kokumin no tomo* had lamented the nation's failure to gain respect. Now, on the eve of the Sino-Japanese War, when China seemed to be offering provocation in Korea, Tokutomi urged that Japan seize the opportunity to demonstrate her strength and gain the respect due her civilization and her status as a nation. A week before Japan declared war, Tokutomi proclaimed the moment favorable for Japan "to build the foundation for national expansion in the Far East, . . . to thrust aside the obstacles to expansion, . . . and to take her place alongside the other great expansionist powers of the world."[11]

Unlike many Japanese, Tokutomi did not advance defensive or economic arguments for war with China. Nor did he justify the war, as Fukuzawa and others did, as a mission to reform Korea and to awaken China to the blessings of civilization. He favored a "splendid little war" to establish a proud national identity that the world would acknowledge. Japan's rival was not so much China as the world—and above all the Western world.

War was declared on August 1, 1894. "We must remember," Tokutomi wrote in the September 13 issue of *Kokumin no tomo*,

that we are fighting before the whole world. Why do some Japanese say we fight in order to reform Korea, or to vanquish Peking, or to establish a huge indemnity? They should realize that we are fighting to determine once and for all Japan's position in the world. . . . If our country achieves a brilliant victory, all previous misconceptions will be dispelled. The true nature of our country and of our national character will suddenly emerge like the sun breaking through a dense fog.[12]

Tokutomi observed that since the Restoration the Japanese had come to know the world, but the world did not yet know Japan. Worse, the Japanese did not yet know themselves.

Tokutomi's alienation from Japanese tradition had been so extreme that reconciliation was hard. The Christian influence on his thinking was too deep to permit an easy acceptance of traditional values as a source of identity. Even during the war, he still expressed disdain for the cultural elements that Miyake could identify with, and for the natural environment that Shiga stressed. The Japanese, he wrote, had encouraged a superficial view of themselves among foreigners. The world was familiar with Japanese enamel, the drawings of Hokusai, the prints of Utagawa, and the natural beauty of Japan. For Tokutomi this kind of cultural identity was frivolous; it implied that Japan's "only mission was to serve as the world's playground."[13]

In his search for a link to the Japanese past, he emphasized instead the enduring quality of Japan's sovereignty. "The vitality of a nation," he said, "cannot transcend its history."[14] Countries like India and Korea were being overrun because they had histories of defeat and submission; Japan, he insisted, had a proud heritage. To personify the national character, he singled out Kōbō Daishi, Fujiwara Kamatari, Minamoto Yoritomo, Minamoto Yoshitsune, Ashikaga Takauji, Oda Nobunaga, Toyotomi Hideyoshi, Tokugawa Ieyasu, Mizuno Tadakuni, Ii Naosuke, Saigō Takamori, and Ōkuma Shigenobu. These were the great historical figures who seemed to him worthy of emulation; in them he found qualities of reason, spirit, and courage that could rival those of Cavour or Palmerston.[15]

But it was clear that Tokutomi himself was not yet wholly convinced that Japan's heritage was a proud one. It was a heritage that was yet to be demonstrated—both to the world and to the Japanese themselves. "If we succeed in this great venture, our three thousand years of history will become living truth. Our historical heroes will become living heroes. But if we lose, we shall not only bring disaster on ourselves, we shall efface our history and betray our heroes."[16] For Tokutomi, the war would determine not only Japan's future, but her past as well!

IV

The general opinion among Western powers was that China's immense resources, together with her navy and the powerful fortifications she had constructed under foreign supervision, would prevail. Almost at once events belied this expectation. The Japanese army pressed immediately to a series of victories, and the navy won a decisive engagement off the Yalu six weeks after hostilities began. Shortly after, Port Arthur fell, and losses to the Japanese were light.

Japan's success in the war brought Tokutomi the national pride he had been seeking. He later recalled the war, which had begun in his thirty-second year, as "the great turning point" in his life.[17] During the early war months he spoke repeatedly of the great *seishinteki gedatsu*—"spiritual release," or "spiritual deliverance"—that the war was producing in Japan.[18] "Gedatsu" was originally a Buddhist term signifying escape from worldly cares, achievement of a peaceful state of mind, and attainment of Nirvana. Tokutomi's use of the word testifies both to the extent of his earlier mental turmoil and to his new spiritual assurance. This assurance owed partly to the new respect that Westerners now accorded Japan. Tokutomi's essays during the war months contained many quotations from American and English newspapers expressing surprise and new esteem for Japanese capabilities. "Now," he exulted in December 1894,

we are no longer ashamed to stand before the world as Japanese. ... The name "Japanese," like the names Satsuma and Chōshū after the Boshin War, like the name of the returned explorer Stanley and the name of Wellington after Waterloo, now signifies honor, glory, courage, triumph, and victory. Before, we did not know ourselves, and the world did not yet know us. But now that we have tested our strength, we know ourselves and we are known by the world. Moreover, we *know* we are known by the world![19]

Besides giving Tokutomi's evolving national identity the

assurance deriving from an impressive national achievement and the reassuring praise of Western nations, the war also helped Tokutomi to overcome the personal isolation he had increasingly felt in the early 1890's, when receptivity to his reformist proposals had rapidly declined. In his autobiography he wrote that he had plunged into the war with his "whole body and spirit."[20] The Min'yūsha dispatched thirty war correspondents to the continent, which was more, he said, than any other group had sent.[21] The daily circulation of *Kokumin shimbun* increased threefold to around 20,000.[22]

Tokutomi recalled that, prior to the war, military and government leaders had expressed a strong dislike for the Min'yūsha and had considered him and his associates scarcely better than traitors. But his changed ideas and his zeal for the war effort brought the opposing groups together. While interviewing military leaders, he became a close friend of Kawakami Soroku, the Satsuma warrior who had risen to become Deputy Chief of the General Staff.* Through Kawakami, who had been the target of Tokutomi's previous antimilitarist views, he established new friendships with other military and government leaders.[23] Soon after the war broke out, the Emperor and several government leaders moved to Hiroshima to be closer to the front; Tokutomi and many others of the Min'yūsha followed. Hiroshima became the center of wartime planning and diplomacy. The Diet met there, and, in an unprecedented display of unity with the oligarchy, voted a huge war appropriation. After the long years of discord the newfound unity was exhilarating. For Tokutomi the personal strain and isolation were past. He recalled in his autobiography, "the period I spent in Hiroshima from early autumn of 1894 to the end of the winter in 1895 was one of the happiest times of my life."[24]

With victory in the war certain, Tokutomi wrote an essay

---

* Nearly a half-century later, during the Pacific War, Tokutomi wrote a biography of Kawakami.

in December 1894 entitled "The Real Meaning of the War with China," in which he argued that the greatest benefit of the war was self-knowledge and confidence.[25] The opening of the country forty years earlier had destroyed self-respect, he explained, because it had been compelled by foreign intimidation rather than by the free choice of Japan. It had been a "humiliating experience," a "blot" on the nation's history that "could not easily be erased." The Japanese, as a consequence, had "stood in awe" of Westerners.

More humiliating for Tokutomi than Japanese self-effacement had been the apparent contempt in the Western attitude toward Japan. Westerners had regarded Japan as having no political significance, ranking her even lower than China. They thought of Japan as a Chinese tributary, like Korea, Annam, or Siam. Japanese visiting the West, said Tokutomi, were often called Chinese by children on the streets. He told of a friend traveling in Europe who had been asked by a lady he had met what province of China Japan belonged to. These instances were examples of the world's ignorance of Japan's "individuality" (*dokuji ikko*). Other Westerners, who knew more of Japan, were nevertheless scornful because Japan had adopted institutions and practices from the West:

They regard the Japanese as a race close to monkeys, or as monkeys who are almost human.... They regard Japan's great reform of thirty years ago as a kind of sleight of hand. Regarding us as savages who have suddenly imitated civilization, they are impressed only by Japanese skill in imitating.... They overlook the fact that we have nurtured elements of civilization for three thousand years.

Tokutomi did not say what these elements were. He did emphasize that Japan had assimilated and not merely imitated. Consciously or not, Tokutomi was repudiating his own earlier ideas, for he too had disparaged the Japanese past by urging that all elements of traditional Japan be supplanted by forms adopted from Western civilization. With the impressive victories against China and the elimination of extraterritoriality, he could take new pride in a Japanese identity, and could scorn the kinds of assumptions he himself had made a decade earlier.

In this essay, Tokutomi sought to define the "special nature" (*tokusei*) of the Japanese and to show cause for national confidence by pointing out three characteristics demonstrated in the war with China. First, the Japanese demonstrated a patriotic spirit unsurpassed in the world. While China was forced to depend on foreign loans for her war expenses, the Japanese Diet confidently approved huge appropriation bills. Not even the English, who boasted of their patriotism, could match the Japanese for unity and self-sacrifice. (During the Crimean War, said Tokutomi, English merchants had put their selfish interests ahead of the national cause.) Second, the Japanese exhibited a special talent for applying and assimilating modern civilization (*kinsei no bummei*). By their brilliant use of modern technology and strategy the Japanese demonstrated that they must also be adept in mastering borrowed political systems, academic theory, literary skills, and manufacturing and commerical techniques. Third, the war revealed the methodical precision and reliability of the Japanese in achieving their goals.

This view of Japan's special nature was still insufficient to prove her equality with the West, for Tokutomi's continuing emphasis on Japan's talent for assimilation implicitly acknowledged that "civilization" had, at least in great measure, developed in the West. He now, however, took a step beyond his previous ideas to deal with this obstacle to his growing Japanese pride. He spoke of a "civilization sickness" (*bummei byō*) that corrupted simple, rugged, frugal virtues and produced self-indulgence, extravagance, and effeminacy. He emphasized that during the period of so-called civilized progress the sturdy qualities of Restoration heroes like Yoshida Shōin had disappeared from society. It is likely that Tokutomi had in mind his earlier disillusionment with the rural landlord class, whose

thrifty, enterprising virtues he had envisioned as the base for
the new society; the city had destroyed these qualities, he believed, and the "country gentlemen" had grown extravagant
and decadent. Tokutomi concluded, however, that the war
with China was now reviving rugged characteristics in the Japanese people. After the war, as we shall see, he returned to this
theme of "civilization sickness" and further developed it.

v

The war lasted only eight months. The uninterrupted successes of the Japanese army, the total destruction of the Chinese fleet, and the surrender of Weihaiwei convinced China
of the futility of further resistance. On March 30, 1895, an
armistice was concluded, and Li Hung-chang, China's leading
diplomat, hastened to Shimonoseki to negotiate with Itō and
Mutsu.

Toward the end of the war, the Japanese government decided that Prince Komatsu should preside over the transfer
of the Imperial War Headquarters from Hiroshima to Port
Arthur. In early April, with the help of his new friends in the
government, Tokutomi gained permission to board ship for
Port Arthur with the Prince and his staff.[26]

En route to Port Arthur, Tokutomi heard news of the signing of the Treaty of Shimonoseki, which ceded the Pescadores,
Formosa, and the Liaotung Peninsula to Japan, recognized
Korean independence, and obliged China to pay a large indemnity, open additional ports, and negotiate a commercial
treaty. The peace treaty satisfied the war ambitions Tokutomi
had expressed the previous autumn, i.e., that annexation of
Taiwan was necessary, because the island was the natural
"footing for the expansion of Greater Japan"; thus the path of
trade and exploration that his Japanese ancestors had followed
three hundred years earlier in the southern Pacific and in
Southeast Asia would again be open.[27] At the same time, Tokutomi had emphasized that Japan must occupy Port Arthur,

because from it Japan "could control the destiny of China as well as of Korea." On the other hand, in the hands of an enemy, he had said, it would jeopardize Japan's security.

The landing at Port Arthur was momentous for Tokutomi.

My trip to the Liaotung Peninsula was the first time I had set foot off Japanese soil, and it was quite exciting. . . . It was late April, and spring had just arrived. The great willows were budding; the flowers of North China were at the height of their fragrance. Fields stretched out before the eye; a spring breeze was blowing. As I traveled about and realized that this was our new territory, I felt a truly great thrill and satisfaction.[28]

Even as Tokutomi made his short tour of the Peninsula, savoring the new Japanese territory, it was wrested from under his feet. On April 23, Germany, Russia, and France urged the Japanese government to renounce possession of the Liaotung Peninsula "in the interests of the peace in the Far East." Yielding completely to the demands of the Triple Intervention, the Japanese government on May 5 agreed to retrocede the Peninsula. When Tokutomi returned to Port Arthur from his tour, he was informed of the reversal. "Vexed beyond tears" and disdaining to remain on the lost territory, Tokutomi returned at once to Japan. But before embarking from Port Arthur he scooped a handful of earth into a handkerchief, and he returned to Japan with this "souvenir of what had been, for a time, Japanese territory." For years he kept it beside his desk in the Min'yūsha offices as a reminder to himself of the importance of national power.[29]

The Triple Intervention strengthened the ideas Tokutomi had been formulating. In 1913 he wrote that "as a result of the Triple Intervention I was baptized to the gospel of power."[30] And in his autobiography he recorded: "The retrocession of Liaotung shaped the destiny of my whole life; after I heard of it I was spiritually a different person."[31] The Triple Intervention completed his disillusionment; he now considered his previous ideas bookish and theoretical. "Previously I had learned from books, but during the 1894–95 war I learned for the first time from reality. . . . The influence of this war completely transcended the influence of Spencer, Cobden, and Bright."[32] The realization that industrial and commercial competition among nations was not supplanting armed conflict, and there- fore that military institutions remained an important and ne- cessary part of a society, greatly altered his earlier Spencerian view of social evolution as an inevitable progression from a barbarous or military phase to a purely industrial phase.

With the new value Tokutomi attached to power and with the new evidence of Japanese capabilities came an increased conviction of national destiny. Writing in July 1895, after his return from Port Arthur, he compared Japan to Imperial Rome, arguing that the Japanese had a mission to "extend the blessings of political organization throughout the rest of East Asia and the South Pacific, "just as the Romans had once done for Europe and the Mediterranean."[33] Rome had brought its vast territories equal laws, human rights, civilization, progress and peace. Japan could do the same, because among East Asian peoples "only the Japanese have the ability for political organ- ization; only the Japanese understand the concept of the na- tion-state."

In another article written in July 1895, Tokutomi amplified his new attitude toward the West. The adoption of Western civilization no longer represented unqualified progress to him. During the war he had denied the absolute worth he had previ- ously ascribed to Western civilization, saying it had weakened the vigorous qualities on which national power depended. Now he added that there was value outside of "civilization": there was an important quality that a nation must preserve from its past. The lesson the Sino-Japanese War had given the world, he now wrote, was that "the union of barbaric vigor [yaban no genki] and civilized learning is the greatest force in the world."[34] Japanese soldiers had stunned the world not solely by their clever, precise use of modern Prussian military tactics, but by their fearlessness, vigor, endurance, and daring as well. "Civilization is not an unmixed blessing," Tokutomi emphasized, "nor is barbarism wholly detrimental." The civilizing process could have baneful effects; by replacing human labor with artificial power it weakened man's resistance to such stimuli as cold, heat, and hunger. Tokutomi argued that Europeans had maintained their vitality and spirit only by preserving barbaric customs such as dueling, hunting, mountain climbing, and horse racing. Europeans failed to realize, however, that their rising standard of living was decaying their vigorous, barbaric spirit. By discovering this flaw in the process of civilization, Tokutomi made Japanese pride and equality with the West possible. Because Japanese possessed and cherished the same rugged qualities that Europeans were losing, Japan could compete with the Western powers, fulfill her destiny of national expansion, and carry the benefits of civilization to less able countries.*

Another article written shortly after his return from Port Arthur further indicated the weakening commitment to his earlier reform proposals. Tokutomi had hitherto argued that national progress depended upon improving the livelihood of each individual citizen. After the war, however, he argued that Japanese should preserve a simple livelihood lest they lose their sturdy physical qualities. Furthermore, Japanese national

---

* At the same time Lafcadio Hearn was drawing a similar conclusion. The Sino-Japanese War had raised uncertainty in his mind over the fitness of Westerners to survive: "Wherein consists the fitness for survival? In the capacity of self-adaptation to any and every environment; in the instantaneous ability to face the unforeseen; in the inherent power to meet and master all opposing natural influences. . . . Now in this simple power of living, our so-called higher races are immensely inferior to the races of the Far East. Though the physical energies and the intellectual resources of the Occidental exceed those of the Oriental, they can be maintained only at an expense totally incommensurate with the racial advantage. For the Oriental has proved his ability to study and to master the results of our science upon a diet of rice, and on as simple a diet can learn to manufacture and to utilize our most complicated inventions. But the Occidental cannot even live except at a cost sufficient for the maintenance of twenty Oriental lives. . . . It may be that the Western Races will perish—because of the cost of their existence. Having accomplished their uttermost, they may vanish from the face of the world—supplanted by peoples better fitted for survival." See *Out of the East* (1895), in Hearn, VII, 184–85.

character found expression in a distinctive, selfless patriotism, a readiness to sacrifice one's personal interests to the good of the community:

The special nature of the Japanese is their concern for the welfare of the whole country rather than for personal well-being . . . . Because of the vitality of this spirit, Japan is the strongest country in the Far East and can compete with the other nations of the world. We admire not those who are intent on their own interests at the expense of the state, but men of high purpose [*shishi*], who disregard their own advantage and devote all their energies to the nation.[35]

A stirring national victory had helped Tokutomi overcome his cultural alienation. But at the same time the identity Tokutomi had formulated for Japan had a precarious, demanding quality. In 1916, reflecting on the Sino-Japanese War, he wrote, "We came to know ourselves for the first time; knowing ourselves was knowing our power and knowing our mission."[36] Japan's identity depended on the continuing proof of national power, and in the years after the war Tokutomi became an increasingly intense advocate of national expansion, for to him pride and identity required it.

VI

Although the great stress Tokutomi put on national power as the prime source of Japanese self-esteem differed from the cultural nationalism espoused by Seikyōsha writers, he nonetheless had, in his own way, reconciled himself to Japan's cultural tradition. His renunciation of Westernism, which ended the long debate between the two groups, reflected a transformation of attitudes that had occurred in the nation during the years we have studied. One finds prevalent among writers at the end of the Sino-Japanese War a more critical attitude toward Western culture than had previously existed, a renewed interest in the Japanese past, and a new sense of national pride and confidence.[37]

These new attitudes seemed to signify the attainment of the Seikyōsha's original goals; the group was no longer forced to contend with Westernism. It was perhaps partly for this reason that Shiga left *Nihonjin* for an active career in government and politics.[38] Miyake, who continued as editor of the magazine, discovered, however, that in this changed climate of thought Seikyōsha ideas were being challenged and preempted by a style of narrow nationalist sentiment that was more conservative and exclusive in its definition of the Japanese character than Shiga, Miyake, and Kuga had ever been. The Seikyōsha's concept of "preserving the national essence" was now being employed by opponents of social reform and adopted by bureaucrats to oppose political reform and to sanction authoritarian government. In short, the Seikyōsha's original ideals were being distorted and used to stigmatize not merely Westernism but reformism in general. Miyake often found himself in disagreement with this orthodox style of thought. He stressed that his wish to preserve an independent cultural tradition did not represent opposition to social and political reform or to selective borrowing from the West. Accordingly, in the years after 1895 he opened the columns of *Nihonjin* to contributions from such reform-minded writers as Kōtoku Shūsui, Katayama Sen, Sakai Toshihiko, Shimada Saburō, and Taguchi Ukichi.

Kuga likewise found himself out of step with the march of postwar nationalist sentiment. Professor Maruyama has sought to distinguish Kuga's "Japanism" from the orthodox nationalism emerging in Japan at the end of the century.[39] He regards Kuga's thought as a fusion of liberalism and nationalism. Like the advocates of People's Rights, Kuga favored representative government, a responsible cabinet system, and an extension of the voting franchise; he was a steadfast opponent of "absolutism and bureaucratic nationalism" and was dismayed by the growth of militarism and jingoism in Japan. At the same time, according to Maruyama, he had a sense of historical reality, recognizing that liberalism in Japan could exist only if national independence were preserved; he thus eschewed the abstract idealism of the People's Rights Movement and called for a "proper balance" between concern for individual rights and concern for national power. Maruyama, whose father was associated with the Seikyōsha, regards Kuga as a proponent of "progressive," "healthy," "liberal" nationalism.*

In contrast with Miyake and Kuga, who were often no more comfortable with orthodox nationalism than they had been with the once prevalent adulation of Western culture, Tokutomi found that his new nationalist views and his support for Japanese imperialism put him in the mainstream of public sentiment—much as his Westernism had put him in the mainstream a decade earlier. His justification of Japanese militant expansionism as an expression of national character accorded with the jingoism and militarism that typified popular sentiment at the turn of the century.

Tokutomi's acceptance after the war of a high position in government, however, disrupted the Min'yūsha.[40] In July 1897 he joined the Matsukata-Ōkuma government, assuming responsibilities that chiefly involved the cabinet's press relations. The cabinet, which at first included party members from the Diet as well as oligarchs, soon split; Ōkuma and his Progressive Party (*Shimpotō*) followers resigned. Tokutomi's decision to remain in the government despite the withdrawal of the Progressives was interpreted in the press as a submission to the oligarchy and a betrayal of the party movement that he had hitherto supported. Although he defended his action as one serving the nation rather than faction, he became the object of much criticism. Attention was drawn to his desertion of his earlier views, and he was called "unprincipled" and "oppor-

---

* Although plagued by illness, Kuga edited *Nihon* for several years after the Sino-Japanese War; and following his death in 1907, the staffs of *Nihon* and *Nihonjin* merged to form the magazine *Nihon oyobi Nihonjin* (Japan and the Japanese), which Miyake edited until 1923.

tunistic."[41] His loss of popularity was reflected in the decreased circulation of *Kokumin no tomo*, which finally ceased publication in August 1898.[42]

VII

It would be impossible to understand the metamorphosis that Tokutomi's thought had undergone apart from the altered circumstances and mood of the nation. During the decade between the publication of *Youth of the New Japan* and the Sino-Japanese War, the climate of thought had shifted radically. Tokutomi had been notably sensitive to this change of climate and had responded to it, for he was by nature neither dogmatic nor detached. Nor was he disposed to cling in solitude to abstract principles. Rather, he was a political journalist who delighted in assessing and leading public opinion. He later defended his position against those who had criticized him for changing his views: "As a participant in public affairs it was only natural to act in accord with the trend of the times [*taisei*] and to try to lead it."[43]

To his critics, Tokutomi seemed to have no fixed ideals; one, writing in 1898, considered him merely clever in discerning trends and in changing with them.[44] Tokutomi's own explanations of his behavior lend some credence to this view. Defending himself from the attacks directed at him for joining the oligarchs, he emphasized that his views had changed with the changed conditions in Japan after the Sino-Japanese War and with the realization that "the trend of the world was toward imperialism."[45] Again in 1916 he discussed his change: "And what should I regret or apologize for? Although I am embarrassed that I could not perceive in 1885 and 1886 what the situation would be ten years later, in 1895 and 1896 I followed a path that continued to be the trend [*jisei*] in 1905–6 and 1915–16. Regardless of the criticism from all quarters, this gave me the greatest pleasure."[46] It is worth recalling that Tokutomi's original ideas concerning Westernization had in part been predicated on his belief that they represented the inescapable trend of the times. As he came to realize that the trend was not in the direction he had once thought, it was easier for him to dispose of his previous views than it would have been had there been no such pragmatism in his original motives.

Tokutomi's changed ideas, emerging as they did shortly after he passed thirty, can perhaps also be attributed to a natural onset of conservatism with maturing years.[47] We have seen that Westernism among youth involved their wish to assert their independence from the adult generation; this kind of self-assertiveness diminished with advancing years. Moreover, experience had demonstrated to Tokutomi the difficulties of achieving the social reforms that he had hoped for as a youthful idealist. As years passed, Tokutomi came to look back on his early writings as a youthful aberration. He pointed out that he had been in his early twenties when he wrote his first important essays. "It was only natural," he concluded, "that they should have many blemishes."[48]

Perhaps. But the fundamental cause of his metamorphosis lay in his need to ease the tensions generated by a conflict of cultural and national loyalties. These tensions were not peculiar to Tokutomi but were widely felt by the new generation. They were in good measure responsible for the dramatic shift in the climate of thought throughout Japan in the years we have been studying.

Chapter Nine

JAPAN'S HISTORICAL PREDICAMENT

SOMEWHERE in the terrain of the late 1880's and early 1890's lies a major watershed in modern Japanese history. On one side lies a Japan occupied with domestic reform; a curious, self-critical, uncertain Japan; a Japan still in the making, preparing for the future, impelled by a robust and often naïve optimism; above all, an experimental Japan, open to the world, trying new institutions, testing new values, intent on reordering her society and government. On the other side lies a Japan with a renewed sense of order and discipline in her national life; a Japan less tractable, less hospitable to social reform, less tolerant of new values; a self-esteeming Japan, advertising her independence and destiny; above all, a Japan with a heightened sense of her own unity and exclusiveness. We may be overdoing the contrast, but anyone who studies this period must be impressed by the profound psychological change that took place.[1] In the present study this change is vividly reflected in the metamorphosis in Tokutomi's thinking.

What caused so profound a change? How was it that an open, experimental era gave way so suddenly to an era of narrow-minded, aggressive nationalism? I have not attempted a full explanation of this change in spirit—a "technical near-impossibility,"[2] in any case. A variety of proximate factors were involved. Among them were international tensions, which ultimately performed a unifying function; the establishment of a constitutional order after two decades of groping for a new political system, which greatly narrowed the range of political debate and diminished the experimental temper of society; and the Meiji leadership's efforts to propagate a new national ideology designed to overcome the dissensions of the early Meiji period, recreate the once familiar order of social life, and elicit support for the new governmental institutions.

In a larger sense, the new spirit of Japanese life after about 1890 is perhaps best understood as a reaction to the dislocations and uncertainties created by a generation of breathtaking change. In the present study I have concentrated on one aspect of this reaction: the intense need felt by the Japanese for a national identity in the modern world. This need was born of the coupling of an extended period of perplexing and humiliating cultural subservience to the West with a time of unprecedented national consciousness.

I

Building a powerful industrial nation involved Japan in a historical predicament from which many of her leading thinkers sought to free her. In little more than a generation, from 1868 through the turn of the century, Japan made the transition from a predominantly agrarian to an industrializing economy. The revolutionary measures of the 1870's, which laid the basis for industrialization, encountered relatively little overt resistance from established thought and institutions. Old forms of behavior and habits of mind remained deeply rooted beneath the newly implanted ideas and institutions; but lacking a practical and coherent defense, they could provide at first comparatively little restraint on the pace of change. The Meiji leadership was able therefore to meet the challenge of Western power by building a new order along Western lines. But as the transition to an industrial economy progressed and as techniques and practices borrowed from the West supplanted established wisdom and skills, Japanese began to feel painful historical and cultural dislocations. "Unless we totally discard everything old and adopt the new," Natsume Sōseki wrote in 1892 while a student at Tokyo University, "it will be difficult to attain equality with Western countries." Yet for the Japanese to give up so much of their own substance—his mind circled about on itself—would "soon weaken the vital spirit we have inherited from our ancestors [and leave us] cripples."[3] Like many other young intellectuals, Natsume was looking for ways to reconcile the conflicting needs of cultural borrowing and national pride, to be both modern and Japanese.

He continued to brood on the dilemmas of Japan's historical position. In a speech at Wakayama two decades later, at the end of the Meiji period, he observed with despair that there really was no escape from the predicament. Japan, he said, was running a race with Western history; only by reaching the Western nations' advanced stage of development could she regain cultural autonomy and control of her own destiny. And yet Japan could be truly independent and self-respecting only if she were no longer "impelled from without" (gaihatsu-teki no kaika), no longer compelled to borrow from the West, no longer forced to follow an already broken path rather than a self-determined course (naihatsuteki no kaika). To Natsume, Japan seemed fated to run an interminable losing race. He saw only two ways, both unsatisfactory, to try to close the gap: Japan could continue "mechanically imitating" the West (in gaihatsu fashion), a shortcut that destroyed integrity and self-esteem and produced a superficial civilization; or she could strive to catch up by progressing along an independent Japanese course (in naihatsu fashion) in hopes of reaching the West's stage of development in a fraction of the time it had taken the Western nations. But the latter alternative was unthinkable, for it would require an effort so consuming and strenuous that it would lead inexorably to "nervous collapse." The "bitter truth," he concluded, was that Japan must continue in her wretched course, following abjectly in the train of Western development.[4]

Others of a less gloomy disposition explored various ways of extricating Japan from her historical predicament. Our study has considered two of these ways. One way, for which the Min'yūsha was a representative spokesman, sought to minimize the issue of cultural autonomy by arguing that progress was unilinear, that the place of origin of civilization was fortuitous, that the course of Western civilization represented the universal path of progress for all nations, and that Japanese therefore need feel no compunction about Westernization. This view accorded with the experiences and expectations of young Japanese in the new generation, and in the 1880's found striking receptivity among them. During the decade we have studied, however, difficulties encountered in reforming traditional patterns of thought and behavior began to force upon members of the unilinear school awareness of the limits that history placed on the scope and pace of change in Japanese society. Moreover, in a period of rapidly mounting national consciousness many Japanese were increasingly uncomfortable with the unilinear view, with its implied indifference to Japan's own history and traditions. The treaty revision controversy, we have seen, laid bare the self-doubt inherent in Westernization and demonstrated the psychological need for a distinct cultural identity.

The Seikyōsha school of thought, representing a different way of trying to deal with the historical predicament, opposed the unilinear concept on two grounds. First, it was degrading because of the failure it imputed to the Japanese and their civilization. Second, it was unrealistic because of its expectation that a Western society could be created in Japan, an expectation that failed to account for the influence exercised on social change by differences of environment and history.

The Seikyōsha advanced the concept of an evolving world civilization, in which progress was achieved through competition and diversity among nations, each learning from the special strengths of others and in turn developing and improving its own special talents. The Seikyōsha writers set out to find elements of their cultural heritage that need not be sacrificed in the course of modern development, factors in Japan's history and geographical position that could be considered special strengths, things that the world would esteem and that would bring pride to modern Japanese. This approach offered no total solution to Japan's predicament; it did not attempt to evade the reality of her historical position, and it acknowledged that continued borrowing from the West would be necessary. It sought to make the predicament less painful, however, by arguing that civilized progress was compatible with a diversity of cultures, that the assimilation of borrowings to the unique traditions and spirit of the nation was possible. In trying to reconcile cultural autonomy and cultural borrowing, to combine an openness to change with a reassuring sense of Japanese individuality, to make national progress and national pride compatible, Seikyōsha members engendered no small amount of conflict and confusion among themselves over what constituted the essential traditions and preservable elements in the Japanese heritage.

A third way of trying to extricate Japan from her historical predicament, a far more conservative brand of nationalism, first became prominent during the 1890's. It was a style of thought, set forth by both intellectuals and government leaders, that offered sweeping solutions to problems of cultural identity. Although in its professed aim of preserving the Japanese national character it bore resemblance to the Seikyōsha views, it was nonetheless distinct in its style. In defining Japanese nationality it was more assertive and unhesitating, more explicit and exclusive, than the Seikyōsha philosophy. This new style of thought, in short, offered total solutions to Ja-

pan's predicament. It claimed to put an end to cultural subservience to the West by asserting the distinctiveness and superiority of the Japanese way of life. It claimed to settle
problems of cultural identity by defining a unique Japanese
political order and social morality based on immutable principles. Like extreme forms of nationalism elsewhere, it erect-
ed "a myth of distinctive national virtues flourishing within
a framework of completely separate national identity"; it set
forth "the mystic idea of an entire people supernaturally
bound together by the common heritage of a national soul."[5]

Takayama Chogyū (1871–1902), editor of the widely read
new magazine *Taiyō* and one of the leading spokesmen for
this new nationalism, credited the Seikyōsha writers with
prompting reflection on the dangers of indiscriminate borrowing from the West, but said they had failed to provide a
clear concept of Japanese nationality.[6] He regarded his own
philosophy of "Japanism" (*Nihonshugi*) as superseding Seikyōsha ideas and expressing a forthright style of nationalism
that "by the end of the Sino-Japanese War had vanquished
the long-entrenched Westernism."[7] Almost identical with the
official ideology of the Meiji regime, Takayama's Japanism
proclaimed national solidarity, harmony between ruler and
people, loyalty, filial piety, and colonial expansion as inherent in the national character. It stressed that all spiritual authority was encompassed in the Japanese state, and therefore
opposed Christianity and Western liberalism as "totally incompatible with our national polity and national character."[8]

Such ideas had clearly gained sway by 1895. Language gives
us one of the best indications we have of the altered mood of
the nation.[9] Terms such as "Japanism," "national polity," and
"preservation of national character" gained currency and became shibboleths expressing a heightened sense of national
unity and exclusiveness. More and more they became clichés,
convenient for dismissing new ideas and avoiding the troublesome and complex reality of Japanese society. After reading

the charter of the Greater Japan League, organized in 1897 by several nationalist intellectuals including Takayama Chogyū and Inoue Tetsujirō, one cynic likened its glib language to "an advertisement for a cure-all."[10]

The widespread acceptance of this style of thought was indicative of the psychological change the nation was undergoing. The Meiji leadership was formulating and propagating a national ideology that would justify its monopoly of power and the sacrifices required to achieve the nation's industrial and military goals. In education, in military training, in public media—everywhere the government reasserted the old values of loyalty and obligation, solidarity and duty to superiors, and propagated the political myths of imperial sanctity and the family state.

But more important than the effectiveness of government indoctrination as an explanation for the success of this view was the remarkable receptivity to this official effort by people outside the government. The pressure to conform to this national orthodoxy, Marius Jansen points out, came not so much from the government as from "forces within Japanese society. Colleagues, neighbors, publicists, relatives—these were the people who hounded the Kumes, the reformers, and the liberals."[11] This receptivity to a national ideology that reasserted familiar ideals represented perhaps a natural reaction to the sense of uprootedness, the emotional stress and dislocation produced by the rapid change of the first two decades of the Meiji period. By apotheosizing traditional ideals and by providing a new basis for unity, the national ideology helped Japanese to recover, or at least compensate for, their lost sense of security. Sacred symbols provided comfort and relief from the mental stress that rapid social change had produced. Writing in 1916, Tokutomi Sohō advised Japanese youth to make service to the nation "not only their ideal but their religion as well." Because of his own experience he could understand the mental turmoil they experienced growing up in the modern period; but "if they would love the Japanese Empire and give themselves wholly to it, they would have no anxiety, no discontent."[12]

By 1895 the tide of conservative nationalist ideas had swept by the Seikyōsha, obscuring its position in a flood of rhetoric. Miyake, highly perceptive of the changed use of words, was dismayed by the consequent blurring of the original intent of Seikyōsha ideas. In an 1899 *Nihonjin* editorial he complained that the "strange nationalism" that had "swept the nation" distorted the Seikyōsha's concept of Japanese individuality, replacing it with a narrow conservatism that sought indiscriminately to preserve traditional things.[13] Writing later in his autobiography, Miyake recalled that from the time in 1888 when Seikyōsha writers had first used the term "kokusui hozon" (preservation of nationality) it had become the subject of increasing misinterpretation, an excuse for slothfulness, a catchword for conservatism, and a pretext for opposing needed reforms and maintaining the status quo.[14] Seikyōsha writers observed that the vocabulary of Western liberalism had lost its vogue; yet they deplored the prevailing disposition to stigmatize concepts of individual human rights and responsible cabinet government as alien to the national character. "Words too have a life," Miyake wrote in 1900, "and if the language of People's Rights is already dead, let us revive the same spirit through new words."[15]

Other Seikyōsha adherents were equally distressed. Maruyama Kanji, for instance (the father of the intellectual historian), warned in a 1913 article in *Nihon oyobi Nihonjin* of the kind of national pride that could lead Japanese to isolate themselves spiritually from the rest of the world. It was "dangerous, truly dangerous," he said, to think "that the Japanese nation is sacred, that Japanese possess an inborn love of country unique in the world, that Japanese have a distinct character of selflessness inconsistent with individualism, and therefore that Japanese politics need not be patterned after the

politics of the West.''[16] Hasegawa Nyozekan, a disciple of the
Seikyōsha founders who perhaps best represents the further
development of the Seikyōsha style of thought during the pre–
World War II period, contended that the formation of national character should be thought of as a continuing process.
Character was the product of both heredity and environment;
and in an age of rapidly developing world communications
Japan's environment was changing. He argued against any
conception of the Japanese character as finished, fixed, immutable, and isolated from developments in the rest of the world.
Above all, as time passed and the national ideology became
still more narrow, Hasegawa and others of the Seikyōsha school
resisted self-aggrandizement and the tendency inherent in Japanese nationalism to regard the Japanese state as a moral en-
tity, the ultimate source of ethical value. Hasegawa wrote of his
circle in 1919 that although they considered themselves nation-
alists, they could not agree that "our nation is absolute and un-
equaled" or that it "possesses unique moral values that transcend the interests of other nations."[17] His book *The Japanese
Character*, published in 1938, argued against the narrow,
closed nationalism of the 1930's, emphasizing that receptivity
to new ideas and institutions was a fundamental part of the
national character.[18]

  The Seikyōsha, occupying as it did a middle ground between the unilinear view and the conservative nationalist outlook, tried on the one hand to stimulate such necessary
changes in society as could be made without causing self-destructive doubt and shame, and on the other hand to provide a
sense of cultural independence without producing a distorted
self-esteem and a spiritual isolation from the outside world.
Critics like Takayama Chogyū complained that the Seikyōsha
offered only a vague definition of the Japanese essence that
its members sought to preserve. There was truth in this com-
plaint. We have seen that Seikyōsha members found it hard to
agree on a clear, precise definition of national identity. But this

difficulty was less a result of the shortcomings of Miyake, Shiga, and Kuga than an indication of their essential moderation in trying to deal with the dilemmas of Japan's historical position. How could the Japanese character be defined except by an appeal to the history and traditions from which so many Japanese felt uprooted? In particular, how could a Japanese identity based on pride and conviction be formulated for a generation alienated from its cultural heritage? How could continued innovation and borrowing from the West, which Seikyō-sha members recognized as necessary, be reconciled with their aim of preserving cultural autonomy? There were no easy answers to these questions; and it was to the credit of Miyake, Shiga, and Kuga that they were aware of their predicament, confronted it openly, and did not on the whole resort to extreme solutions. They neither cut themselves off from the past as the unilinear school did, nor embraced a simplified and distorted solution as the nationalist orthodoxy did. Nor did they follow the tendency of many young Japanese after the turn of the century to retreat from the concerns of the nation. On the whole, the Seikyōsha members with whom we have dealt chose to grapple with the uncertainties and complexities of Japan's historical predicament in search of genuine self-knowledge.

II

On the surface, concern with problems of Japanese identity appeared to subside after the mid-1890's. In part this was because through the spiritual conflicts of the decade we have studied, Japanese had found various formulas for easing the painful stresses created by rapid cultural change. In part, too, concern with problems of Japanese identity receded not so much because the questions involved had been satisfactorily answered as because the altered circumstances and mood of the nation made the issues raised earlier seem less urgent. The imminent end of extraterritoriality gave tangible cause for increased self-confidence; and military victories, territorial acquisition, and wartime unity helped relieve anxieties over cultural identity.

We have seen, for example, how heavily Tokutomi relied on the achievements of national power as a source of pride and equivalence with the West. Unlike an Okakura Tenshin or the Seikyōsha writers, who found cause for pride in elements of the Japanese cultural heritage and in Japan's history as an Asian nation, Tokutomi's alienation from Japanese culture had been so deep and pervasive that he could find no traditional cultural elements sufficient to give reassuring substance to his intense national consciousness. He could not say with Okakura: "Fain would we remain barbarians, if our claim to civilization were to be based on the gruesome glory of war. Fain would we await the time when due respect shall be paid to our art and ideals."[19] For Tokutomi national pride was a matter of military victories, territorial acquisition, and the revival of martial values.

How many others depended upon the achievements of national power to overcome their feelings of cultural alienation and to inspire pride in their nation? We cannot know, but there were surely many like Tokutomi. The journalist and reformer Kinoshita Naoue observed after the Russo-Japanese War that Japanese intellectuals had been "seduced" into false national pride by military victories and the acclaim they brought Japan from abroad; those who fell victim to this temptation had earlier been humiliated at the thought that "since the opening of the country the Japanese people have done nothing but import and copy foreign things."[20] Miyake Setsurei cautioned his countrymen that "although a modern nation must depend first of all on military strength, the true measure of its worth is determined mostly by its cultural elements."[21] And Natsume Sōseki observed in 1911 that Japanese no longer resorted to "such foolishness as saying to foreigners, 'My country has Mount Fuji.' But since the [Russo-Japanese] war one hears boasting everywhere that we have become a first-class country." Sensitive to what he regarded as Japan's

cultural subservience, Natsume felt it "frivolous" to claim
equality with the West on the basis of military victories.[22] But
imperialism did find increasing support after 1895, partly because many Japanese, consciously or otherwise, felt the exercise of national power necessary to sustain their newly acquired self-esteem and identity.

Although problems of identity appeared to subside after
1895, often beneath the surface of events perplexity over the
same issues persisted. The national ideology was too superficial to command the wholehearted belief of sensitive minds.
Often protestations of belief masked inner conflict and uncertainty. Takayama Chogyū provides a striking example. At the
very time the young editor was gaining recognition as one of
the leading advocates of the new nationalism, his faith was
ebbing. He confessed to a friend that his philosophy of Japanism could not satisfy his spirit, that it "represented only my
superficial side," and that he felt overwhelmed by "contradic-
tions" and "anguish."[23]

Many young Japanese, Yamaji Aizan observed, were becoming "bored to death" by hollow nationalist pieties.[24] After the
turn of the century, young people in numbers significant
enough to attract considerable attention lost interest in national issues and retreated into the private concerns of their
own lives. This indifference to national politics was particularly noticeable at the time of the Russo-Japanese War. In a
series of *Kokumin shimbun* editorials, Tokutomi expressed
dismay that so many young Japanese should be "interested
in the gossip of *sōshi*-drama rather than in the fierce battle
fought at Liaoyang."[25] Behind this apathy the poet Ishikawa
Takuboku (1885–1912) perceived "exactly the same discontent that had motivated the attempted rebellion against traditional morality, thought, and customs."[26] But although
young Japanese after the mid-1890's felt a cultural alienation similar to that of their counterparts in the 1870's and
1880's, they reacted very differently.

In the early Meiji period there had been few restraints upon

national self-criticism, and nearly all thinkers had been critical of their cultural heritage. Issues of cultural change were
openly confronted and debated. In such an open, experimental atmosphere, young Japanese like Tokutomi, despite their
extreme cultural alienation, were not despairing and frustrated. Growing up in a period of extraordinary receptivity
to reform and change, they had confidence in the future, believing they could complete the reformation of society. History and the trend of the times, they thought, were on their
side.

Only when the social order began to harden and seem un-
malleable, when the burden of the past appeared inescapable,
when orthodox nationalism became oppressive, did cultural
alienation breed frustration and despair. Young Japanese by
the turn of the century had lost much of their predecessors'
optimism about reforming society. Many felt powerless before
a political and social order that seemed to them immutable.
"The atmosphere that surrounds us youth," Ishikawa wrote,
"is suffocating. The influence of authority pervades the entire
country. The existing social organization reaches into every
nook and cranny." Oppressed by the increasing power of the
bureaucracy and the routinization of life, finding little room
for self-expression in national affairs, young Japanese felt "de-
prived of a future."[27]

One source of their frustration lay in the way the goals of
Japanese education had been recast by the 1890's. In addition
to the original Meiji objective of providing practical training
for careers in the new industrial society, schools had assumed
the burden of inculcating the traditional values of loyalty,
obligation, and social solidarity on which the national ideology rested. This task was not easily reconciled with the original objective. An educational system designed to promote science and technology tended to encourage qualities of mind
inimical to indoctrination in the Japanese political myth.
Kinoshita Naoue, reading Tokutomi's editorials criticizing

young Japanese for their lack of patriotism, pointed out that the nationalist education Tokutomi's paper supported was responsible for the very attitudes he deplored. "The duty of students in an age of scientific education," Kinoshita wrote, "is to be skeptical, to investigate, and to understand."[28] The indifference of many students to national issues was therefore symbolic of their inner resistance to indoctrination: they could not readily accept ideas on faith. Miyake likewise criticized the "empty formalism" of patriotic education and argued that the way to overcome the indifference of the young was to encourage independent thought, debate, and open confrontation on politcial issues in the schools.[29]

Japanese youth were victims of the underlying conflict of objectives in the educational system. Even while revivifying values found in pre-industrial life, education by its commitment to science and technology was helping to create an industrial society that was increasingly at odds with traditional values. This conflict of purpose bespoke the ultimate failure of the national ideology to extricate Japan from her historical predicament. In narrowly defining Japanese identity in terms of traditional values, it offered a self-image that was increasingly outmoded and difficult to reconcile with the conditions of industrial society.

Although less apparent after 1895, cultural alienation persisted, often concealed by apathy or halfhearted protestations of belief in the national orthodoxy. Whether from a sense of futility, social pressure, or some other inhibition, or as a result of censorship, this alienation less frequently produced the open discussion and debate typical of the early Meiji period. One supposes that alienation was frequently internalized and lay hidden in men's minds, aggravating existing tensions and frustrations. From time to time, however, it came to the surface, and one has a glimpse of how deeply felt cultural alienation still was.

Consider as an instance an occurrence in 1909, when the

novelist Nagai Kafū, having recently returned to Japan after several years in Europe and America, attracted attention with his severe criticism of Japanese civilization.[30] Ishikawa Takuboku responded with an anonymous essay in the poetry magazine *Subaru* expressing distaste for Nagai's "enchantment with Western ideas" and his "scorn of everything Japanese."[31] Ishikawa confessed that he himself, along with many other Japanese intellectuals, shared Nagai's feelings of estrangement from his cultural heritage: "In his [Nagai's] dissatisfaction with the moral formalism that most Japanese maintain I am of the same mind. In his dissatisfaction with the Japanese state and with Japanese society I am of the same mind. I myself once went through a stage when I thought my greatest misfortune was having been born in Japan."[32] But Ishikawa asserted that one could not repudiate Japanese culture without at the same time disparaging one's own national identity: "Ultimately we are Japanese. No matter where we go, we are Japanese. What then is accomplished by scorning one's own country?"

Ishikawa wanted Japanese intellectuals to face up to the implications of their cultural alienation and to choose between their cultural and their national loyalties. He himself had come to realize that "I must decide: 'Should I live in Japan or should I leave?' " Nagai, with his attachment to French culture, ought to go and live in Paris. But those who chose to remain in Japan should actively concern themselves with improving Japanese society. Indifference was irresponsible. Ishikawa concluded his essay with an abrupt and enigmatic reference to Tokutomi: "I myself have recently for the first time been able to discover a certain connection between the early and the late Tokutomi Sohō."[33]

Ishikawa's remark is an example of the puzzled interest that the dramatic shift in Tokutomi's thought has continued to attract. Apparently the "certain connection" referred to Tokutomi's unwavering concern with the fate of the nation throughout his career. Although Tokutomi had begun by urging a radical rejection of Japanese culture, he had nonetheless been motivated by the kind of passionate commitment to the nation that Ishikawa found lacking among many intellectuals by 1910. Ishikawa may have concluded that Tokutomi too had faced the question "Should I live in Japan or should I leave?" and come to the same realization that he must choose between his cultural and national allegiances. In the early Meiji period the tensions betwen cultural alienation and patriotism had not been strong. After 1890, circumstances combined to bring Westernism more and more into conflict with national allegiance; and the compulsion to choose between opposing loyalties greatly increased.

In the flux at the beginning of the decade we have studied, Japan was confronted with the need for a new conception of herself. Disoriented by the accelerated process of history, she required some meaningful way of relating her past to the present and future, some clear perspective and sense of direction that would function as a binding and integrative force, enabling her people to act in concert and deal effectively with her domestic and international problems. The task of formulating a viable self-image proved profoundly difficult: on the one hand, it had to be forged from the vestiges of the national past; on the other hand, it had to be responsive to the progress of knowledge and the changing conditions of industrial society. The refractory nationalist spirit that had gained sway at the end of the decade signified the failure of most Japanese to strike such a balance.

NOTES

NOTES

The newspapers and magazines most relevant to this study are given in the Notes with the following abbreviations:

KMSB	Kokumin shimbun
KMNT	Kokumin no tomo
TKZZ	Tōkyō keizai zasshi
NH	Nihon
NHJ	Nihonjin

References to sources listed in the Bibliography have also been abbreviated in the Notes; in such cases, see pp. 225–32 for complete authors' names, titles, and publication data.

INTRODUCTION

1. Jacob Burckhardt, *Force and Freedom* (New York, 1955), p. 238, quoted in C. Vann Woodward, "The Age of Reinterpretation," *American Historical Review*, LXVI, 1 (1960), 19.

2. Chamberlain, pp. 1–2. My attention was called to this quotation by John Whitney Hall, "Changing Conceptions of the Modernization of Japan," in Jansen, *Changing Attitudes*, p. 7.

3. Tanabashi Ichirō, "Kokkyō o mokuru no hitsuyō o ronzu," *NHJ*, pp. 370–83.

4. *Ibid.*, pp. 370–71.

5. R. R. Palmer and Joel Colton, *A History of the Modern World* (New York, 1961), p. 554.

6. Lafcadio Hearn, *Glimpses of Unfamiliar Japan*, in Hearn, VI, 367.

CHAPTER 1

1. "Shin Nihon no seinen oyobi shin Nihon no seiji," *KMNT*, Oct. 7, 1887.

2. Ozaki Yukio, *Shōnen ron*, in Ozaki, II, 629–57; the quoted passage is from p. 641.

3. Tanabashi Ichirō, "Kokkyō o mokuru no hitsuyō o ronzu," *NHJ*, Apr. 18, 1888.

4. Concerning problems of generational change, I have found the following essays particularly useful: Karl Mannheim, *Essays on the Sociology of Knowledge* (London, 1952), chap. 7, "The Problem of Generations"; Karl Mannheim, *Diagnosis of Our Time* (New York, 1944), chap. 3, "The Problem of Youth in Modern Society"; S. N. Eisenstadt, *From Generation to Generation* (London, 1956); Seymour Martin Lipset, "The Political Behavior of University Students in Developing Nations" (mimeo., 1964); Erik H. Erikson, ed., *Youth: Change and Challenge* (New York, 1963). With regard to youth in modern Japanese society there are two particularly illuminating essays by Robert Jay Lifton: "Youth and History," in Erikson, *ibid.*, pp. 260–90; and "Individual Patterns in Historical Change: Imagery of Japanese Youth," *Comparative Studies in Society and History*, IV, 4 (1964), 369–83. Since I wrote this chapter, an essay covering some of the same ground has appeared in Japanese: Okawada Tsunetada, "Seinen ron to sedai ron," *Shisō*, 514 (1967), 37–57.

5. See the passage on the Tokugawa family system in Dore, *City Life*, pp. 91–110.

6. *Ibid.*, p. 113.

7. For a useful interpretation of the roles of family and formal education in cultural change in early American society, see Bernard Bailyn, *Education in the Forming of American Society* (New York: Vintage Books, 1965).

8. Smith, "Japan's Aristocratic Revolution," p. 383.

9. "Seinen dokuritsu no konnan," *TKZZ*, Dec. 15, 1888, in Taguchi, VIII, 167–74.

10. Fukuzawa Yukichi, *Gakumon no susume*, in Fukuzawa, *Zenshū*, III, 29.

11. Matsuzaki Minoru, *Bummei inaka mondo*, in Yoshino, XX, 277; translated in Dore, *City Life*, p. 195.

12. Smith, "Japan's Aristocratic Revolution," p. 383.

13. Bailyn, *Education in the Forming of American Society*, pp. 22–23. Professor Bailyn's discussion of the way in which education may influence generational change, though cast in a different setting, is suggestive of what was taking place in Meiji Japan.

14. Yamaji Aizan, *Gendai kinken shi*, in Yamaji, *Aizan shū*, pp. 44–45. For a discussion of the difficulties involved in producing capable teachers for the new school system in early Meiji Japan, see Passin, pp. 75–80.

15. Fukuzawa, *Autobiography*, pp. 90–91.

16. Ozaki, II, 638–39, 649.

17. Ryan, pp. 17–18, 34–36.

18. See Dore, *Education*, p. 313; and R. P. Dore, "The Legacy of Tokugawa Education," in Jansen, *Changing Attitudes*, pp. 126–27.

19. Ebina, p. 54. See also Notehelfer, p. 11.

20. Natsume, V, 532; the translated passage is in Smith, *Agrarian Origins,* pp. 206–7.

21. Tokutomi Iichirō, *Shin Nihon no seinen,* in Tokutomi Iichirō, *Shū,* p. 7.

22. See Hearn's letter to Basil Hall Chamberlain dated June 4, 1894, in Hearn, XVI, 190–93.

23. Of the adult generation Robert Bellah observes: "It is interesting that the generation of the great enlighteners grew up in Tokugawa times. These men all came to know who they were when the traditional order was intact. This provided the fundamental personality stability which carried them through all the vicissitudes of later years." In Jansen, *Changing Attitudes,* p. 422.

24. *Ibid.*

25. H. Stuart Hughes, *Consciousness and Society* (New York: Vintage Books, 1961), p. 338.

26. Bailyn, *Education in the Forming of American Society,* p. 36.

27. Kozaki, pp. 36–37.

28. Mathy, pp. 1–20.

29. Tokutomi Iichirō, *Jiden,* pp. 109–11.

30. Makoto Sangu, ed., *Lafcadio Hearn: Editorials from the Kobe Chronicle* (Tokyo, 1960), p. 23.

31. Baelz, p. 17.

32. Chamberlain, p. 3.

33. Levenson, *Modern China,* p. 164.

CHAPTER 2

1. "Zuikan zuiroku," *KMNT,* Oct. 7, 1887.

2. Masamune Hakuchō, "Fukuzawa Ō jiden dokugokan," in Masamune, IX, 85–89. Masamune writes that by the Meiji twenties Fukuzawa's early writings had lost their appeal; because of the rapid progress of knowledge about the West, they had become dated. It was Min'yūsha publications, he said, that captivated youth. Also, concerning the attitude of the youthful Tokutomi when he met Fukuzawa, see Tokutomi Iichirō, *Jiden,* pp. 187–89.

3. Fukuzawa sympathized with those who were dismayed by the brashness of the new generation, but he disagreed with the argument that instituting moral education would effectively deal with the problem. Fukuzawa Yukichi, "Tokuiku ikan," in Fukuzawa, *Zenshū,* V, 349–64.

4. See the text of a speech given Nov. 10, 1890, reprinted in Yamaji, *Aizan shū,* pp. 247–50.

5. "Tōyōryū no kifū o dassezaru bekarazu," *KMNT,* June 15, 1887.

6. Owing to the prominence of his lineage group, there is an unusual wealth of biographical material available on Tokutomi. Two of the best sources for his early life are his autobiography, *Sohō jiden,* and an essay

by Irokawa Daikichi, "Tokutomi Sohō ron." This and several useful, related essays are incorporated into Professor Irokawa's book *Meiji seishinshi*. Valuable material about Tokutomi's youth is also found in the writings about and by his brother, especially Maedakō Kōichirō, *Roka den*; and Tokutomi Roka, *Takezaki Junko, Omoide no ki*, and *Fuji*, all three of which are contained in *Roka zenshū*. See also Matsumoto, "Tokutomi Sohō."

7. "Immitsu naru seijijō no hensen," *KMNT*, Feb. 17, 1888.

8. Tokutomi Iichirō, *Jiden*, pp. 204–5.

9. For Yokoi's life, see Yamazaki. See also Miyauchi.

10. See Tokutomi's introduction to Yamazaki. See also Tokutomi Iichirō, *Jiden*, pp. 13–18, 204–5.

11. *Ibid.*, pp. 39–40, 640.

12. Notehelfer, "Ebina Danjō," makes use of a considerable amount of material on the school.

13. Tokutomi Iichirō, *Jiden*, pp. 63–64.

14. Notehelfer, p. 35.

15. *Ibid.*, p. 33.

16. Kozaki, p. 23.

17. Tokutomi Iichirō, *Jiden*, pp. 64–65.

18. *Ibid.*, pp. 101–2.

19. Quoted in Ienaga Saburō, "Niijima Jō to Uchimura Kanzō," in Sakisaka, *Kindai Nihon no shisōka*, p. 108.

20. Tokutomi Iichirō, *Jiden*, pp. 149–52.

21. Miyazaki, *Sanjūsannen no yume*, contains a description of Tokutomi's school, where Miyazaki was a student.

22. Tokutomi Iichirō, *Jiden*, pp. 149–52.

23. For Baba's influence on Tokutomi, see Soviak, pp. 201–2. For Tokutomi's own account of his activities in the People's Rights Movement, see Tokutomi Iichirō, *Jiden*, pp. 176–81.

24. *Dai jūku seiki Nihon no seinen oyobi sono kyōiku* was the original title. *Shin Nihon no seinen* is contained in Tokutomi Iichirō, *Shū*, pp. 3–53.

25. *Ibid.*, pp. 7, 46.

26. *Ibid.*, pp. 15–25.

27. A translation of the preamble is found in Passin, pp. 209–11.

28. Tokutomi Iichirō, *Shū*, p. 6.

29. *Ibid.*, pp. 28–29.

30. *Ibid.*, p. 29.

31. *Ibid.*, p. 43.

32. *Ibid.*, pp. 7–9.

33. Tokutomi Iichirō, *Jiden*, p. 209.

34. See Tokutomi Iichirō, *Shū*, p. 405. Tokutomi says in this tribute to Taguchi Ukichi that *Shōrai no Nihon* was inspired by Taguchi's *Nihon kaika shōshi*, which will be discussed in Chapter 4 below, and by Spen-

cer's "Political Institutions," which was a section of *Principles of Sociology*.

35. Herbert Spencer, *Principles of Sociology* (New York, 1884), II, chap. 17.

36. *Ibid.,* II, 573.

37. *Ibid.,* II, chap. 18.

38. *Shōrai no Nihon* is contained in Tokutomi Iichirō, *Shū,* pp. 54–128. Tokutomi gives Spencer little credit, even though several passages of *Shōrai no Nihon* appear to be almost direct translations of *Principles of Sociology.*

39. Tokutomi Iichirō, *Shū,* p. 106.

40. *Ibid.,* p. 122.

41. *Ibid.,* p. 125.

42. *Ibid.,* p. 103.

43. *Ibid.,* p. 109.

44. Tokutomi Iichirō, *Jiden,* pp. 217–19. Tokutomi had succeeded to the family headship in 1883. *Ibid.,* p. 199.

45. For the founding of the Min'yūsha and *Kokumin no tomo,* see Tokutomi Iichirō, *Jiden,* pp. 221–24; Ienaga, "Kokumin no tomo"; Uete, "Kokumin no tomo—Nihonjin"; and Tokutomi Iichirō, "Min'yūsha."

46. "Aa Kokumin no tomo umaretari," *KMNT,* Feb. 15, 1887.

47. "Shin Nihon no seinen oyobi shin Nihon no seiji," *KMNT,* July 15, Aug. 15, Sept. 15, Oct. 7, 1887. (Many of the lead articles in *KMNT* are unsigned. Japanese scholars often attribute these to Tokutomi on the assumption that he was responsible for all opinion in these articles. This assumption is probably safe, but throughout this study I have avoided attributing the unsigned lead articles to Tokutomi unless they contain clear internal evidence that they are his or unless they are included in one of the anthologies of his works published during his lifetime.)

48. See the description of heiminshugi by Takekoshi Yosaburō, an early Min'yūsha member, in his *Shin Nihon shi,* contained in Matsushima, 169.

49. Nishida, p. 206. The early issues of *KMNT* contain charts showing the circulation. It is well to remember that at that time individual copies of magazines were shared much more than they are now. Thus the circulation figures may be but a fraction of the actual readership.

50. Kitamura, II, 250.

51. See the interview with Masamune in *Kindai Nihon shisōshi kōza: geppo,* Sept. 1959.

52. Masamune, VI, 149.

53. *Ibid.,* p. 152.

54. See Konishi.

55. Conversation with Professor Maruyama.

56. Maruyama Kanji, "Sohō to Setsurei," *Nihon hyōron,* June 1941.

57. Ryan, pp. 116–17.

58. See the introduction to Ienaga, *Nihon kindai shisōshi kenkyū,* and Ienaga's introduction to vol. I of the reprint series of *KMNT* (Tokyo, 1966).

59. See Yoshino, XXI, 345–49. See also Tanaka, p. 72.

60. Sakai, VI, 101.

61. Suekane; Hasegawa, *Aru kokoro no jijoden,* p. 9; interview with Masamune Hakuchō, *Kindai Nihon shisōshi kōza: geppo,* Sept. 1959.

62. "Immitsu naru seijijō no hensen," *KMNT,* Mar. 2, 1888.

63. "Aa Kokumin no tomo umaretari," *KMNT,* Feb. 15, 1887.

64. Tokutomi Iichirō, *Shū,* pp. 117–18.

CHAPTER 3

1. Sansom, p. 378.

2. Henry Steele Commager, *The Search for a Usable Past* (New York, 1967).

3. Ienaga, "Kokumin no tomo," p. 40.

4. "Ikani shite Nihonkoku o Nihonkoku tarashimu beki ya," *KMNT,* Oct. 21, 1887.

5. "Yamato minzoku no sanseiryoku," *NHJ,* July 3, 1888.

6. For a complete list of writings by and about Shiga, see *Kindai bungaku kenkyū sōsho,* compiled by Shōwa Joshi Daigaku Kindai Bungaku Kenkyūshitsu (Tokyo, 1967), XXVI, 141–213. There are several good discussions of Shiga's life and thought: Iwai; Matsuda; and Motoyama, "Meiji nijūnendai." In addition, Shiga (along with Uchimura Kanzō and Nitobe Inazō) has been studied in a recent doctoral dissertation: Kimitada Miwa, "Crossroads of Patriotism in Imperial Japan" (Princeton University, 1967).

7. Shiga, VII, 153.

8. *Ibid.,* III, 3.

9. *Ibid.,* p. 107.

10. *Ibid.,* p. 7.

11. *Ibid.,* pp. 54–55.

12. *Ibid.,* pp. 102–3.

13. *KMNT,* Oct. 21, 1887.

14. Miyake wrote two autobiographical pieces: *Daigaku konjaku tan* and *Jibun o kataru.* There are also two biographies: Yanagida, *Miyake Setsurei*; and Hasegawa, "Miyake Setsurei." See also two essays by Motoyama: "Miyake Setsurei" and "Meiji nijūnendai." The latter deals with the thought of Kuga and Shiga as well as Miyake.

15. Miyake Setsurei, "Jibun no shisō no yurai," *Gakan,* Sept. 1925. This is one of a series of autobiographical essays first published in *Gakan* and later collected into one volume entitled *Jibun o kataru.*

16. Miyake Setsurei, "Jibun no kyōshi," *Gakan,* Sept. 1926, in *Jibun o kataru.*

17. Chisolm, pp. 39–40.

18. Miyake, *Daigaku konjaku tan*, p. 129.

19. Miyake, "Jibun no shisō no yurai," *Gakan*, Sept. 1925, in *Jibun o kataru*.

20. Seppō Kōji, "Nihon jimmin koyū no seishitsu," *Tōyō gakugei zasshi*, Jan. and Feb. 1883. I am indebted to Professor Yanagida Izumi for telling me of this essay. See also Yanagida, *Miyake Setsurei*, p. 18.

21. Seppō Kōji, "Nihon jimmin koyū no seishitsu."

22. *Ibid.*

23. *Ibid.*

24. *Ibid.*

25. Yanagida, *Miyake Setsurei*, p. 17.

26. For the founding of the Seikyōsha and *Nihonjin*, see Izumi; Uete, "Kokumin no tomo—Nihonjin"; Matsumoto, "Nihon oyobi Nihonjin."

27. See the sources cited in the preceding note and the remarks of Tanabashi Ichirō in "Seikyōsha kaiko zadankai," *Nihon oyobi Nihonjin*, Apr. 1, 1938.

28. *NHJ*, Apr. 3, 1888.

29. "Nihon shūkyō ron," *NHJ*, Apr. 3, 1888.

30. "Nihon seiji shakai no ichi shin genshō," *NHJ*, May 3, 1888.

31. "Kokkyō o mokuru no hitsuyō o ronzu," *NHJ*, Apr. 18, 1888.

32. "Meiji shisō no hensen," in Takayama, IV, 424–25. See also "Kokusuihozonshugi to Nihonshugi," *ibid.*, pp. 384–403.

33. "Nihon zento no ni daitōha," *NHJ*, June 18, 1888, in Shiga, I, 26–31.

34. "Yamato minzoku no sanseiryoku," *NHJ*, July 3, 1888.

35. "Nihonjin ga kaihō suru tokoru," *NHJ*, Apr. 18, 1888, in Shiga, I, 1–7.

36. "Yamato minzoku no sanseiryoku," *NHJ*, July 3, 1888.

37. "Kokusuishugi no honkyo ikan (2)," *NHJ*, Jan. 3, 1889.

38. "Kokusuishugi no honkyo ikan (1)," *NHJ*, Nov. 18, 1888.

39. "Yohai kokusuishugi o shōdō suru," *NHJ*, May 18, 1889.

40. Joseph Levenson makes this point in his study of Chinese intellectuals. See Levenson, *Liang Ch'i-ch'ao*, p. 143.

41. Miyake, "Jibun no kyōshi," *Gakan*, Sept. 1925, in *Jibun o kataru*; Miyake, "Hi kokushu hozon," *NHJ*, June 5, 1899.

42. See, for example, Suekane; Ise Tokio, "Nihon kongo no kokuze," *KMNT*, July 20, 1888.

43. Quoted from *Gendai Nihon kyōkai shiron* in Motoyama, "Tani Kanjō," p. 111.

44. See "Hi kokushu hozon," *NHJ*, June 5, 1899. See also Yanagida, *Miyake Setsurei*, p. 34.

45. The best biography of Kuga is Yanagida, "Kuga Katsunan." See also Uete, "Kuga Katsunan"; Yasui.

46. *Tōkyō dempō*, June 9, 1888.

47. *Ibid.*, June 12, 1888.
48. *Ibid.*, June 9, 1888.
49. *Ibid.*, June 12, 1888.
50. *Ibid.*, June 13, 1888.

CHAPTER 4

1. Ise Tokio, "Nihon kongo no kokuze," *KMNT*, July 20, 1888. Yokoi Tokio was adopted into the Ise family after his father's death.
2. Tokutomi Iichirō, *Jiden*, p. 287. See also Tokutomi Iichirō, "Min'-yūsha," p. 122. My information about the personal relationship between Miyake and Tokutomi came from a conversation with Professor Yanagida.
3. Marc Bloch, *The Historian's Craft*, translated by Peter Putnam (New York: Vintage Books, 1965), p. 185.
4. Suekane.
5. Yamaji, *Aizan shū*, pp. 247–50.
6. "Seijishugi ni kansuru kanken," in Uemura, II, 122, 126–27.
7. Sakai, VI, 101.
8. Conversation with Dr. Hasegawa.
9. Conversation with Professor Maruyama Masao.
10. Washio, p. 48.
11. Katō, p. 320.
12. Smith, *Political Change*, p. 44.
13. See Shibusawa Keizō, *Meiji bunka shi: seikatsu hen,* in Kaikoku, V, 449–59.
14. A discussion of psychic mobility is found in Daniel Lerner, *The Passing of Traditional Society* (Glencoe, Ill., 1958), pp. 47–49. See also the same author's "Toward a Communication Theory," in Lucian Pye, ed., *Communications and Political Development* (Princeton, N.J., 1963), pp. 332–33.
15. Hearn, VII, 283.
16. Katō, pp. 320–21.
17. *Ibid.*, p. 322.
18. Tokutomi Iichirō, *Jiden,* pp. 84–87. See also John F. Howes, "Japanese Christians and American Missionaries," in Jansen, *Changing Attitudes,* pp. 337–68.
19. "Gaijin no yugen hatashite ikubaku no kachi aru," *KMNT,* June 22, 1889.
20. "Nihon kokumin no kifū ni kanshite," *KMNT,* Oct. 5, 1888.
21. *KMNT,* June 22, 1889.
22. Arnold, pp. 240–43.
23. Chamberlain, pp. 3–5.
24. Tokutomi Iichirō, *Taishō,* pp. 234–35.
25. Tokutomi Iichirō, *Shū,* p. 405.
26. Ienaga, *Nihon no kindai shigaku,* pp. 68–70; Shigakkai, II, 1291–1326; Akagi, pp. 75–140.
27. Taguchi's history, *Nihon kaika shōshi,* was published serially be-

tween 1877 and 1883. In 1885 he published in book form *Nihon kaika no seishitsu*; in 1886 he published a sequel, *Nihon no ishō oyobi jōkō*. Both had appeared earlier in *Tōkyō keizai zasshi*. All are found in Taguchi, II.

28. Taguchi, II, 127.
29. *Ibid.*, pp. 118 et seq.
30. *Ibid.*, pp. 127–31.
31. *Ibid.*, pp. 158–60.
32. "Seiyō to Nihon," *TKZZ*, Apr. 21, 1888, in Taguchi, II, 520–23.
33. "Seiyō to Nihon," *KMNT*, May 4, 1888.
34. "Yamato minzoku no sanseiryoku," *NHJ*, July 3, 1888.
35. Sakisaka, *Kindai Nihon no shisōka*, p. 100.
36. "Kinji seironkō," *NH*, July 20–Aug. 30, 1890, in Kuga, *Bunroku*, pp. 73–151; for the quoted passage, see p. 147.
37. For the founding of *NH*, see Hirao, pp. 587–94; Kawabe, pp. 47–80; Yanagida, "Kuga Katsunan," pp. 138–48.
38. *TKZZ*, Feb. 23, 1889.
39. "Nihon," *NH*, Feb. 11, 1889, in Kuga, *Bunshū*, p. 1.
40. "Shimbun kisha," *NH*, Oct. 22, 1890, in Kuga, *Bunshū*, pp. 161–88; the quoted passage is from p. 183.
41. "Nihon," *NH*, Feb. 11, 1889, in Kuga, *Bunshū*, pp. 2–3.
42. "Kinji seironkō," *NH*, July 20–Aug. 30, 1890, in Kuga, *Bunroku*, p. 148.
43. *Ibid.*, p. 137.
44. "Kinji kempō kō"; serialized in *Tōkyō dempō* and *NH*, Dec. 28, 1888–Feb. 28, 1889, in Kuga, *Bunroku*, pp. 1–56.
45. *Ibid.*, p. 4.
46. *Ibid.*, p. 2.
47. *Ibid.*, p. 40.
48. "Mori daijin," *TKZZ*, Feb. 16, 1889; "Nihon kisha," *TKZZ*, Feb. 23, 1889.
49. "Shūkyōjō no enaku," *NH*, Feb. 20, 1889. See also *NH*, Feb. 27, 1889.
50. "Jiyūshugi ikan," *NH*, Jan. 15–20, 1890, in Kuga, *Bunroku*, pp. 57–72.
51. "Kokuminteki no kannen," *NH*, Feb. 12, 1889, in Kuga, *Bunshū*, pp. 9–13.
52. See Joseph Levenson's comments in "'History and Value': The Tensions of Intellectual Choice in Modern China," in Arthur F. Wright, ed., *Studies in Chinese Thought* (Chicago, 1953), p. 173.

CHAPTER 5

1. Quoted in Jones, p. 80.
2. Quoted in Dore, *City Life*, pp. 159–60.
3. Tani's writings are collected in Tani, *Kanjō ikō*. See also Hirao; Motoyama, "Tani Kanjō"; Teters, "The Genro-In."
4. Motoyama, Tani Kanjō," pp. 92–93.

5. A translation of Tani's memorial on treaty revision is found in *Trans. Asiatic Society of Japan*, XLII, 1 (1914), 596–604.

6. *Ibid.*, p. 599.

7. Besides his memorial on treaty revision, Tani submitted a lengthy statement denouncing government policies.

8. Inoue Kiyoshi, p. 121.

9. Motoyama, "Tani Kanjō," p. 109.

10. Inoue Kiyoshi, writing in a Marxian vein, felt that if the anti-treaty movement had developed further these youths would have formed the core of a revolutionary army. Inoue Kiyoshi, p. 122.

11. *Ibid.*, pp. 125–26.

12. "Gaikō no urei wa soto ni arazushite uchi ni ari," *KMNT*, Mar. 1887, in Tokutomi Iichirō, *Bunsen*, pp. 21–34.

13. "Hoshuteki handō no taisei," *KMNT*, Oct. 21, 1887.

14. *Ibid.* A part of this quoted passage appears in Sansom, p. 372.

15. "Shin hoshutō," *KMNT*, Nov. 4, 1887.

16. "Shin hoshutō no tame ni," *KMNT*, June 22, 1889; "Meiji nenkan no sakoku ron," *KMNT*, Mar. 12, 1889.

17. See Kuga's essay "Kinji seironkō," *NH*, July 20–Aug. 30, 1890, in Kuga, *Bunroku*, p. 148.

18. *KMNT*, June 22, 1889.

19. Inoue Kiyoshi, pp. 147–48.

20. Ōshima.

21. This essay is contained in Yoshino, VI, 471–520.

22. *Ibid.*, p. 475.

23. *Ibid.*, p. 508.

24. Miyake, *Shū*, p. 219. See below, Chapter 7.

25. For social Darwinism in Japan, see Nagai, "Herbert Spencer." See also a revision of this article by the same author: "Supensashugi no ryūkō," *Shisō*, 393 (1957), 49–58.

26. Katō Hiroyuki, *Zakkyo shōsō ron* (Tokyo, 1893); Oka, "Jōyaku kaisei rongi"; Matsumoto Sannosuke, "Katō Hiroyuki ni okeru shinka ron no juyō," *Tōkyō Kyōiku daigaku kyōyō kiyō*, IX (1962). For a good example of Katō's views, see the text of his speech before Tōyō Gakkai, reprinted in the fourth and fifth issues of *NHJ*.

27. For a good example of this viewpoint, see "Shinajin no naichi zakkyo o ronsu," *NHJ*, Nov. 18, 1889.

28. Nihon Kōdōkai, I, 728.

29. Yoshino, VI, 363–408.

30. "Kyoryūchi seido to naichi zakkyo," in Taguchi, V, 59–75.

31. "Naichi zakkyo no kiyū," *TKZZ*, July 13, 1889.

32. Text of the speech is contained in Yoshino, VI, 351–63.

33. "Jōyaku kaisei," *KMNT*, July 2, 1889.

34. Inoue Kiyoshi, p. 152.

35. See the chart reprinted from *NH* in Inoue Kiyoshi, p. 153.

36. "Jōyaku kaisei," *KMNT*, July 2, 1889; "Hijōyaku kaisei ha," *KMNT*, Sept. 2, 1889.

37. *Ibid.*

38. Inoue Kiyoshi, pp. 149–50.

39. "Naichi kanshō ron," *NH*, Aug. 22–Sept. 5, 1889, in Kuga, *Bunroku*, pp. 561–62.

40. *Ibid.*, p. 563.

41. "Kokuminteki seishin," *NH*, July 5, 1889.

42. "Gaikokujin ron," *NH*, June 22–23, 1889, in Kuga, *Bunroku*, pp. 385–93.

43. See the conclusion to "Kokusai ron," *NH*, Apr. 3–22, 1893, in Kuga, *Bunroku*, pp. 301–10.

44. *Ibid.*, pp. 267–68.

45. Inoue Kiyoshi, pp. 151–61.

46. *Ibid.*, p. 161.

47. Tanabashi Ichirō, "Jōyaku kaisei ron," *NHJ*, Nov. 3, 1889.

CHAPTER 6

1. Tokutomi Iichirō, *Jiden*, pp. 86, 109–11.

2. Tokutomi Iichirō, *So Ō kammeiroku*, pp. 72–73.

3. For background on the drafting of the Rescript, see Shively, "Motoda Eifu," and "Nishimura Shigeki."

4. Quoted in Passin, p. 85.

5. *Ibid.*, p. 151.

6. Smith, *Agrarian Origins*, p. 210; see also the same author's "Old Values."

7. Levenson, *Modern China*, p. 160.

8. "Shakai reishū ron," *NH*, Jan. 3, 1892.

9. Ōkubo, "Yugamerareta rekishi," pp. 42–51.

10. *Ibid.*

11. "Shintō ronsha no kikō," *NH*, Apr. 4, 1892.

12. For Kuga's attack on the "merchant princes," see "Ku shinshō geki," *NH*, Apr. 26–30, 1890, in Kuga, *Bunshū*, pp. 80–98; for his critique of politicians, see "Gensei," *NH*, Mar. 6–22, 1893, in Kuga, *Bunroku*, pp. 179–224.

13. "Seishin," *NH*, Jan. 5, 1891, in Kuga, *Bunshū*, pp. 194–99.

14. "Gensei," *NH*, Mar. 6–22, 1893, in Kuga, *Bunroku*, pp. 179–224; "Jinzai ron," *NH*, Aug. 22–24, 1890, in Kuga, *Bunshū*, pp. 120–34.

15. "Seishin," *NH*, Jan. 5, 1891, in Kuga, *Bunshū*, pp. 194–99.

16. "Shidō ron," *NH*, Nov. 3, 1890.

17. *Ibid.*

18. *Ibid.*

19. Inoue Tetsujirō, *Chokugo engi.*

20. Quoted in Minamoto, pp. 183–91.

21. *Ibid.* For the quoted passage, see pp. 194–96.

22. Hearn, XV, 42–43.

23. Inoue Tetsujirō, *Kyōiku to shūkyō no shōtotsu.*
24. Takayama, IV, 430.
25. *Ibid.*, IV, 430–31. Takayama, a former student of Inoue's, wrote that nationalism had won out and that from that point on the influence of Christianity and Westernism had greatly diminished. *Ibid.*, IV, 332.
26. "Kyōiku to shūkyō," *NH*, Sept. 16–20, 1893.
27. "Heimin no dōtoku," *KMNT*, Oct. 23, 1892.
28. "Shōgaku no tokuiku," *KMNT*, June 3, 1890.
29. *Ibid.*
30. "Kyōiku hōshin no chokugo," and "Shigeno Yasutsugu shi ayamareri," *KMNT*, Nov. 13, 1890.
31. Quoted from *KMSB*, Apr. 7, 1893, in Kano, pp. 13–14.
32. "Kokumin no genki to kyōka no hyōjun," *KMNT*, Apr. 13, 1893.
33. Tokutomi Iichirō, *Jiden*, p. 318.
34. "Kazokuteki sensei," *KMNT*, June 23, 1893.
35. "Yo Jiyū kisha," *NH*, July 8–11, 1893.
36. "Idai naru kokumin," *KMNT*, May 23, 1891.
37. "Meiji no seinen to hoshutō," *KMNT*, May 3, 1891, in Tokutomi Iichirō, *Bunsen*, pp. 151–60.
38. "Chūtō kaikyū no daraku," *KMNT*, Nov. 13, 1892, in Tokutomi Iichirō, *Bunsen*, pp. 174–82.
39. "Meishin," *KMNT*, Oct. 3, 1892.
40. "Ishin kakumei shi no hammen," *KMNT*, Nov. 3, 1893. For a discussion of this and other Min'yūsha historical essays, see Ōkubo, "Min'yūsha no ishin ron."

CHAPTER 7

1. Inoue Kaoru wrote: "Constitutional government was not created simply to satisfy the desires of the people. Those in the government also believed that it was imperative to create a constitutional regime to expedite the revision of treaties and the restoration of equal rights." Ōkuma agreed. See Akita, "Meiji Constitution," p. 42.
2. Miyake, *Shū*, p. 215.
3. "Kokusai ron," *NH*, Apr. 3–22, 1893, in Kuga, *Bunroku*, pp. 230–31.
4. "Meiji nijūsannen," *KMNT*, Jan. 3, 1890.
5. "Kokumin mizukara sono chōjō," *KMNT*, Feb. 23, 1891.
6. "Idai naru kokumin," *KMNT*, May 23, 1891.
7. Quoted in Matsumoto, "Kokuminteki shimeikan," p. 95.
8. This editorial is found in Fukuzawa, *Zenshū*; for the quoted passage, see X, 238–40.
9. "Kinji seironkō," *NH*, July 20–Aug. 30, 1890, in Kuga, *Bunroku*, pp. 142–43.
10. "Shinnen ni sasshi Nihonjin no chii," *NHJ*, Jan. 6, 1891.
11. *Shin-zen-bi Nihonjin* is found in Miyake, *Shū*, pp. 215–38.
12. "Shin-zen-bi Nihonjin," *TKZZ*, June 6, 1891.
13. Yanagida, *Miyake Setsurei*, p. 60.

14. Maruyama Kanji, "Miyake Setsurei ron," *Nihon hyōron*, June 1937.

15. "Nihonjin," *KMNT*, Mar. 23, 1891.

16. "Tōhō kyōkai hōkoku hatsuda no riyū," *Tōhō kyōkai hōkoku*, May 31, 1891; "Tōhō kyōkai no setsuritsu," *NH*, May 9, 1891.

17. "Tōhō kyōkai hōkoku hatsuda no riyū," *Tōhō kyōkai hōkoku*, May 31, 1891.

18. *Ibid.*

19. The best book on this subject is Irie, *Meiji nanshin shikō*.

20. "Hankai yumemonogatari," in Sugiura, pp. 29–40.

21. Shiga, III, 1–157.

22. Quoted in Iwai, 186 (1960), p. 16.

23. Fukumoto Nichinan, *Kaikoku seidan* (Tokyo, 1892).

24. See Miyake's own description of the trip in *Daigaku konjaku tan*, pp. 142–43.

25. Irie, pp. 116–17.

26. *Nihon fūkei ron* is found in Shiga, IV, 1–194.

27. Shiga, IV, 52–53.

28. Yanagida Kunio, *Japanese Manners and Customs in the Meiji Era*, translated by C. S. Terry (Tokyo, 1957), p. 277.

29. Ubukata, p. 103.

30. Kojima Torimizu's Introduction to Shiga Shigetaka, *Nihon fūkei ron* (Tokyo: Iwanami Bunko, 1963), p. 5.

31. Yoshino Sakuzō, "Shiga Shigetaka sensei," in Shiga, VIII, 228–31.

32. "Idai naru kokumin," *KMNT*, May 23, 1891.

33. "Gendai Nihon no kaika," in Natsume, XIII, 379.

CHAPTER 8

1. "Waga Tōyō mondai no kiin," *NH*, Nov. 12–14, 1894, in Kuga, *Bunroku*, pp. 726–42.

2. Miyake, *Shikon*, p. 548.

3. "Nihon kokumin no dōkaryoku," *KMNT*, Oct. 23, 1893.

4. "Nihon kokumin no hinkaku," *KMNT*, June 23, 1893.

5. For the "strict enforcement movement," see Inoue Kiyoshi, pp. 199–211; Yamamoto, pp. 510–11.

6. Tokutomi Iichirō, *Jiden*, pp. 284–85.

7. *Ibid.*, p. 287.

8. "Heiminteki shimposhugi to kokuminteki seishin," *KMNT*, Apr. 3, 1894; "Minshin no tōitsu," *KMNT*, Feb. 23, 1894.

9. Jones, p. 149.

10. "Nihon kokumin no bōchōsei," *KMNT*, June 3, 1894, in Tokutomi Iichirō, *Bunsen*, pp. 293–98.

11. "Kōki," *KMSB*, July 23, 1894.

12. "Sekai ni okeru Nihon kokumin no ichi," *KMNT*, Sept. 13, 1894.

13. *Ibid.*

14. "Sei-Shin no shin igi," *KMSB*, Dec. 5, 1894, in Tokutomi Iichirō, *Bunsen*, pp. 312–42.
15. "Sekai ni okeru Nihon kokumin no ichi," *KMNT*, Sept. 13, 1894.
16. *Ibid.*
17. Tokutomi Iichirō, *Jiden*, p. 293.
18. "Sei-Shin no shin igi," *KMSB*, Dec. 5, 1894, in Tokutomi Iichirō, *Bunsen*, pp. 312–42.
19. *Ibid.*
20. Tokutomi Iichirō, *Jiden*, p. 302.
21. *Ibid.*, pp. 294–95.
22. *Ibid.*, pp. 301–2.
23. *Ibid.*, pp. 295 et seq.
24. *Ibid.*, p. 304.
25. "Sei-Shin no shin igi," *KMSB*, Dec. 5, 1894, in Tokutomi Iichirō, *Bunsen*, pp. 312–42.
26. Tokutomi Iichirō, *Jiden*, pp. 305–8.
27. "Senshō yogen," *KMSB*, Nov. 27, 1894.
28. Tokutomi Iichirō, *Jiden*, pp. 308–9.
29. *Ibid.*, p. 311; Tokutomi Iichirō, *Jimu ikkagen*, p. 15.
30. Tokutomi Iichirō, *Jimu ikkagen*, pp. 15–16.
31. Tokutomi Iichirō, *Jiden*, p. 310.
32. Tokutomi Iichirō, *Jimu ikkagen*, p. 14.
33. Tokutomi Iichirō, *Bunsen*, pp. 391–97.
34. *Ibid.*, pp. 387–91.
35. Quoted in Matsumoto, "Kokuminteki shimeikan," pp. 101–2.
36. Tokutomi Iichirō, *Taishō*, p. 223; also quoted in Matsumoto, "Kokuminteki shimeikan," p. 98.
37. See Matsumoto, "Kokuminteki shimeikan," pp. 84–85; Jansen, *Changing Attitudes*, pp. 74–76; Oka, "Ni-Shin sensō."
38. Iwai, 194 (1961), pp. 40–43 describes Shiga's activities in the postwar period and the change in his thought. Shiga tended more toward support of expansionism and militarism than before. Iwai believes that Shiga maintained some ties with the Seikyōsha; but he was no longer an editor or a frequent contributor for *Nihonjin*.
39. Maruyama, "Kuga Katsunan to kokuminshugi."
40. Asukai, "Min'yūsha saha to Ni-Shin sensō" argues that several young members of the Min'yūsha who were still concerned with problems of social reform appear to have left the group, owing to their disagreement with Tokutomi's new determination to subordinate domestic concerns to expansionist goals.
41. Tokutomi Iichirō, *Jiden*, pp. 337 et seq.; Matsumoto, "Tokutomi Sohō."
42. See Ienaga, "Kokumin no tomo"; Uete, "Kokumin no tomo–Nihonjin."
43. Tokutomi Iichirō, *Jiden*, p. 294.
44. Toyabe, pp. 97–109.

45. "Yamaji Aizan ni atau," in Tokutomi Iichirō, *Shū*, pp. 419–23.
46. Tokutomi Iichirō, *Taishō*, p. 7.
47. Masamune, VI, 150.
48. Tokutomi Iichirō, *Taishō*, pp. 6–7.

CHAPTER 9

1. Henry Steele Commager has formulated a similar "watershed of the nineties" for American intellectual history. See his *The American Mind* (New Haven, 1950), chap. 2.
2. "The paradoxical truth is that the discovery of the spirit of the times is at once a technical near-impossibility and the intellectual historian's highest achievement." H. Stuart Hughes, *Consciousness and Society* (New York: Vintage Books, 1961), p. 8.
3. "Chūgaku kairyō ron," quoted in Ino, p. 198.
4. "Gendai Nihon no kaika," in Natsume, XIII, 352–80.
5. For a useful discussion of the difficulties of studying national character and the obstacles nationalism has created, see David M. Potter, *People of Plenty* (Chicago: Phoenix Books, 1954), chap. 1. The quoted passage is from p. 25.
6. "Kokusuihozonshugi to Nihonshugi," in Takayama, IV, 384–403.
7. "Meiji shisō no hensen," in Takayama, IV, 404–49; the quoted passage is from p. 436.
8. "Kakko ichinen no kokumin shisō," in Takayama, IV, 449–68; the quoted passage is from p. 461.
9. See the discussion of "loading the language" in R. J. Lifton, *Thought Reform and the Psychology of Totalism* (New York: Norton Library, 1963), pp. 429–30.
10. Ōnishi Hajime, quoted in Tōyama, *Kindai Nihon shisōshi*, II, 305.
11. Jansen, *Changing Attitudes*, pp. 80–81.
12. Tokutomi Iichirō, *Taishō*, p. 567.
13. "Hi kokushu hozon," *NHJ*, June 5, 1899.
14. "Jibun no kyōshi," *Gakan*, Sept. 1925, in Miyake, Jibun o kataru.
15. "Jiyūshugi no kikazaru no yuen," *NHJ*, July 5, 1900.
16. Quoted in Matsumoto, "Kokuminteki shimeikan," p. 111.
17. "Ōsaka Asahi kara Warera e," *Warera*, Feb. 1919.
18. Hasegawa Nyozekan, *Nihonteki seikaku* (Tokyo, 1938). An English translation by John Best was published in 1965 under the title *The Japanese Character*.
19. Okakura Kakuzō, *The Book of Tea* (New York, 1906), p. 7.
20. Kinoshita Naoue, "Nihon kokumin no daiyūwaku," in Kinoshita, p. 337.
21. Miyake Setsurei, "Waga Nihonjin no shokubun," *Nihon oyobi Nihonjin*, Jan. 1907. Quoted in Matsumoto, "Kokuminteki shimeikan," p. 110.
22. "Gendai Nihon no kaika," in Natsume, XIII, 379.
23. Takayama, V, 393, 400; Kōsaka Masaaki, *Meiji bunka shi: Shisō*

genron hen, in Kaikoku, IV, 306–10. See also Kōsaka, *Japanese Thought*, pp. 299–312.

24. Yamaji Aizan, *Gendai Nihon kyōkai shiron* (Tokyo, 1906), in Yamaji, *Shiron shū*; the quoted passage is from p. 400. See also Masao Maruyama, "Patterns of Individuation and the Case of Japan: A Conceptual Scheme," in Jansen, *Changing Attitudes*, p. 511. Confirmation of Yamaji's impressions is found in Abe Yoshishige, "Meiji shisōkai no chōryū," in *Iwanami kōza—Nihon bungaku* (Tokyo, 1931–33).

25. Tokutomi Sohō, "Seinen no fūki," *KMSB*, Sept. 25, 1904, in Tokutomi Iichirō, *Bunsen*, pp. 785–91. The translation is from Maruyama, "Patterns of Individuation," in Jansen, *Changing Attitudes*, p. 511. For observations of youthful indifference by Miyake Setsurei, see "Dorei konjō to gimushin" and "Kōgai otoroete hammon okoru," in Miyake, *Shikon*, pp. 546–52, 579–84.

26. Ishikawa Takuboku, "Seikyū na shisō," in Ishikawa, IV, 465–71. See also Kōsaka, pp. 362–63.

27. Ishikawa Takuboku, "Jidai heisoku no genjō," in Ishikawa, IV, 539–55.

28. Kinoshita Naoue, "Aikokushin ketsubō no gen'in," in Kinoshita, pp. 358–59. See also Maruyama, "Chūsei to hangyaku," p. 451.

29. Miyake Setsurei, "Kokumin shisō no taitō o fusegu no benpō," in Miyake, *Shikon*, pp. 522 et seq. See also Maruyama, "Chūsei to hangyaku," p. 450.

30. For examples of Nagai's feelings, see Seidensticker, pp. 28–33.

31. Ishikawa Takuboku, "Hyakkai tsūshin," in Ishikawa, IV, 368–70.

32. *Ibid.*

33. Ishikawa Takuboku, "Kiregire ni kokoro ni ukanda kanji to kaisō," in Ishikawa, IV, 438–40.

GLOSSARY

This selective list provides characters for many of the names and terms used in the text.

Baba Tatsui　馬場辰猪
Dōshisha　同志社
Ebina Danjō　海老名彈正
Fukumoto Nichinan　福本日南
Fukuzawa Yukichi　福澤諭吉
Futabatei Shimei　二葉亭四迷
gaihatsuteki no kaika　外發的の
　開化
gōnō　豪農
Hasegawa Nyozekan　長谷川如
　是閑
heiminshugi　平民主義
Inagaki Manjirō　稲垣滿次郎
Inoue Enryō　井上圓了
Inoue Kaoru　井上馨
Inoue Tetsujirō　井上哲次郎
Ishikawa Takuboku　石川啄木
Itagaki Taisuke　板垣退助
Itō Hirobumi　伊藤博文
Katō Hiroyuki　加藤弘之
kenryoku no henchō　權力の偏
　重
Kikuchi Kumatarō　菊池熊太郎
Kinoshita Naoue　木下尚江
Kitamura Tōkoku　北村透谷

Kojima Kazuo　古島一雄
Kokumin no tomo　國民之友
kokusui hozon　國粹保存
Kōtoku Shūsui　幸德秋水
Kozaki Hiromichi　小崎弘道
Kuga Katsunan (Minoru)　陸
　羯南（實）
Kume Kunitake　久米邦武
Kunikida Doppo　國木田獨步
Kunitomo Shigeaki　國友重章
Maruyama Kanji　丸山幹治
Maruyama Masao　丸山眞男
Masamune Hakuchō　正宗白鳥
Min'yūsha　民友社
Miyake Setsurei (Yūjirō)　三宅
　雪嶺（雄二郎）
Mori Arinori　森有禮
Mori Ōgai　森鷗外
Motoda Eifu　元田永孚
Nagai Kafū　永井荷風
naichi zakkyo　內地雜居
naihatsuteki no kaika　內發的の
　開化
Nakae Chōmin　中江兆民
Natsume Sōseki　夏目漱石

Niijima Jō　新島襄
Nishimura Shigeki　西村茂樹
Okakura Tenshin　岡倉天心
Ōkuma Shigenobu　大隈重信
Ozaki Yukio　尾崎行雄
Sakai Toshihiko　堺利彦
Seikyōsha　政教社
seishinteki gedatsu　精神的解脱
Shiga Shigetaka　志賀重昂
Shimada Saburō　島田三郎
Shin-zen-bi Nihonjin　眞善美日
　本人
Sugiura Jūgō　杉浦重剛
Taguchi Ukichi　田口卯吉
Taiyō　太陽
Takayama Chogyū　高山樗牛

Tanabashi Ichirō　棚橋一郎
Tani Kanjō　谷干城
Tōhō Kyōkai　東邦協會
Tokutomi Roka　德富蘆花
Tokutomi Sohō (Iichirō)　德富
　蘇峰（猪一郎）
Torio Koyata　鳥尾小彌太
Uemura Masahisa　植村正久
Yamaji Aizan　山路愛山
Yanagida Izumi　柳田泉
Yanagida Kunio　柳田國男
Yano Fumio　矢野文雄
Yokoi Shōnan　横井小楠
Yokoi Tokio　横井時雄
Yoshino Sakuzō　吉野作造

BIBLIOGRAPHY

The richest source material for this study consists of Meiji newspapers and magazines, an excellent guide to which is Nishida's *Meiji jidai no shimbun to zasshi*. Some of these periodicals, including *Kokumin no tomo* and *Nihonjin*, are now being collected and reprinted and will be more readily available for use in research.

The best collection of periodicals is found in the Library of Meiji Newspapers and Magazines (Meiji shimbun zasshi bunko); Mr. Nishida, who was its director, was very helpful to me. I also used the extensive collections at the Waseda University Library and the National Diet Library.

The periodicals of which I made the most use are *Ajia, Gakan, Jiyū shimbun, Kokumin no tomo, Kokumin shimbun, Nihon, Nihonjin, Nihon oyobi Nihonjin, Tōhō kyōkai hōkoku, Tōkyō dempō, Tōkyō keizai zasshi*, and *Tōyō gakugei zasshi*.

The collected writings and memoirs of principals in this study are another valuable source of primary material. This bibliography includes the collected works and memoirs I have cited. Such collections continue to appear, providing the intellectual historian of the Meiji period with a wealth of material. The massive *Meiji bungaku zenshū* now being published, for example, will provide a convenient source of writings from this period.

I should mention in addition conversations I had with Dr. Hasegawa Nyozekan and Professor Yanagida Izumi, both of whom began their professional careers as disciples of Miyake Setsurei; and with Professor Maruyama Masao, whose father was a Seikyōsha adherent who wrote for both *Nihon* and *Nihonjin*.

Akagi Kensuke. *Nihon shigakushi*. Tokyo, 1947.

Akita, George. Foundations of Constitutional Government in Modern Japan, 1868–1900. Cambridge, Mass., 1967.

—— "The Meiji Constitution in Practice: The First Diet," *Journal of Asian Studies*, XXII, 1 (1962), 31–46.

Arima, Tatsuo. Failure of Freedom. Ph.D. thesis, Harvard University, 1962.

Arnold, Edwin. Seas and Lands. London, 1891.

Asahi jānaru, compiler. Nihon no shisōka. Tokyo, 1962–63. 3 vols.

Asukai Masamichi. "Min'yūsha saha to Ni-Shin sensō," *Bungaku,* XXVII, 8 (1959), 21–32.

Baba Tatsui. *See* Soviak.

Baelz, Erwin. Awakening Japan: The Diary of a German Doctor. Translated by Eden Paul and Cedar Paul. New York, 1932.

Beasley, W. G., and E. G. Pulleyblank, eds. Historians of China and Japan. London, 1961.

Beckmann, George M. The Making of the Meiji Constitution. Lawrence, Kans., 1957.

Bellah, Robert N. "Japan's Cultural Identity: Some Reflections on the Work of Watsuji Tetsurō," *Journal of Asian Studies,* XXIV, 4 (1965), 573–94.

―――― Tokugawa Religion: The Values of Pre-Industrial Japan. Glencoe, Ill., 1957.

Benedict, Ruth. The Chrysanthemum and the Sword. Boston, 1946.

Blacker, Carmen. The Japanese Enlightenment: A Study of the Writings of Fukuzawa Yukichi. Cambridge, Eng., 1964.

Brown, Delmer M. Nationalism in Japan. Berkeley, Calif., 1955.

Chamberlain, Basil Hall. Things Japanese. London, 1891.

Chisolm, Lawrence W. Fenollosa: The Far East and American Culture. New Haven, Conn., 1963.

Conroy, Hilary. The Japanese Seizure of Korea: 1868–1910. Philadelphia, 1960.

Craig, Albert M. Chōshū in the Meiji Restoration. Cambridge, Mass., 1961.

Dore, R. P. City Life in Japan. Berkeley, Calif., 1958.

―――― Education in Tokugawa Japan. Berkeley, Calif., 1965.

――――, ed. Aspects of Social Change in Modern Japan. Princeton, N.J., 1967.

Ebina Danjō. Kirisutokyō gairon mikankō: waga shinkyō no yurai to keika. Tokyo, 1937.

―――― *See also* Notehelfer.

Etō, Jun. "Natsume Sōseki: A Japanese Meiji Intellectual," *American Scholar,* XXXIV, 4 (1965), 603–19.

Fenollosa, Ernest. *See* Chisolm.

Fukuzawa Yukichi. The Autobiography of Yukichi Fukuzawa. Translated by Eiichi Kiyooka. New York, 1966.

―――― Fukuzawa Yukichi zenshū. Compiled by Keiō Gijuku. Tokyo, 1958–64. 21 vols.

―――― *See also* Blacker.

Hasegawa Nyozekan. Aru kokoro no jijoden. Tokyo, 1950.

―――― The Japanese Character. Translated by John Best. Tokyo and Palo Alto, Calif., 1965.

——— "Miyake Setsurei," in Sandai genronjin shū. Tokyo, 1963, V, 237–336.
Hearn, Lafcadio. The Writings of Lafcadio Hearn. Boston, 1923. 16 vols.
Hirao Michio. Shishaku Tani Kanjō den. Tokyo, 1935.
Hoshino Tōru. Mimpōten ronsō shi. Tokyo, 1944.
Ienaga Saburō. Gairai bunka no sesshu shiron. Tokyo, 1948.
——— "Kokumin no tomo," Bungaku, XXIII, 1 (1955), 38–44.
——— Nihon dōtoku shisōshi. Tokyo, 1954.
——— Nihon kindai shisōshi kenkyū. Tokyo, 1953.
——— Nihon no kindai shigaku. Tokyo, 1957.
Ike, Nobutaka. The Beginnings of Political Democracy in Japan. Baltimore, 1950.
Ino Kenji. "Natsume Sōseki: kindaika to chishikijin no ummei," in Nihon no shisōka. Compiled by Asahi jānaru. Tokyo, 1963, II, 196–214.
Inoue Kaoru Kō denki hensan kai, compiler. Segai Inoue Kō den. Tokyo, 1933–34, 5 vols.
Inoue Kiyoshi. Jōyaku kaisei. Tokyo, 1955.
Inoue Tetsujirō. Chokugo engi. Tokyo, 1891.
——— Kyōiku to shūkyō no shōtotsu. Tokyo, 1893.
——— See also Ōshima.
Irie Toraji. Meiji nanshin shikō. Tokyo, 1943.
Irokawa Daikichi. Meiji seishinshi. Tokyo, 1964.
——— "Tokutomi Sohō ron," Rekishi hyōron, 94 (1958), 37–59; 96 (1958), 32–43; 97 (1958), 2–18.
Ishida Takeshi. Meiji seiji shisōshi kenkyū. Tokyo, 1954.
Ishikawa Takuboku. Ishikawa Takuboku zenshū. Tokyo, 1928–29. 5 vols.
Iwai Tadakuma. "Shiga Shigetaka ron," Ritsumeikan bungaku, 186 (1960), 1–22; 194 (1961), 28–46; 198 (1961), 35–56.
Izumi Aki. "Nihonjin," Bungaku, XXIII, 4 (1955), 91–97.
Jansen, Marius B. The Japanese and Sun Yat-sen. Cambridge, Mass., 1954.
——— Sakamoto Ryōma and the Meiji Restoration. Princeton, N.J., 1961.
———, ed. Changing Japanese Attitudes Toward Modernization. Princeton, N.J., 1965.
Jones, F. C. Extraterritoriality in Japan. New Haven, Conn., 1931.
Kaigo Tokiomi. Nishimura Shigeki, Sugiura Jūgō (Nihon kyōiku bunko, XLIV). Tokyo, 1937.
Kaikoku hyakunen kinen bunka jigyōkai, compiler. Meiji bunka shi. Tokyo, 1953–57. 14 vols.
Kano Masanao. "Inaka shinshitachi no ronri." Rekishigaku kenkyū, 249 (1961), 5–15.
Katayama Sen. See Kublin.
Katō Hidetoshi. "Meiji nijūnendai nashonarizumu to komyunikeishon," in Sakata Yoshio, ed., Meiji zenhanki no nashonarizumu. Tokyo, 1958, pp. 311–42.
Kawabe Shinzō. Katsunan to Sohō. Tokyo. 1943.

Kawashima Takeyoshi. Ideorogī to shite no kazoku seidō. Tokyo, 1957.
Kindai Nihon shisōshi kōza. Tokyo, 1959– . 8 vols. planned.
Kinoshita Naoue. Kinoshita Naoue shū (Meiji bungaku zenshū, XLV).
    Edited by Yamagiwa Keiji. Tokyo, 1965.
Kitamura Tōkoku. Tōkoku zenshū. Edited by Katsumoto Seiichirō. To-
    kyo, 1950–60. 3 vols.
——— See also Mathy.
Kojima Kazuo. Kojima Kazuo seidan. Compiled by Mainichi shimbun.
    Tokyo, 1951.
——— See also Washio.
Konishi Shirō. "Yamaji Aizan: kokuminteki rekishikan," in Nihon no
    shisōka. Compiled by Asahi jānaru. Tokyo, 1962, I, 269–85.
Kōsaka Masaaki. Japanese Thought in the Meiji Era. Translated by
    David Abosch. Tokyo, 1958.
Kōtoku Shūsui. See Tanaka.
Kozaki Hiromichi. Reminiscences of Seventy Years. Translated by Nari-
    aki Kozaki. Tokyo, 1933.
Kublin, Hyman. Asian Revolutionary: The Life of Sen Katayama.
    Princeton, N.J., 1964.
Kuga Katsunan (Minoru). Katsunan bunroku. Edited by Suzuki Torao.
    Tokyo, 1938.
——— Katsunan bunshū. Edited by Kajii Mori. Tokyo, 1910.
——— See also Kawabe; Maruyama; Uete; Yanagida; Yasui.
Levenson, Joseph R. Liang Ch'i-ch'ao and the Mind of Modern China.
    Cambridge, Mass., 1953.
——— Modern China and Its Confucian Past: The Problem of Intel-
    lectual Continuity. Garden City, N.Y., 1964.
Lifton, Robert Jay. "Youth and History," in Erik H. Erikson, ed., Youth:
    Change and Challenge. New York, 1963, pp. 260–90.
Maedakō Kōichirō. Roka den. Tokyo, 1938.
Maruyama Masao. "Chūsei to hangyaku," in Kindai Nihon shisōshi kōza.
    Tokyo, 1960, VI, 377–471.
——— "Kuga Katsunan to kokuminshugi," in Minkenron kara nasho-
    narizumu e (Meijishi kenkyū sōsho, IV). Compiled by Meiji shiryō
    kenkyū renrakukai. Tokyo, 1957, pp. 192–209.
——— "Meiji kokka no shisō," in Nihon shakai no shiteki kyūmei.
    Compiled by Rekishigaku kenkyūkai. Tokyo, 1949, pp. 183–236.
——— Nihon no shisō. Tokyo, 1961.
——— Nihon seiji shisōshi kenkyū. Tokyo, 1952.
——— Thought and Behavior in Modern Japanese Politics. Edited by
    Ivan Morris. New York, 1963.
———, ed. Nihon no nashonarizumu. Tokyo, 1953.
Masamune Hakuchō. Masamune Hakuchō zenshū. Tokyo, 1965–68. 13
    vols.
Mathy, Francis. "Kitamura Tōkoku: The Early Years," Monumenta Nip-
    ponica, XVIII, 1–4 (1963), 1–44.

Matsuda Michio. "Shiga Shigetaka: Meiji no kokkashugi," in Nihon no shisōka. Compiled by *Asahi jānaru*. Tokyo, 1963, II, 21–40.

Matsumoto Sannosuke. Kindai Nihon no seiji to ningen. Tokyo, 1966.

—— "Kokuminteki shimeikan no rekishiteki hensen," in Kindai Nihon shisōshi kōza. Tokyo, 1961, VIII, 81–136.

—— "Meiji zenki hoshushugi shisō no ichi dammen," in Sakata Yoshio, ed., Meiji zenhanki no nashonarizumu. Tokyo, 1958, pp. 129–64.

—— "Nihon oyobi Nihonjin," *Bungaku*, XXIV, 4 (1956), 91–97.

—— "Tokutomi Sohō: jidai no nagare to genronjin," in Nihon no shisōka. Compiled by *Asahi jānaru*. Tokyo, 1963, II, 41–58.

Matsushima Eiichi, ed. Meiji shiron shū (1) (Meiji bungaku zenshū, LXXVII). Tokyo, 1965.

Meiji bunka kenkyūkai, compiler. Meiji bunka zenshū. Tokyo, 1955–59. 16 vols.

Minamoto Ryōen. "Kyōiku chokugo no kokkashugiteki kaishaku," in Sakata Yoshio, ed., Meiji zenhanki no nashonarizumu. Tokyo, 1958, pp. 165–212.

Miyake Setsurei (Yūjirō). Daigaku konjaku tan. Tokyo, 1946.

—— Dōjidai shi. Tokyo, 1950. 6 vols.

—— Jibun o kataru. Tokyo, 1950.

—— Meiji shisō shōshi. Tokyo, 1913.

—— Miyake Setsurei shū (Gendai Nihon bungaku zenshū, V). Tokyo, 1931.

—— Shikon. Tokyo, 1916.

—— *See also* Hasegawa; Motoyama; Yanagida.

Miyauchi, Dixon Yoshihide. Yokoi Shōnan: A Pre-Meiji Reformist, Ph.D. thesis, Harvard University, 1957.

Miyazaki Tōten. Sanjūsannen no yume. Tokyo, 1943.

Motoda Eifu. *See* Shively.

Motoyama Yukihiko. "Meiji nijūnendai no seiron ni arawareta nashonarizumu," in Sakata Yoshio, ed., Meiji zenhanki no nashonarizumu. Tokyo, 1958, pp. 37–84.

—— "Miyake Setsurei: zaiya no nashonarisuto," in Nihon no shisōka. Compiled by *Asahi jānaru*. Tokyo, 1963, II, 59–76.

—— "Tani Kanjō no seiji shisō ni tsuite," *Jimbun gakuhō*, VI (1956), 87–114.

Nagai Kafū. *See* Seidensticker.

Nagai, Michio. "Herbert Spencer in Early Meiji Japan," *Far Eastern Quarterly*, XIV (1954), 55–64.

—— "Mori Arinori," *Japan Quarterly*, XI, 1 (1964), 98–105.

Natsume Sōseki. Sōseki zenshū. Tokyo, 1936. 19 vols.

—— *See also* Etō; Ino.

Nihon Kōdōkai, compiler. Hakuō Nishimura Shigeki den. Tokyo, 1933. 2 vols.

Nishida Taketoshi. Meiji jidai no shimbun to zasshi. Tokyo, 1961.

Nishimura Shigeki. *See* Kaigo; Nihon Kōdōkai.

Notehelfer, Fred. "Ebina Danjō: A Christian Samurai of the Meiji Period," in Albert Craig and J. K. Fairbank, eds., Harvard Papers on Japan. Cambridge, Mass., 1963, II, 1–56.

Oka Yoshitake. "Jōyaku kaisei rongi ni arawareta tōji no taigai ishiki," Kokka gakkai zasshi, LXVII (1953), 1–24, 183–206.

———— "Ni-Shin sensō to tōji ni okeru taigai ishiki," Kokka gakkai zasshi, LXVIII (1954–55), 101–29, 223–54.

Ōkubo Toshiaki. "Min'yūsha no ishin ron," Nihon rekishi, 77 (1954), 8–16.

———— "Yugamerareta rekishi," in Sakisaka Itsurō, ed., Arashi no naka no hyakunen. Tokyo, 1952, pp. 35–78.

Ōmachi Keigetsu and Igari Shizan. Sugiura Jūgō sensei. Tokyo, 1924.

Ōshima Yasumasa. "Inoue Tetsujirō: chishiki to shissaku no bunri," in Nihon no shisōka. Compiled by Asahi jānaru. Tokyo, 1963, II, 94–110.

Ozaki Yukio. Ozaki Yukio zenshū. Tokyo, 1926–27. 10 vols.

Passin, Herbert. Society and Education in Japan. New York, 1965.

Pittau, Joseph. Political Thought in Early Meiji Japan, 1868–1889. Cambridge, Mass., 1967.

Ryan, Marleigh Grayer. Japan's First Modern Novel: Ukigumo. New York, 1967.

Sakai Toshihiko. Sakai Toshihiko zenshū. Compiled by Chūō kōron. Tokyo, 1933. 6 vols.

Sakamoto Ryōma. See Jansen.

Sakata Yoshio, ed. Meiji zenhanki no nashonarizumu. Tokyo, 1958.

Sakisaka Itsurō, ed. Kindai Nihon no shisōka. Tokyo, 1954.

———— Arashi no naka no hyakunen. Tokyo, 1952.

Sandai genronjin shū. Tokyo, 1962–63. 8 vols.

Sansom, George B. The Western World and Japan. New York, 1950.

Scalapino, Robert A. Democracy and the Party Movement in Prewar Japan. Berkeley, Calif., 1953.

Seidensticker, Edward. Kafū the Scribbler. Stanford, Calif., 1965.

Shiga Shigetaka. Shiga Shigetaka zenshū. Compiled by Shiga Shigetaka zenshū kankōkai. Tokyo, 1927–29. 8 vols.

———— See also Iwai; Matsuda.

Shigakkai, compiler. Hompō shigakushi ronsō. Tokyo, 1939.

Shimada Kō. "Kokumin no tomo to junbungaku rinen," Bungaku, XXX (1962), 1003–19.

Shively, Donald H. "Motoda Eifu: Confucian Lecturer to the Meiji Emperor," in D. S. Nivison and A. F. Wright, eds., Confucianism in Action. Stanford, Calif., 1959.

———— "Nishimura Shigeki: A Confucian View of Modernization," in Marius B. Jansen, ed., Changing Japanese Attitudes Toward Modernization. Princeton, N.J., 1965.

Smith, Thomas C. The Agrarian Origins of Modern Japan. Stanford, Calif., 1959.

———— "Japan's Aristocratic Revolution," Yale Review, L, 3 (1961), 370–83.

—— "Landlords' Sons in the Business Elite," *Economic Development and Cultural Change*, IX, 1, pt. 2 (1960), 93–186.

—— "Old Values and New Techniques in the Modernization of Japan," *Far Eastern Quarterly*, XIV, 3 (1955), 355–63.

—— Political Change and Industrial Development in Japan: Government Enterprise, 1868–1880. Stanford, Calif., 1955.

Soviak, Eugene. "The Case of Baba Tatsui," *Monumenta Nipponica*, XVIII, 1–4 (1963), 191–235.

Spencer, Herbert. *See* Nagai.

Suekane Yaokichi. Kokumin no tomo oyobi Nihonjin. Tokyo, 1888.

Sugiura Jūgō. Tendai dōshi chosakushū. Edited by Igari Matazō. Tokyo, 1916.

—— *See also* Kaigo; Ōmachi.

Taguchi Ukichi. Teiken Taguchi Ukichi zenshū. Compiled by Teiken Taguchi Ukichi zenshū kankōkai. Tokyo, 1928–29. 8 vols.

Takayama Chogyū. Chogyū zenshū. Tokyo, 1905. 5 vols.

Tanaka Sōgorō. Kōtoku Shūsui. Tokyo, 1955.

Tani Kanjō. Tani Kanjō ikō. Edited by Shimanouchi Toshie. Tokyo, 1912.

—— *See also* Hirao; Motoyama.

Teters, Barbara Joan. The Conservative Opposition in Japanese Politics, 1877–94. Ph.D. thesis, University of Washington, 1955.

—— "The Genro-In and the National Essence Movement," *Pacific Historical Review*, XXI (1962), 359–78.

—— "A Liberal Nationalist and the Meiji Constitution," in Robert K. Sakai, ed., Studies on Asia. Lincoln, Neb., 1965, VI, 105–23.

Tokutomi Roka. Roka zenshū. Compiled by Roka zenshū kankōkai. Tokyo, 1928–29. 20 vols.

—— *See also* Maedakō.

Tokutomi Sohō (Iichirō). Dai-Nihon bōchō ron. Tokyo, 1894.

—— Jimu ikkagen. Tokyo, 1913.

—— "Min'yūsha to 'Kokumin no tomo,'" in Nihon bungaku kōza. Tokyo, 1934, XI, 117–29.

—— Seishi yoroku. Tokyo, 1924.

—— Sohō bunsen. Compiled by Kusano Shigematsu and Namiki Sentarō. Tokyo, 1915.

—— Sohō jiden. Tokyo, 1935.

—— So Ō kammeiroku. Tokyo, 1944.

—— Taishō no seinen to teikoku no zento. Tokyo, 1916.

—— Tokutomi Sohō shū (Gendai Nihon bungaku zenshū, V). Tokyo, 1930.

—— Yoshida Shōin. Tokyo, 1893.

—— *See also* Irokawa; Kawabe; Matsumoto.

Toyabe Sentarō. Meiji jimbutsu hyōron. Tokyo, 1898.

Tōyama Shigeki. "Mimpōten ronsō no seijishiteki kōsatsu," in Minkenron kara nashonarizumu e (Meijishi kenkyū sōsho, IV). Compiled by Meiji shiryō kenkyū renrakukai. Tokyo, 1957, pp. 247–90.

———— et al. Kindai Nihon shisōshi. Tokyo, 1956–57. 4 vols.

Ubukata Toshirō. Meiji Taisho kembun shi. Tokyo, 1926.

Uemura Masahisa. Uemura Masahisa chosakushū. Tokyo, 1966–67. 7 vols.

Uete Michiari. "Kokumin no tomo—Nihonjin," Shisō, 452 (1962), 112–22.

———— "Kuga Katsunan: nashonarizumu to genronjin," in Nihon no shisōka. Compiled by Asahi jānaru. Tokyo, 1962, I, 238–52.

Ward, Robert E., and Dankwart A. Rustow, eds. Political Modernization in Japan and Turkey. Princeton, N.J., 1964.

Washio Yoshinao, ed. Kojima Kazuo. Tokyo, 1949.

Watsuji Tetsurō. See Bellah.

Yamaji Aizan. Shiron shū. Tokyo, 1958.

———— Yamaji Aizan shū (Meiji bungaku zenshū, XXXV). Edited by Ōkubo Toshiaki. Tokyo, 1965.

———— See also Konishi.

Yamamoto Shigeru. Jōyaku kaisei shi. Tokyo, 1943.

Yamazaki Masatada. Yokoi Shōnan. Tokyo, 1938.

Yanagida Izumi. "Kuga Katsunan," in Sandai genronjin shū. Tokyo, 1963, V, 123–235.

———— Tetsujin Miyake Setsurei. Tokyo, 1956.

Yasui Tatsuo. "Kuga Katsunan ni okeru nashonarizumu," Shakai kagaku kiyō (Tōkyō Daigaku kyōyō gakubu), 8 (1959).

Yokoi Shōnan. See Miyauchi; Yamazaki.

Yoshida Shōin. See Tokutomi Sohō (Iichirō).

Yoshino Sakuzō, ed. Meiji bunka zenshū. Tokyo, 1927–30. 24 vols.

INDEX

INDEX